NEW DIRECTIONS
FOR TEACHING PRACTICE AND RESEARCH

Edited by

Hersholt C. Waxman
University of Houston

and

Herbert J. Walberg
University of Illinois at Chicago

McCutchan Publishing Corporation
P.O. Box 774, 2940 San Pablo Ave., Berkeley, CA 94702

ISBN 0-8211-2274-6
Library of Congress Catalog Card Number 99-61326

Copyright © 1999 by McCutchan Publishing Corporation. All rights reserved

Printed in the United States of America

Contents

Contributors   vii
Introduction and Overview, *Hersholt C. Waxman and Herbert J. Walberg*   1

Part I: Reviews and Syntheses of Research on Teaching

1. Analyzing and Improving Teaching
   Allan C. Ornstein   17
2. Toward a Knowledge Base for School Learning
   Margaret C. Wang, Geneva D. Haertel, and Herbert J. Walberg   63
3. Productive Teaching
   Herbert J. Walberg   75

Part II: Research on Classroom Instruction

4. Classroom Observation Research and the Improvement of Teaching Practices
   Hersholt C. Waxman and Shwu-Yong L. Huang   107
5. Effective Instruction in Effective Schools
   Bert P. M. Creemers   131
6. Interpersonal Relationships Between Teachers and Students in the Classroom
   Theo Wubbels, Mieke Brekelmans, Jan van Tartwijk, and Wilfried Admiraal   151
7. Effective Instructional Practices for English Language Learners
   Yolanda N. Padrón and Hersholt C. Waxman   171
8. Improving Classroom Teaching and Learning: What American Educators Can Learn from International Research
   Lorin W. Anderson   205

Part III: Constructivist Perspectives on Teaching

9. Narrative, Teaching, and Teacher Thinking
   Linda S. Behar-Horenstein   229

10	Perspectives on Classroom Management in Learning-Centered Classrooms	
	Caroline M. Evertson and Catherine H. Randolph	249
11	Social-Constructivist Perspectives on the Teaching of Science	
	Kenneth Tobin	269
12	"Grain Sizes" in Learning Environment Research: Combining Qualitative and Quantitative Methods	
	Barry J. Fraser	285
13	Technology's Role in Student-Centered Classrooms	
	Barbara Means and Kerry Olson	297
Index		319

Contributors

Wilfried Admiraal, Utrecht University
Lorin W. Anderson, University of South Carolina
Linda S. Behar-Horenstein, University of Florida
Mieke Brekelmans, Utrecht University
Bert P. M. Creemers, Gion Institute for Educational Research
Caroline M. Evertson, Vanderbilt University
Barry J. Fraser, Curtin University
Geneva D. Haertel, Temple University
Shwu-Yong L. Huang, University of Houston
Barbara Means, SRI International
Kerry Olson, SRI International
Allan C. Ornstein, Loyola University of Chicago
Yolanda N. Padrón, University of Houston
Catherine H. Randolph, Vanderbilt University
Kenneth Tobin, University of Pennsylvania
Jan van Tartwijk, Utrecht University
Herbert J. Walberg, University of Illinois at Chicago
Margaret C. Wang, Temple University
Hersholt C. Waxman, University of Houston
Theo Wubbels, Utrecht University

Introduction and Overview

Hersholt C. Waxman
and
Herbert J. Walberg

One of the major challenges in education today is improving the quality of classroom instruction for all students. In recent years, many social, school, and classroom factors have been investigated in order to improve student learning. Some educators, for example, pointed out that macrolevel or distal variables (e.g., poverty, crime, drug abuse, and unemployment) have caused the deterioration of some schools. Although such economic and social variables are serious problems, they are not the direct causes of classroom learning that educators can easily alter. Furthermore, educators focusing on such external conditions may divert "energy and attention from the circumstances within schools and classrooms that can have a positive impact on the experiences of students—even those who face social, demographic, or economic circumstances that place them 'at risk' of school failure" (Phelan, Davidson, and Cao, 1992, p. 696).

On the other hand, a growing body of research shows that proximal or "alterable" educational variables are directly and highly related to improved outcomes for students (Wang, Haertel and Walberg, 1993). One such alterable variable that promotes the academic achievement of students is the quality of classroom instruction. Improved classroom instruction leads to improved cognitive and affective outcomes for students. In fact, one of the best ways to improve schools is to provide them with effective teachers who provide superior classroom instruction and maintain a supportive learning environment (Pierce, 1994; Wang, Reynolds, and Walberg, 1995; Waxman and Huang, 1997; Waxman,

Huang, Anderson, and Weinstein, 1997; Waxman, Huang, and Padrón, 1995).

The accumulated evidence about classroom instruction, however, has not always been widely acknowledged by the research community. A few decades ago, one of the major concerns among educators was that instructional practices were often based on unexamined assumptions with little empirical data supporting what was done in the classroom. Furthermore, a number of criticisms about the quality and quantity of research on teacher effectiveness were made by reviewers in the mainstream, as well as by those outside the field. Some educators even argued that the lack of a body of research knowledge about teacher effectiveness was one of the major obstacles that prevented us from changing or improving teaching.

About fifteen years ago, we synthesized the reviews of process-product research (Waxman and Walberg, 1982). At that time, we acknowledged that the research on teacher effectiveness and the process-product paradigm was characterized as "chaotic," "disappointing," and "fruitless." We also found that the reviews of research on the process-product paradigm had a "great number of serious flaws in search and selection procedures, validity assessments, and summarization of empirical results" (p. 118). We concluded, nonetheless, that the magnitude of results in the primary studies were sufficient to have produced "a substantial body of reasonably consistent, hard-won knowledge about the associations of teaching processes and student learning" (p. 118). Since then, other reviews and syntheses of the research on teacher effectiveness have similarly shown the importance of the quality of classroom instruction on student outcomes (Brophy and Good, 1986; Rosenshine, 1995; Walberg, 1986, 1995).

Now, nearly two decades later, we have seen considerable progress in the field. The process-product paradigm is no longer the dominant paradigm or approach to research on teaching. Research on teaching has become more qualitative, and the new paradigms on teacher effectiveness have shifted from focusing primarily on the teacher to focusing on student- or learner-centered perspectives. These newer approaches also focus on improving students' higher-level outcomes rather than just focusing on improving students' basic skills or lower-level cognitive outcomes (Waxman, Padrón, and Knight, 1991). This book highlights some of the recent work of researchers in the field of classroom instruction and teacher effectiveness. More specifically, this book

Introduction and Overview 3

examines some of the traditional research approaches and methods that have been used in the field, as well as newer approaches to research on effective teaching.

OVERVIEW OF THE BOOK

The chapters in this volume address some of the current research on effective teaching. The book is divided into three parts. Part One, "Reviews and Syntheses of Research on Teaching," includes a historical overview of the field and a discussion of new approaches or paradigms in the field. Part One also includes two state-of-the-art reviews. Part Two, "Research on Classroom Instruction," includes some different ways that researchers view classrooms in order to examine effective teaching. Part Three, "Constructivist Perspectives on Teaching," includes five chapters that examine teaching from a variety of constructivist approaches.

Part One: Reviews and Syntheses of Research on Teaching

Allan Ornstein's chapter, "Analyzing and Improving Teaching," presents a historical overview of the research on effective teaching. The framework for this chapter is the five basic components of teaching that can be analyzed: (a) teacher style, (b) teacher interactions, (c) teacher characteristics, (d) teacher effects, and (e) teacher contexts. The first section on teacher styles presents this line of research from a historical context and then follows with specific research on teacher styles, using the work of Ned Flanders as an example. The next section examines research on teacher-student interaction, where several classic studies focusing on verbal and nonverbal communication in the classroom are described. The next two sections focus on research on teacher expectations, self-fulfilling prophecies, labeling of students, and teacher characteristics. The section on teacher effects summarizes research that examines the effects of teacher processes on student outcomes. Several conceptual models of this research are also presented. The fifth and final basic way of analyzing teaching, teacher contexts, is presented as a new paradigm. Ornstein describes this new approach as one focusing on the personal and practical knowledge of teachers, the culture of teaching, and the language and thoughts of teachers. This work includes research that uses concepts like metaphors, stories, biographies and autobiographies, voice, and the expert teacher.

In their chapter, "Toward a Knowledge Base for School Learning," Margaret Wang, Geneva Haertel, and Herb Walberg describe a set of large-scale surveys to estimate the effects of teaching and other educational practices. The sources are a national survey of educational practitioners and leading educational researchers, a content analysis of reviews of educational research, and calculations of the sizes of effects of teaching methods and other educational practices. From the results of these surveys, the authors rank order the various estimates of the effects. These estimates can serve as a basis for future research and theory, for educational practitioners to choose among alternative educational policies and teaching methods, and for teacher educators to design preservice and in-service programs.

Herb Walberg provides a summary of the research syntheses that have been conducted in the areas of teaching and instruction in his chapter, "Productive Teaching and Instruction: Assessing the Knowledge Base." He begins with the effects of the psychological elements of teaching and then discusses methods and patterns of teaching. Next, he examines systems of instruction that require special planning, student grouping, and materials. He then describes effects that are unique to reading, writing, science, and mathematics. Finally, he discusses results concerning special students and techniques, and effects of training on teachers.

Part Two: Research on Classroom Instruction

The chapter by Hersh Waxman and Shwu-Yong Huang, "Classroom Observation Research and the Improvement of Teaching Practices," describes research that has employed systematic classroom observation techniques in order to investigate effective teaching at the elementary, middle, and high school levels. This chapter describes the use of classroom observation methods to investigate instructional processes and behaviors that occur in classrooms. The authors review some of the ways classroom observation has contributed to the research knowledge in the field and discuss some of the important implications for the improvement of teaching and student learning. Four specific areas where systematic classroom observation has been found to be especially useful for educational practice are highlighted in the chapter: (1)

Introduction and Overview

describing instructional practices, (2) investigating instructional inequities for different groups of students, (3) improving teacher education programs, and (4) improving teachers' classroom instruction based on feedback from individual classroom profiles. Some of the criticisms and cautions related to the use of structured observation techniques are also described. Finally, some new directions for observational research are reported and one specific technique, "shadowing," is described.

Bert Creemers's chapter, "Effective Instruction in Effective Schools," begins by describing the school effectiveness movement and how initial research typically did not distinguish differences between school levels and classroom levels in order to demonstrate that schools do matter. He explains that while current research focuses on teachers and classrooms, educational effectiveness is more than just effectiveness at the classroom level. Creemers then describes a theory on effective instruction that is based on empirical evidence of research on learning and instruction. He presents his conceptual model of quality of instruction by explicitly summarizing three major components: (1) the curriculum, (2) grouping arrangements, and (3) teacher behavior. The next two sections focus on conditions for effectiveness at the school level such as quality, time, and opportunity, and the formal criteria of important conditions that are necessary for effectiveness at the school level (i.e., consistency, cohesion, constancy, and control). The final section describes future research in the field of educational effectiveness, including studies that link with theories on educational effectiveness, a variety of types of research, more refined operationalization of variables, studies that include more than one level of educational system, experimental designs, and international comparative research.

In the next chapter, "Interpersonal Relationships Between Teachers and Students in the Classroom," Theo Wubbels and his colleagues from Utrecht University in the Netherlands describe their research on teacher-student interpersonal relationships in the classroom. Their work analyzes effective teaching from the "interpersonal" or affective dimension, which focuses on the actions teachers use to create and maintain a working classroom climate. First, they introduce a systems approach to communication, and then they propose a theory developed by Timothy Leary that focuses on a language for interpersonal relationships that divides discourse into eight categories that can be presented in a two-dimensional plane, proximity and influence. The next section of the chapter describes characteristics of interpersonal relationships and provides examples of how students derive the interpersonal significance of teacher behavior from both verbal and nonverbal signals. They also describe some of their research on the development and use of the Questionnaire on Teacher Interaction (QTI), which measures eight different aspects of teacher behavior. Next, they report on some of their research that examined the relations between teacher interpersonal behavior and instructional strategies and management techniques, and asked students to complete the QTI on their best teachers and their worst. The final two sections focus on implications for professional development and teacher education. In particular, Wubbels and his colleagues describe changes that occur in the teacher-students interpersonal relationships during teachers' professional career and discuss how teacher education programs could incorporate this research in preparing teachers.

Yolanda Padrón and Hersh Waxman's chapter, "Effective Instructional Practices for English Language Learners," focuses on the educational problems of learners whose primary language is not English. Latinos constitute the largest group of English language learners (ELLs), but they often have the lowest levels of education and the highest dropout rates. The chapter begins with a focus on several of the critical problems associated with the education of ELLs, namely, instructional programs that have not been effective in meeting the educational needs of ELLs, the shortage of adequately qualified teachers, and instructional approaches that predominantly focus on a basic skills/mastery orientation that generally leads to student compliance but passive resentment and teacher burn out. In response to the concerns about current instructional practices used with ELLs, several educators have advocated alternative teaching approaches that emphasize more active student learning and change the role of teachers from deliverers of knowledge to facilitators of learning. The following five research-based instructional approaches all stress this changing model of classroom instruction, and they all have been found to be previously successful for ELLs: cognitively guided instruction, culturally responsive teaching, technology-enriched instruction, cooperative learning, and instructional conversation. The following sections of the chapter briefly describe each of these approaches, explaining why they may be especially successful for ELLs. The final two sections focus on implications for teacher education and future research.

Lorin Anderson's chapter, "Improving Classroom Teaching and Learning: What American Educators Can Learn from International Research," describes a conceptual framework that integrates the results of international studies of classroom teaching and learning. The centerpiece of the conceptual framework is the lesson, and the five components of lessons are (1) purpose or objective of the lesson, (2) time allocated to the lesson and the pace with which students move through the lesson, (3) activities or events engaged in by the students, (4) roles and responsibilities of teachers and students, and (5) ways in which lesson progress is assessed and evaluated. The chapter uses the conceptual framework for discussing the results of international studies of classroom teaching and learning. The chapter concludes by highlighting six of the most important generalizations of the research. In addition, Anderson discusses what American educators can learn from international classroom researchers. He argues that this research provides a mirror by which we can more clearly see ourselves as well as identify collaborative research efforts and methodologies that could be used to address our most critical and fundamental educational problems.

Part Three: Constructivist Perspectives on Teaching

In her chapter, "Narrative, Teaching, and Teacher Thinking," Linda Behar-Horenstein examines the legitimacy of narrative inquiry as an educational research method for analyzing teachers and teacher thinking. She begins by describing conceptions of story or narrative forms of inquiry. She compares story and musical compositions and then draws parallels to narrative inquiry, which is defined as an ethnographic form of qualitative research that involves telling or recounting. The next section of the chapter discusses conceptual frameworks for narrative inquiry and its advantages and disadvantages. She discusses epistemological issues such as the assumptions underlying interpretation and the conceptual roots of story. The concluding section argues that story research makes knowledge about teachers' expertise accessible and provides perspectives on teaching and learning that cannot be found in other forms of inquiry. Behar-Horenstein also discusses how to make story research available by building large databases of multiple stories and categorizing themes in relation to demographic teacher variables and school variables.

"Perspectives on Classroom Management for Learning-Centered Classrooms," by Carolyn Evertson and Catherine Randolph, starts out by establishing a definition and conceptualization of management. The authors argue for a view of management that encompasses all that teachers must do to encourage learning in their classrooms, including setting up an environment that encourages learning, discourages wasted time, and orchestrates instruction in ways that promote and maintain student engagement. The next sections describe the history and current direction of classroom management research and focus on contributions of sociocultural studies that show that students are highly active in interpreting when and how they participate in classrooms. The authors' sociocognitive perspective allows us a view of classrooms from a student-centered perspective, the expectations participants have of each other, and the definitions of teaching and learning that ultimately evolve in the setting. Evertson and Randolph present a table that highlights the different tasks of teachers and students when instruction changes from recitation to teacher-led discussion to student-led discussion. Some vivid examples of these changes are provided as well as a detailed example from the Schools for Thought project at Peabody College. The next section describes flawed beliefs about classroom management. Three major conclusions are drawn from this chapter: (1) good classroom management practices are inseparable from good instructional practices; (2) as teachers move from traditional teacher-centered approaches to more student-centered approaches, principles of good management do not change; and (3) developing a classroom management system is not just a matter of enacting a few rules and procedures. The chapter concludes by discussing directions for future research.

Ken Tobin's chapter, "Social-Constructivist Perspective on the Teaching of Science," explores some of the applications of social constructivism to the practice of teaching and learning science. He begins by discussing what science and scientific knowledge are and then discusses the notion of learning science through a shared language that can be assessed by all participants to communicate with one another. The next few sections focus on why teachers should examine naive theories or incorrect knowledge held by students, small-group and whole-class activities, and the assessment role of fair judgment that constructivist teachers often assume. Finally, the value of portfolio assessment is discussed as a method of bringing teaching, learning, and assessment closer together.

Barry Fraser's chapter, "Grain Sizes in Learning Environment Research: Combining Qualitative and Quantitative Methods," explicitly addresses the need for different research studies to focus on different levels of analyses, or "grain sizes." He begins by summarizing the field of learning environment research and specifically the advantages of using students' perceptions of their classroom learning environment. He specifically points out the value of using learning environment measures as criteria for effectiveness in the evaluation of educational innovations. He shows that student perceptions consistently account for appreciable amounts of variance in student learning even after statistically controlling for student achievement and background variables. In the next part of the chapter, Fraser describes an intensive qualitative and quantitative study of a tenth-grade science teacher. Six university-based researchers collaborated with a teacher-researcher in developing an extensive database consisting of interviews, classroom observations, video recording, student diaries, and a modified version of the Constructivist Learning Environment Survey. The results from this study are reported, interpreted, and discussed at various grain sizes. The chapter concludes with advice about determining the appropriate grain size for a particular study in conceptualizing, planning, and reporting studies of classroom learning environment.

Barbara Means and Kerry Olson's chapter, "Technology's Role in Student-Centered Classrooms," focuses on ways that technology can be used as a tool to support student thinking and productivity. They introduce the constructivist view of learning that focuses on (a) teaching basic skills within authentic contexts, (b) modeling expert thought processes, and (c) providing opportunities for collaboration that enable students to achieve intellectual accomplishments. Most of the chapter describes a case study of a fifth/sixth-grade classroom with predominantly ethnically and linguistically diverse students in an inner-city school that illustrates the positive role that technology can have in supporting student thinking and productivity. In particular, they describe the Computer-Supported Intentional Learning Environments (CSILE) model, which is a networked multimedia environment consisting of eight Macintosh computers in each classroom. Students are allowed to generate "notes" within CSILE, which other students may comment on. This exchange often leads to meaningful dialogues about topics under study. Means and Olson illustrate how CSILE helped teachers adopt a new attitude toward economically disadvantaged learners, reshaped the curriculum, and applied new instructional strategies. The next section focuses on the relationship of technology to constructivist teaching. The authors described how CSILE supports collaborative learning and a "community of learners," where it is acceptable for different students to make different contributions. In addition, they point out how the computer provides a safe channel for communication that makes it easier for linguistically diverse students to engage in the dialogue. The concluding section focuses on implications for teachers, including the new role for classroom teachers that focuses on orchestrating multiple groups of students as well as on diagnosing individual learning problems and providing feedback.

CONCLUSIONS

The purpose of this book is to make available information for improving our understanding of some new directions for research on effective teaching. This book also illustrates several ways we can use research on classroom instruction to improve student learning. Ideally, research should influence all aspects of education, including that of teaching and learning in schools. We maintain that research can play a critical role in improving the role of teachers and classroom instruction. Although recognition of the uniqueness of each school and classroom situation will always need to be considered, the accumulation of research evidence over time and across studies provides consistent findings that enhance our understandings of effective classroom instruction. In other words, more and better research in this field may allow us to change and improve the education of teachers and consequently improve the education of students.

The general public and policymakers have often not had confidence in the research findings of educational researchers because of the contradictory conclusions often presented by different studies using different analytic methods or research methods. Although research syntheses and meta-analyses have alleviated many of these concerns, researchers must still explain the advantages, disadvantages, and appropriate uses of the paradigms and methods they employ. Examining research methods and paradigms in the area of teacher effectiveness is important because in educational research, the answers we develop are shaped by the form of questions we ask and by the methods we use to resolve them (Clark, 1979).

Unfortunately, investigators' personal commitments to a given research methodology have sometimes guided and shaped the research process by affecting their choice of design, instrumentation, and interpretation of data (Dunkin and Biddle, 1974). In other words, the selection of the research method is often related to the theoretical or ideological commitments or beliefs of the investigator (Shulman, 1981). Awareness of a variety of research methodologies and paradigms can broaden our approaches and perspectives on research problems and change our ways of thinking about what we can study and how we can study it (Kerlinger, 1977). Only then will educators understand the complicated role that methodology has in educational research. Given the large number of appropriate methodological options that researchers now have in designing their studies, we may start to see more and better research on teaching that contributes to educational improvements for students. We hope at the same time that policymakers will further employ education research in formulating policies that effectively support improvements in schools and classrooms. Research is a vehicle that can enhance educational change, but we must be aware that in order to impact practice, research must be effectively communicated and disseminated.

Improving research on teaching, however, will take more than just awareness of the wide range of research methods and paradigms in the field. Methodological rigor and sophistication are only one component of excellence in education (Walker, 1992). We will also need a commitment to quality research and collaboration among educators who have different perspectives about research in the field. A broad, interdisciplinary research agenda will need to be collaboratively developed and carried out. It will need to include both basic and applied research as well as both quantitative and qualitative data. It should also include more experimental and longitudinal studies. Furthermore, in order to capture all the processes and nuances that occur in classrooms, triangulation procedures are needed to collect data from multiple perspectives (Evertson and Green, 1986). Collecting multiple measures or indicators of classroom processes may help alleviate some of the concerns and criticisms of prior research and provide us with a more comprehensive picture of effective classroom instruction.

REFERENCES

Brophy, J. E., and Good, T. L. (1986). Teacher behavior and student achievement. In M. C. Wittrock (ed.), *Handbook of research on teaching* (3rd ed., pp. 328–375). New York: Macmillan.

Clark, C. M. (1979). Five faces of research on teaching. *Educational Leadership, 37*(1), 29–32.

Dunkin, M., and Biddle, B. J. (1974). *The study of teaching.* New York: Holt, Rinehart & Winston.

Evertson, C., and Green, J. (1986). Observation as inquiry and method. In M. C. Wittrock (ed.), *Handbook of research on teaching* (3rd ed., pp. 162–207). New York: Macmillan.

Kerlinger, F. N. (1977). The influence of research on education practice. *Educational Researcher, 6*(8), 5–11.

Phelan, P.; Davidson, A. L.; and Cao, H. T. (1992). Speaking up: Students' perceptions on school. *Phi Delta Kappan, 73,* 695–704.

Pierce, C. (1994). Importance of classroom climate for at-risk learners. *Journal of Educational Research, 88,* 37–42.

Rosenshine, B. (1995). Advances in research on instruction. *Journal of Educational Research, 88,* 262–268.

Shulman, L. S. (1981). Disciplines of inquiry in education: An overview. *Educational Researcher, 10*(6), 5–12.

Walberg, H. J. (1986). Synthesis of research on teaching. In M. C. Wittrock (ed.), *Handbook of research on teaching* (3rd ed., pp. 214–229). New York: Macmillan.

Walberg, H. J. (1995). Generic practices. In G. Cawelti (ed.), *Handbook of research on improving student achievement* (pp. 7–19). Arlington, Va.: Educational Research Services.

Walker, D. F. (1992). Methodological issues in curriculum research. In P. W. Jackson (ed.), *Handbook of research on curriculum* (pp. 98–118). New York: Macmillan.

Wang, M. C.; Haertel, G. D.; and Walberg, H. J. (1993). Toward a knowledge base for school learning. *Review of Educational Research, 63,* 249–294.

Wang, M. C.; Reynolds, M. C.; and Walberg, H. J. (1995). Inner-city students at the margins. In M. C. Wang and M. C. Reynolds (eds.), *Making a difference for students at risk: Trends and alternatives* (pp. 1–26). Thousand Oaks, Calif.: Corwin.

Waxman, H. C., and Huang, S. L. (1997). Classroom instruction and learning environment differences between effective and ineffective urban elementary schools for African American students. *Urban Education, 32*(1), 7–44.

Waxman, H. C.; Huang, S. L.; Anderson, L.; and Weinstein, T. (1997). Investigating classroom processes in effective/efficient and ineffective/inefficient urban elementary schools. *Journal of Educational Research, 91,* 49–59.

Waxman, H. C.; Huang, S. L.; and Padrón, Y. N. (1995). Investigating the pedagogy of poverty in inner-city middle level schools. *Research in Middle Level Education, 18*(2), 1–22.

Waxman, H. C.; Padrón, Y. N.; and Knight, S. L. (1991). Risks associated with students' limited cognitive mastery. In M. C. Wang, M. C. Reynolds, and H. J. Walberg (eds.), *Handbook of special education: Emerging programs* (Vol. 4, pp. 235–254. Oxford, England: Pergamon.

Waxman, H. C., and Walberg, H. J. (1982). The relation of teaching and learning: A review of reviews of process-product research. *Contemporary Education Review, 1*, 103–120.

Part I
Reviews and Syntheses of Research on Teaching

1
Analyzing and Improving Teaching

Allan C. Ornstein

In this chapter, we present an overview of the research on effective teaching and five components of teaching that can be analyzed: teacher style, teacher interactions, teacher characteristics, teacher effects, and teacher contexts. In the early stages of research, up to the mid-1970s, the theorists were concerned with *teacher processes*—that is, what the teacher was doing while teaching. They attempted to define and explain good teaching by focusing on teacher styles, teacher interactions, and teacher characteristics. From about 1975 to 1990, researchers shifted their concerns to *teacher products*—that is, student outcomes—and the assessment focused on teacher effects. More recently, theorists are attempting to analyze the culture, language, and thoughts of teachers, combine (rather than separate) teaching and learning processes, and use qualitative methods to assess what they call *teacher contexts*.

Theorists are also searching for ways to improve teaching. Beginning teachers in particular should expect to encounter some problems and frustrations in the classroom, but with proper assistance they should be able to improve their technical skills over time. Improvement is linked to teacher feedback and evaluation, including peer evaluation, self-evaluation, and reflective evaluation.

REVIEW OF THE RESEARCH ON TEACHING

Over the years, thousands of studies have been conducted to identify the behaviors of successful teachers and of unsuccessful teachers. However, teaching is a complex act; what works in some situations with some students may not work in different school settings with different subjects, students, and goals. There will always be teachers who break many of the rules, procedures, and methods and yet are profoundly successful. There will always be teachers who follow the rules and are unsuccessful.

Biddle and Ellena (1964) maintain that we cannot distinguish between "good" and "poor" or "effective" and "ineffective" teachers, that no one knows for sure or agrees what the competent teacher is, that few authorities can "define, prepare for, or measure teacher competence" (p. 3). They point out that disagreement over terms, problems in measurement, and the complexity of the teaching act are major reasons for the negligible findings in judging teacher behavior. The result is, according to Jackson (1968) and Ornstein (1993), that much of the data have been confusing, contradictory, or confirmations of common sense (a democratic teacher is a good teacher), and that so-called acceptable findings have often been repudiated. The more complex or unpredictable one views teaching as being, the more one is compelled to conclude that it is difficult to agree on generalizations about successful teaching.

Other researchers (Brophy, 1986; Gage and Needels, 1989; Prawat, 1992; Schulman, 1988) assert that appropriate teaching behaviors can be defined (and learned by teachers), that good or effective teachers can be distinguished from poor or ineffective teachers, and that the magnitude of the effect of these differences on students can be determined. They conclude that the kinds of questions teachers ask, the ways they respond to students, their expectations of and attitudes toward students, their classroom-management techniques, their teaching methods, and their general teaching behaviors (sometimes referred to as "classroom climate") all make a difference.

However, in some cases the positive effects of teachers upon student performance may be masked or washed out by the relative negative effects of other teachers in the same schools. The teacher may not be the only variable, or even the major one, in the teaching-learning equation, but he or she can make a difference, either positive or negative. Here it should be noted that negative teacher influences have greater impact than do positive ones, in that students can be turned into nonlearners and experience loss of self-concept, composure, and focusing ability in a matter of weeks as a result of a hostile or intimidating teacher.

If teachers do not make a difference, then the profession has problems. For example, if teachers do not make a difference, the notions of teacher evaluation, teacher accountability, and teacher performance are nonworkable, sound educational policy cannot be formulated, and there is little hope for many students and little value in trying to learn how to teach. However, even if we are convinced that teachers have an effect, it is still true that we are unable to assess with confidence the influence a teacher has on student performance because the learning variables are numerous and the teaching interactions are complex.

TEACHER STYLES

Teaching style is a broad dimension or personality type that encompasses teacher stance, pattern of behavior, mode of performance, and attitude toward self and others. Peterson (1979) defines teacher style as how teachers utilize space in the classroom, their choice of instructional activities and materials, and their method of student grouping. Still others (Lytle and Cochran-Smith, 1992; Ornstein, 1990) describe teacher style as an *expressive* aspect of teaching (characterizing the emotional relationship between students and teachers, such as warm or businesslike) and as an *instrumental* aspect (how teachers carry out the task of instruction, organize learning, and set classroom standards).

Regardless of which definition of teacher style you prefer, the notion of stability or pattern is central. Certain behaviors and methods are stable over time, even with different students and different classroom situations. There is a purpose or rationale—a predictable teacher pattern even in different classroom contexts. Aspects of teaching style dictated by personality can be modified by early experiences and perceptions and by appropriate training as a beginning teacher. As years pass, a teacher's style becomes more ingrained, and it takes a more powerful set of stimuli and more intense feedback to make changes. If you watch teachers at work, including teachers in your school, you can sense that each one has a personal style for teaching, for structuring the classroom, and for delivering the lesson.

Research on Teacher Styles

Lippitt and White (1943) laid the groundwork for a more formal classification of what a teacher does in the classroom. Initially, they developed an instrument for describing the "social atmosphere" of children's clubs and for quantifying the effects of group and individual behaviors. The results have been generalized in numerous research studies and textbooks on teaching. The classic study used classifications of authoritarian, democratic, and laissez-faire styles.

The *authoritarian* teacher directs all the activities of the program. This style shares some characteristics with what is now called the *direct teacher*. The *democratic* teacher encourages group participation and is willing to let students share in the decision-making process. This behavior is typical of what is now called the *indirect teacher*. The *laissez-faire* teacher (now often considered to be an *unorganized* or *ineffective* teacher) provides no (or few) goals and directions for group or individual behavior.

One of the most ambitious research studies on teacher styles was conducted by Flanders (1965, 1970) and his associates between 1954 and 1970. Flanders focused on developing an instrument for quantifying verbal communication in the classroom. Every three seconds, observers sorted teacher talk into one of four categories of *indirect* behavior or one of three categories of *direct* behavior. Student talk was categorized as response or initiation, and there was a final category representing silence or when the observer could not determine who was talking. The ten categories are shown in Table 1-1.

Flanders' indirect teacher tended to overlap with Lippitt and White's democratic teacher, and the direct teacher tended to exhibit behaviors similar to their authoritarian teacher. Flanders found that students in the indirect classrooms learned more and exhibited more constructive and independent attitudes and that students in all types of subject classes learned more with the indirect (more flexible) teachers. In an interesting side note, Flanders found that as much as 80 percent of classroom time was consumed in teacher talk.

Table 1-1
Flanders' Classroom Interaction Analysis Scale

I. Teacher Talk
  A. Indirect Influence
    1. *Accepts Feelings.* Accepts and clarifies the tone of feeling of the students in an unthreatening manner. Feelings may be positive or negative. Predicting or recalling feelings are included.
    2. *Praises or Encourages.* Praises or encourages student action or behavior. Jokes that release tension, but not at the expense of another individual, nodding head or saying "um hm?" or "go on" are included.
    3. *Accepts or Uses Ideas of Student.* Clarifying building, or developing ideas suggested by a student. As teacher brings more of his own ideas into play, shift to category 5.
    4. *Asks Questions.* Asking a question about content or procedure, expressing his own ideas, asking rhetorical questions.
  B. Direct Influence
    5. *Lecturing.* Giving facts or opinions about content or procedure, expressing his own ideas, asking rhetorical questions.
    6. *Giving Directions.* Directions, commands, or orders that students are expected to comply with.
    7. *Criticizing or Justifying Authority.* Statements intended to change student behavior from unacceptable to acceptable pattern; bawling someone out; stating why the teacher is doing what he is doing; extreme self-reference.
II. Student Talk
    8. *Student Talk—Response.* Talk by student in response to teacher. Teacher initiates the contact or solicits student statement.
    9. *Student Talk—Initiation.* Talk initiated by students. If "calling on" student is only to indicate who may talk next, observer must decide whether student wanted to talk.
III. Silence
    10. *Silence or Confusion.* Pauses, short periods of silence and periods of confusion in which communication cannot be understood by the observer.

Source: Flanders (1965).

The data obtained from Flanders' system do not show when, why, or in what context teacher-student interaction occurs, only how often particular types of interaction occur. Nonetheless, the system is useful for making teachers aware of their interaction behaviors in the classroom.

The Flanders system can be used to examine teacher-student verbal behaviors in any classroom, regardless of grade level or subject. Someone can observe the verbal behavior of a prospective, the beginning, or even an experienced teacher and show how direct or indirect the teacher is. Most prospective and beginning teachers tend to exhibit direct behavior, since they talk too much. Professors also usually lecture and thus exhibit many direct behaviors while teaching. In fact, education students and student teachers often associate good teaching with some form of lecturing, since most of their recent teaching models are professors who often do a lot of talking—this is the wrong method to use with younger students, who lack the maturity, attentiveness, and focus to cope with a passive learning situation for any length of time. Beginning teachers, therefore, must often unlearn what they have learned in their experiences with their own professors. Table 1-2 helps new teachers supplement their pedagogical knowledge and practices by observing other good teachers. School administrators need to develop a policy that addresses how inexperienced teachers or those who need assistance can see how other teachers organize their classrooms and instruct their students. Table 1-2 provides a list of questions teachers can consider when observing other teachers.

TEACHER INTERACTION

One approach to the study of teacher behavior is based on systematic observation of *teacher-student interaction* in the classroom as, for example, in the work of Flanders, which we have already described. The analysis of interaction often deals with a specific teacher behavior and a series of these behaviors constituting a larger behavior, described and recorded by an abstract unit of measurement that may vary in size and time (for example, every three seconds a recording is made).

Verbal Communication

In a classic study of teacher-student interaction, Arno Bellack and colleagues analyzed the linguistic behavior of teachers and students in the classroom. Most classroom activities are carried out by verbal interaction between students and teachers; few classroom activities can be carried out without the use of language. The research, therefore, focused on language as the main instru-

Table 1-2
Observing Other Teachers to Improve Teaching Practices

Student-Teacher Interaction
- What evidence was there that the teacher understood the needs of the students?
- What techniques were used to encourage students' respect for each others' turn to talk?
- What student behaviors in class were acceptable and which were unacceptable?
- How did the teacher motivate students?
- How did the teacher encourage student discussion?
- In what way did the teacher see things from students' points of view?
- What evidence was there that the teacher responded to students' individual differences?
- What evidence was there that the teacher responded to students' affective development?

Teaching-Learning Processes
- Which instructional methods interested the students?
- How did the teacher provide for transitions between instructional activities?
- What practical life experiences (or activities) were used by the teacher to integrate concepts truly being learned?
- How did the teacher minimize student frustration or confusion concerning the skills or concepts being taught?
- In what way did the teacher encourage creative, imaginative work from students?
- What instructional methods were used to make students think about ideas, options, or answers?
- How did the teacher arrange the groups? What social factors were evident within groups?
- How did the teacher encourage independent (or individualized) student learning?
- How did the teacher integrate the subject matter with other subjects?

Classroom Environment
- How did the teacher use classroom space/equipment effectively?
- What did you like and dislike about the physical environment of the classroom?

---

ment of communication in teaching. Four basic verbal behaviors, or "moves," were labeled.

1. *Structuring moves* focus attention on subject matter or classroom procedures and begin interaction between students and teachers. They set the context for subsequent behavior. For example, beginning a class by announcing the topic to be discussed is a structuring move.

2. *Soliciting moves* are designed to elicit a verbal or physical response. For example, the teacher asks a question about the topic with the hope of encouraging a response from the students.
3. *Responding moves* occur in relation to and after the soliciting behaviors. Their ideal function is to fulfill the expectations of the soliciting behaviors.
4. *Reacting moves* are sometimes occasioned by one or more of the above behaviors, but are not directly elicited by them. Reacting behaviors serve to modify, clarify, or judge the structuring, soliciting, or responding behavior.

These pedagogical moves occur in combinations that Bellack calls *teaching cycles*. A cycle usually begins with a structuring or soliciting move by the teacher, both of which are initiative behaviors; continues with a responding move from a student; and ends with some kind of reacting move by the teacher. In most cases, the cycle begins and ends with the teacher. The investigators' analysis of the classroom also produced several insights:

1. Teachers dominate verbal activities. The teacher-student ratio in words spoken is 3 to 1. (This evidence corresponds with Flanders' finding that teachers' talk is 80 percent of classroom activity.)
2. Teachers and student moves are clearly defined. The teacher engages in structuring, soliciting, and reacting behaviors, while the student is usually limited to responding. (This also corresponds with Flanders' finding that most teachers dominate classrooms in such a way as to make students dependent.)
3. Teachers initiate about 85 percent of the cycles. The basic unit of verbal interaction is a soliciting-responding pattern. Verbal interchanges occur at a rate of slightly less than two cycles per minute.
4. In approximately two-thirds of the behaviors and three-fourths of the verbal interplay, talk is content-oriented.
5. About 60 percent of the total discourse is fact-oriented.

In summary, the data suggest that the classroom is teacher-dominated, subject-centered, and fact-oriented. The student's primary responsibility seems to be to respond to the teacher's soliciting behaviors. To be sure, teachers need to break this cycle of teaching.

In another study, Smith and Meux (1970) focused on the linguistic behavior of the teacher. Teacher linguistic behavior was divided into "episodes" and "monologues." The *teacher episode* is defined as one or more verbal exchanges between two or more speakers. Questions by the teacher and answers by the students constitute the most common episode. The *teacher monologue* consists of a solo performance by a speaker addressing the group; the teacher who gives directions or a command is engaged in a monologue. Effective teachers tend to engage in episodes. The ideal episode seems to be an exchange in which several speakers respond to an original question or statement. Thus the most effective linguistic behavior is not teacher to student or student to teacher, but teacher to several students.

A series of episodes or monologues form a "cycle" that includes one or more of several verbal entries (that is, questions or statements that initiate the exchange):

1. *Defining* entries are concerned with how words are used to refer to objects: "What does the word _____ mean?"
2. *Describing* entries ask for an explanation or description about something: "What did John find out?"
3. *Designating* entries identify something by name: "What mountain range did we see in the film?"
4. *Stating* entries involve statements of issues, proofs, rules, theories, conclusions, beliefs, and so on: "What is the plot of the story?"
5. *Reporting* entries ask for a summary or a report on a book or document: "Can you summarize the major points of the book?"
6. *Substituting* entries require the performance of a symbolic operation, usually of mathematic or scientific value: "Who can write the equation on the chalkboard?"
7. *Evaluating* entries ask for judgment or estimate of worth of something: "Would you like to assess the validity of the argument?"
8. *Opinioning* entries ask for a conclusion, affirmation, or denial based on evidence: "How do you feel President Clinton will be judged by historians?"

Most beginning teachers, and even a large percentage of experienced teachers, interact with their students at the first three levels of verbal entries—that is, defining, describing, and designating. This leads to the teaching of knowledge and facts, not higher-order thinking. Good teaching requires reflection, and it is important for beginning teachers to become aware of these methods of verbal communications and incorporate more-sophisticated questions or statements into their teaching (levels four to eight).

Nonverbal Communication

According to Patterson (1983), nonverbal behavior in the classroom serves five teacher functions: (1) *providing information*, or elaborating on a verbal statement; (2) *regulating interactions*, such as pointing to someone; (3) *expressing intimacy or liking*, such as smiling or touching a student on the shoulder; (4) *exercising social control*, reinforcing a classroom rule, say, by proximity or distance, and (5) *facilitating goals*, as when demonstrating a skill that requires motor activity or gesturing. These categories are not mutually exclusive; there is some overlap, and nonverbal cues may serve more than one function depending on how they are used.

Although the teaching-learning process is ordinarily associated with verbal interaction, nonverbal communication operates as a silent language that influences the process. What makes the study of nonverbal communication so important and fascinating is that some researchers (Siegman and Feldstein, 1978) contend that it constitutes about 65 percent of the social meaning of the classroom communication system. As the old saying goes, "Action speaks louder than words."

In a study of 225 teachers (and school principals) in 45 schools, Stephens and Valentine (1986) observed 10 specific nonverbal behaviors: (1) smiles or frowns, (2) eye contact, (3) head nods, (4) gestures, (5) dress, (6) interaction distance, (7) touch, (8) body movement, (9) posture, and (10) seating arrangements. In general, the first four behaviors are easily interpreted by the observer; some smiles, eye contact, head nods, and gestures are expected, but too many make students suspicious or uneasy. Dress is a matter of professional code and expectation. Distance, touch, body movement, posture, and seating are open to more interpretation, are likely to have personal meaning between communicators, and are based on personalities and social relationships.

Different types of these five behaviors, especially distance, touch, and body movement, can be taken as indications of the degree of formality in the relationship between the communicators, from

Analyzing and Improving Teaching 27

intimate and personal to social and public. Teachers should maintain a social or public relationship—that is, a formal relationship—with their students. Behaviors that are appropriate to, or could be interpreted as indicating, intimate and personal relations must be avoided. It is difficult to define the point in student-teacher relationship where friendliness can be misconstrued. To some extent that point differs for different students and teachers. It is fine to be warm, friendly, and caring—but too much warmth or friendliness in your interaction (distance, touch, body movement, posture) can get you into trouble as a teacher. Teachers need to be aware of the messages they are sending to the students, especially if the students are teenagers and the teachers are in their twenties.

According to Galloway (1968, 1984), when the teacher's verbal and nonverbal cues contradict one another, the students tend to read the nonverbal cues as a true reflection of the teacher's feelings. Galloway developed global guidelines for observing nonverbal communication of teachers, which he referred to as the "silent behavior of space, time, and body."

1. *Space.* A teacher's use of space conveys meaning to students. For example, teachers who spend most of their time by the chalkboard or at their desk may convey insecurity, a reluctance to venture into student territory.
2. *Time.* How teachers use classroom time is an indication of how they value certain instructional activities. The elementary teacher who devotes a great deal of time to reading but little to science is conveying a message about the preference of subjects to the students.
3. *Body awareness.* Nonverbal cues are used by teachers to control students. The raised eyebrow, the pointed finger, the silent stare all communicate meaning.

Galloway suggests that various nonverbal behaviors of the teacher can be viewed as encouraging or restricting. By their facial expression, gestures, and body movements, teachers affect student participation and performance in the classroom. Whether you realize it or not, these nonverbal behaviors—ranging from highly focused to minimal eye contact, a pat on the back to a frown, a supporting to an angry look—all add up to suggest approval and support or irritability or discouragement. In sum, these nonbehaviors influence teacher-student interactions. What teachers should do, both in their personal and professional pursuits, is to become aware of how their mannerisms influence their communication and relations with others.

Teacher Expectations

Teachers communicate their expectations of students through verbal and nonverbal cues. It has been well established that these expectations affect the interaction between teachers and students and, eventually, the performance of students. In many cases, teacher expectations become *self-fulfilling prophecies*; that is, if the teacher expects students to be slow or exhibit deviant behavior, the teacher treats them accordingly, and in response students adopt such behaviors.

The research on teacher expectations is rooted in the legal briefs and arguments Clark (1965) prepared during his fight for desegregated schools in the 1950s and in subsequent descriptions of the problem in New York City's Harlem schools. He pointed out that prophesying low achievement for black students not only provides teachers with an excuse for their students' failure but also communicates a sense of inevitable failure to the students.

Clark's thesis was given empirical support a few years later by Rosenthal and Jacobsen's (1968) *Pygmalion in the Classroom*, a study of students in the San Francisco schools. After controlling for the ability of students, experimenters told teachers there was reason to expect that certain students would perform better— and that expectancy was fulfilled. However, confidence in *Pygmalion* diminished when Thorndike (1968), a respected measurement expert, pointed out that there were several flaws in the methodology and that the tests were unreliable.

Interest in teacher expectations and self-fulfilling prophecy reappeared in the 1970s and 1980s. Cooper (1979) and Cooper and Good (1983) outlined how teachers communicate expectations to students and in turn influence student behavior:

1. The teacher expects specific achievement and behavior from particular students.
2. Because of these different expectations, the teacher behaves differently toward various students.
3. This interaction suggests to students what achievement and behavior the teacher expects from them, which affects their self-concepts, motivation, and performance.

4. If the teacher's interaction is consistent over time, it will shape the student's achievement and behavior. High expectations for students will influence achievement at high levels, and low expectations will produce lower achievement.
5. With time, student achievement and behavior will conform more and more to the original expectations of the teacher.

Beyond the above research summary, the most effective teacher is realistic about the differences between high and low achievers. The teacher who develops a rigid or stereotyped perception of students is likely to have a harmful effect on them. The teacher who understands that differences exist and adapts realistic methods and content accordingly will have the most positive effect on students.

Labeling Students

More recently, Kagan (1990, 1992) outlined a comprehensive model of how teachers (and students) alienate low achievers by making assumptions about their behavior and achievement, thus labeling and tracking them into a second-class status in classrooms and schools. Once a label is attached to a student, according to Kagan, the teacher tends to adjust teaching methods so that they are consistent with the label ("underachiever," "slow learner," "disabled learner"). The anticipation and expectations associated with the label constitute a "rational response" by the teacher in understanding and reacting to the students. This "typing" of students is often reinforced by school specialists, counselors, and psychologists, which in turn has a reinforcing effect on the teacher's perceptions and an overwhelming effect on the student.

It is little wonder, then, that some theorists such as Ogbu (1994, 1995) attribute the academic failure of some black students to an oppositional cultural frame of reference, an oppositional identity, and a continuous distrust of white educators. As some researchers (Knapp and Shields, 1990; Wehlage and Rutter, 1986) point out, dropping out of school for some low achievers and minority students might be regarded as a process of disengagement from school, a means of preserving one's own personal and cultural identity, and a way of alleviating the negative effects associated with low self-concept, low motivation, and low achievement—and only secondarily fulfilling the expectations associated with school failure.

But a dilemma evolves in helping teachers work with low achievers and with culturally diverse students. Generalizations are needed to inform teachers about various instructional methods and techniques that can be applied to students with differing backgrounds. On the other hand, a universal concept of multicultural education exposes teachers to the problems inherent in prejudging individuals on the basis of membership of a particular group (McDiarmid, 1992; Wang, Reynolds, and Walberg, 1995). Thus we raise a number of questions to consider in the context of teacher expectations and views of teaching low achievers or minority groups. How can educators avoid the dangers inherent in generalizing about low achievers or diverse cultural groups? Given educators' own prior experiences, how can they be objective in examining their own view about low achievers or culturally different students? How does the teacher's attitude affect teacher behavior and teacher-student interaction?

TEACHER CHARACTERISTICS

In the reams of research published on teacher behavior, most concerns teacher characteristics. The problem is that researchers disagree on which teacher characteristics constitute successful teaching, on how to categorize characteristics, and on how to define them. In addition, researchers use a variety of terms to name what they are trying to describe, such as "teacher traits," "teacher personality," "teacher performance," or "teacher outcomes." Descriptors or characteristics have different meanings to different people. "Warm" behavior for one investigator often means something different for another, just as the effects of such behavior may be seen differently. For example, it can be assumed that a warm teacher would have a different effect on students depending on the students' age, sex, achievement level, socioeconomic class, and ethnic group and on the subject and classroom context (Ornstein, 1985, 1990).

Such differences tend to operate for every teacher characteristic and to affect every study on teacher behavior. Although a list of teacher characteristics may be suitable for a particular study, the characteristics (as well as results) cannot always be compared with another study. Yet, as Schulman (1986, 1991) points out, researchers of teacher behavior often disregard factors such as the time of day, school year, and content, and combine data from an early observation with the data from a later occasion. Data from the early part of the school term may be combined with the data from the latter part of the term; data from one unit of content (which may require different teacher behaviors or techniques) are combined with those from other units of content. All these aggregations assume that instances of teaching over time can be summed to have equal weights, which is rarely the case. The accuracy issue is further clouded when such studies are compared, integrated, and built on each other to form a theory or viewpoint about which teacher characteristics are most effective.

Despite such cautions, many researchers feel that certain teacher characteristics can be defined, validated, and generalized from one study to another. In turn, recommendations can be made from such generalizations for use in a practical way in the classroom and elsewhere.

Research on Teacher Characteristics

Although researchers have named literally thousands of teacher characteristics over the years, Barr (1958) organized recommended behaviors into a manageable list. Reviewing some fifty years of research, he listed and defined twelve successful characteristics (Table 1-3). Other authorities have made other summaries of teacher characteristics, but Barr's work is considered most comprehensive.

While Barr presented an overview of hundreds of studies of teacher characteristics, the single most comprehensive study was conducted by Ryans (1960). More than 6,000 teachers in 1,700 schools were involved in the study over a six-year period. The objective was to identify through observations and self-ratings the most desirable teacher characteristics. Ryans developed a bipolar list of eighteen teacher characteristics (for example, original versus conventional, patient versus impatient, hostile versus warm). Respondents were asked to identify the approximate position of teachers for each pair of characteristics on a seven-point scale. (A seven-point scale makes it easier for raters to avoid midpoint responses and nonpositions.) The eighteen teacher characteristics were defined in detail and further grouped into three "patterns" of successful versus unsuccessful teachers:

Table 1-3
Characteristics Important for Successful Teaching

1. *Resourcefulness.* Originality, creativeness, initiative, imagination, adventurous, progressiveness
2. *Intelligence.* Foresight, intellectual acuity, understanding, mental ability, intellectual capacity, common sense
3. *Emotional stability.* Poise, self-control, steadfastness, sobriety, dignity, no neuroticism, emotional maturity, adjustment, constancy, loyalty, easygoing realism in facing life, not excitable, stable, integrated character
4. *Considerateness.* Appreciativeness, kindliness, friendliness, courteousness, sympathy, tact, good-naturedness, helpfulness, patience, politeness, thoughtfulness, tolerance
5. *Buoyancy.* Optimism, enthusiasm, cheerfulness, gregariousness, fluency, talkativeness, sense of humor, pleasantness, carefreeness, vivaciousness, alertness, animation, idealism, articulativeness, expressiveness, wit
6. *Objectivity.* Fairness, impartiality, open-mindedness, freedom from prejudice, sense of justice
7. *Drive.* Physical vigor, energy, perseverance, ambition, industry, endurance, motivation, purposefulness, speediness, zealousness, quickness
8. *Dominance.* Self-confidence, forcefulness, decisiveness, courageousness, independence, insensitiveness to social approval, self-sufficiency, determination, thick-skinnedness, self-reliance, self-assertiveness
9. *Attractiveness.* Dress, physique, freedom from physical defects, personal magnetism, neatness, cleanliness, posture, personal charm, appearance
10. *Refinement.* Good taste, modesty, morality, conventionality, culture, polish, well-readness
11. *Cooperativeness.* Friendliness, easy-goingness, geniality, generosity, adaptability, flexibility, responsiveness, trustfulness, warm-heartedness, unselfishness, charitableness
12. *Reliability.* Accuracy, dependability, honesty, responsibility, conscientiousness, painstakingness, trustworthiness, consistency, sincerity

Source: Barr (1958).

1. *Pattern X:* understanding, friendly, and responsive versus aloof and egocentric
2. *Pattern Y:* responsible, businesslike, and systematic versus evading and unplanned, slipshod
3. *Pattern Z:* stimulating, imaginative, and original versus dull and routine

Analyzing and Improving Teaching

These three primary teacher patterns were the major qualities singled out for further attention. Elementary teachers scored higher than secondary teachers on scales of understanding and friendly classroom behavior (Pattern X). Differences between women and men teachers were insignificant in the elementary schools, but in the secondary schools women consistently scored higher in Pattern X and in stimulating and imaginative classroom behavior (Pattern Z), and men tended to exhibit businesslike and systematic behaviors (Pattern Y). Younger teachers (under age forty-five) scored higher than older teachers in patterns X and Z; older teachers scored higher in pattern Y.

A similar but more recent list of teacher characteristics was compiled by Tuckman (1991, 1995a), who has developed a feedback system for stimulating change in teacher behavior. His instrument, which originally contained twenty-eight bipolar items, was expanded to thirty items (for example, creative versus routinized, cautious versus outspoken, assertive versus passive, quiet versus bubbly) on which teachers were also rated on a seven-point scale.

TEACHER EFFECTS

Research on teacher behavior has shown that teacher behaviors, as well as specific teaching principles and methods, affect student achievement. Rosenshine and Furst (1971, 1973) analyzed some forty-two correlational studies in their often-quoted review of process-product research. They concluded that there were eleven teacher processes (behaviors or variables) strongly and consistently related to products (outcomes or student achievement). The first five teacher processes showed the strongest correlation to positive outcomes:

1. *Clarity* of teacher's presentation and ability to organize classroom activities
2. *Variability* of media, materials, and activities used by the teacher
3. *Enthusiasm,* defined in terms of the teacher's movement, voice inflection, and the like
4. *Task orientation* or businesslike teacher behaviors, structures, routines, and academic focus

5. *Student opportunity to learn*, that is, the teacher's coverage of the material or content in class on which students are later tested.

The six remaining processes were classified as promising: using student ideas, justified criticism, using structuring comments, asking appropriate questions suited to students' cognitive levels, probing or encouraging student elaboration, and using challenging instructional materials.

Rosenshine (1979) later reviewed his previous conclusions and found that only two behaviors or processes consistently correlated with student achievement: (1) task orientation (later referred to as *direct instruction*), and (2) opportunity to learn (later referred to as *academic time, academic engaged time,* and *content covered*). On a third behavior, clarity, he wavered, pointing out that it seemed to be a correlate of student achievement for students above the fifth grade. The other eight processes appeared to be less important and varied in importance not only according to grade level but also according to subject matter, instructional groups and activities, and students' social class and abilities. Nevertheless, the original review remains a valuable study on how teacher behaviors relate to student products.

The Gage Model

Gage (1978) analyzed forty-nine process-product studies. He identified four clusters of behaviors that show a strong relationship to student outcomes: (1) *teacher indirectness*, the willingness to accept students' ideas and feelings, and the ability to provide a healthy emotional climate; (2) *teacher praise*, support and encouragement, use of humor to release tensions (but not at the expense of others), and attention to students' needs; (3) *teacher acceptance*, and clarifying, building, and developing students' ideas; and (4) *teacher criticism*, reprimanding students, and justifying authority. The relationship between the last cluster and outcome was negative—where criticism occurred, student achievement was low. In effect, the four clusters suggest the traditional notion that a democratic or warm teacher (a model emphasized for several decades) enhances student achievement.

From the evidence on teacher effects on student achievement in reading and mathematics in the elementary grades, Gage presented successful teaching principles and methods that seem

Analyzing and Improving Teaching

relevant for other grades as well. These commonsense strategies are summarized below. They apply to many grade levels, and most experienced teachers are familiar with them. Nonetheless, they provide guidelines for education students or beginning teachers who say, "Just tell me how to teach."

1. Teachers should have a system of rules that allows students to attend to their personal and procedural needs without having to check with the teacher.
2. A teacher should move around the room, monitoring students' seatwork and communicating an awareness of their behavior while also attending to their academic needs.
3. To ensure productive independent work by students, teachers should be sure that the assignments are interesting and worthwhile, yet still easy enough to be completed by each student without teacher direction.
4. Teachers should keep to a minimum such activities as giving directions and organizing the class for instruction. Teachers can do this by writing the daily schedule on the board and establishing general procedures so that students know where to go and what to do.
5. In selecting students to respond to questions, teachers should call on volunteers and nonvolunteers by name before asking questions to give all students a chance to answer and to alert the students to be called on.[1]
6. Teachers should always aim at getting less academically oriented students to give some kind of response to a question. Rephrasing, giving cues, or asking leading questions can be useful techniques for bringing forth some answer from a silent student, one who says "I don't know," or one who answers incorrectly.
7. During reading group instruction, teachers should give a maximum of brief feedback and provide fast-paced activities of the "drill" type.

---

1. This author disagrees with this item. Most good teachers first ask the question, then call on a student so that everyone in the class is required to listen; hence, no one knows who the teacher will call on.

The Good and Brophy Model

Over the last twenty years, Good and Brophy (1986) have identified several factors related to effective teaching and student learning. They focus on basic principles of teaching, but not teacher behaviors or characteristics, since both researchers contend that teachers today are looking more for principles of teaching than for prescriptions. These principles are

1. *Clarity* about instructional goals (objectives).
2. Knowledge about *content* and ways for teaching it.
3. *Variety* in the use of teaching methods and media.
4. "*With-it-ness*," awareness of what is going on, alertness in monitoring classroom activities.
5. "*Overlapping*," sustaining an activity while doing something else at the same time.
6. "*Smoothness*," sustaining proper lesson pacing and group momentum, not dwelling on minor points or wasting time dealing with individuals, and focusing on all students.
7. *Seatwork* instructions and management that initiate and focus on productive task engagement.
8. Holding students *accountable* for learning; accepting responsibility for student learning.
9. *Realistic expectations* in line with student abilities and behaviors.
10. *Realistic praise*, not praise for its own sake.
11. *Flexibility* in planning and adapting classroom activities.
12. *Task orientation* and businesslike behavior in the teacher.
13. *Monitoring* of students' understanding, providing appropriate feedback, giving praise, asking questions.
14. Providing students the *opportunity to learn* what is to be tested.
15. Making comments that help *structure learning* of knowledge and concepts for students; helping students learn how to learn.

Many of these behaviors are classroom management techniques and structured learning strategies, which suggests that good discipline is a prerequisite for good teaching—at least in the schools in which Good and Brophy conducted their research.

The Emmer and Evertson Model

The Emmer and Evertson model (1994) is similar to that of Good and Brophy (in fact, Evertson has written several papers and articles with Brophy). The models are similar in three ways: (1) teacher effectiveness is associated with specific teaching principles and methods, (2) organization and management of instructional activities is stressed, and (3) findings and conclusions are based primarily on process-product studies.

Nine basic teaching principles represent the core of Evertson's work with Emmer (and, to a lesser extent, with Brophy). Effectiveness is identified as raising student achievement scores.

1. *Rules and procedures.* Rules and procedures are established and enforced and students are monitored for compliance.
2. *Consistency.* Similar expectations are maintained for activities and behavior at all times for all students. Inconsistency causes confusion in students about what is acceptable.
3. *Prompt management of inappropriate behavior.* Inappropriate behavior is attended to quickly to stop it and prevent its spread.
4. *Checking student work.* All student work, including seatwork, homework, and papers, is corrected, errors are discussed, and feedback is provided promptly.
5. *Interaction teaching.* This takes several forms and includes presenting and explaining new materials, question sessions, discussions, checking for student understanding, actively moving among students to correct work, providing feedback, and, if necessary, reteaching materials.
6. *Academic instruction,* sometimes referred to as "academic learning time" or "academic engaged time." Attention is focused on the management of student work.
7. *Pacing.* Information is presented at a rate appropriate to the students' ability to comprehend it, not too rapidly or too slowly.
8. *Transitions.* Transitions from one activity to another are made rapidly, with minimal confusion about what to do next.
9. *Clarity.* Lessons are presented logically and sequentially. Clarity is enhanced by the use of instructional objectives and adequate illustrations and by keeping in touch with students.

The Master Teacher

The national interest in education reform and excellence in teaching has focused considerable attention on teachers and the notion of the master teacher. The direct behaviors suggested by the previous Good, Brophy, and Evertson models corresponded with Doyle's (1985, 1992) description of a master teacher as task-oriented and businesslike. Such teachers "focus on academic goals, are careful and explicit in structuring activities..., promote high levels of student academic involvement and content coverage, furnish opportunities for controlled practice with feedback, hold students accountable for work,... have expectations that they will be successful in helping students learn, [and are] active in explaining concepts and procedures, promoting meaning and purpose for academic work, and monitoring comprehension" (Doyle, 1985, p. 30).

When 641 elementary and secondary teachers were asked to "rate criteria for recognition of a master teacher," they listed, in rank order: (1) knowledge of subject matter, (2) encourages student achievement through positive reinforcement, (3) uses a variety of strategies and materials to meet the needs of all students, (4) maintains an organized and disciplined classroom, (5) stimulates students' active participation in classroom activities, (6) maximizes student instruction time, (7) has high expectations of student performance, and (8) frequently monitors student progress and provides feedback regarding performance (Azumi and Lerman, 1987).

Although the sample of teachers was predominantly female (71 percent), which could support the idea that the recommended behaviors reflect female norms, it must be noted that the teaching profession is predominantly female (67 percent, according to survey data from the National Education Association). Most important, the teachers surveyed were experienced (77 percent had been teaching for at least eleven years) and their rank-order list of criteria corresponds closely to Doyle's notion of master teacher.

Based on a study of several hundred teachers who teach in multiracial and multilinguistic schools, Haberman (1992, 1995) developed a portrait of "star" urban teachers that revealed a host of behaviors and attitudes unlike what many educators say makes master or effective teachers. Star teachers develop an ideology—that is, a pervasive way of believing and acting. These teachers do not use theory to guide their practice; they do not refer to the axioms or principles of Piaget, Skinner, or the like. Star teachers do not consider the research on teacher effectiveness or school effectiveness. They are generally oblivious to and unconcerned with how researchers or experts in various subjects organize the content in their disciplines. Rather, they have internalized their own view of teaching, their own practices through experience and self-discovery. Star teachers reflect on what they are doing in the classroom, why they are doing it, and the best way to do it. These teachers are also guided by the expectations that inner-city and poor children can learn, think, and reflect.

To the casual observer it may seem that teachers generally perform like one another. From the data, we might infer that star teachers or master teachers are different from the average; they have a well-thought-out ideology that gives their performance a different meaning. They appear to be mavericks (or at least atypical) and confident in the way they organize and operate their own classrooms. They are sensitive to their students and teach in ways that make sense to their students, not necessarily according to what researchers or administrators and colleagues have to say about teaching. These teachers seem to be driven by their own convictions of what is right and not by how others interpret the teacher's role and teacher's pedagogy.

Cautions and Criticisms

Although the notions of teacher competencies and teacher effectiveness are often identified as something new in research efforts to identify good teaching, they are nothing more than a combination of teaching principles and methods that good teachers have been using for many years prior to this recent wave of research. What these product-oriented researchers have accomplished is to summarize what we have known for a long time, but often passed on in the form of "tips for teachers" or practical suggestions that were once criticized by researchers as being recipe oriented. They give credibility to teaching practices by correlating teacher behaviors (processes) to student achievement (products). Product-oriented researchers also dispel the notion that teachers have little or no measurable effect on student achievement.

However, there is some danger in this product-oriented research. The conclusions overwhelmingly portray the effective teacher as task-oriented, organized, and structured (nothing more than Ryans' Pattern Y teacher). But the teacher-competency and teacher-effectiveness models tend to overlook the friendly, warm, and democratic teacher; the creative teacher who is stimulating and imaginative; the dramatic teacher who bubbles with energy and enthusiasm; the philosophical teacher who encourages students to play with ideas and concepts; and the problem-solving teacher who requires that students think out the answers. In the product-oriented researchers' desire to identify and prescribe behaviors that are measurable and quantifiable, they overlook the emotional, qualitative, and interpretive descriptions of classrooms, and the joys of teaching. Most of their research has been conducted at the elementary grade levels, where one would expect more social, psychological, and humanistic factors to be observed, recorded, and recommended as effective. A good portion of their work also deals with low achievers and at-risk students—perhaps the reason many of their generalizations or principles coincide with classroom management and structured and controlling techniques.

The teacher-effectiveness models also fail to consider that a good deal of effective teaching may not directly correlate with student achievement. For Greene (1986, 1988) good teaching and learning involve values, experiences, insights, imagination, and appreciation—the "stuff" that cannot be easily observed or measured. For her, teaching and learning are an existential encounter, a philosophical process involving ideas and creative inquiries that cannot be easily quantified.

We might add that much of teaching involves caring, nurturing, and valuing behaviors—attributes that are not easily assessed by evaluation instruments. Eisner (1994) is concerned that what is not measurable goes unnoticed in product-oriented teaching models. By breaking down the teaching act into behaviors and competencies and criteria that can be defined operationally and quantified, educators overlook the hard-to-measure aspects, such as the personal, humanistic, and playful aspects of teaching. To say that excellence in teaching requires measurable behaviors and outcomes is to miss a substantial part of teaching—what some educators refer to as artistry, drama, tones, and flavor.

Teacher behaviors that correlate with measurable outcomes often lead to rote learning, learning "bits" and not wholes, memorization, and automatic responses, and not to higher-order learning. The product models also seem to miss moral and ethical outcomes, as well as social, personal, and self-actualizing factors related to learning and life—in effect, the affective domain of learning and the psychology of being human. In their attempt to observe and measure what teachers do, and to detail whether students improve their performance on reading or math tests, these models ignore the learner's imagination, fantasy, and intuitive thinking—their dreams, hopes, and aspirations—and how teachers affect these hard-to-define but very important aspects of the student's life. Learning experiences that deal with character, spiritual outlook, and philosophy are absent (Ornstein, 1991, 1995a).

The new and popular teacher-effectiveness models lock us into a narrow mold that misses many nuances of teaching. Many of these prescriptions (which the researchers call principles) themselves are old ideas bottled under new labels such as "with-it-ness," "smoothness," or "clarity." They seem to confirm what effective teachers have been doing for many years, but the confirmation is needed so that beginning teachers have a better yardstick or starting point.

TEACHER CONTEXTS: NEW PARADIGMS

For the last fifty years or more, research on teacher behavior has been linear and category-based, focused on specific teacher styles, interactions, characteristics, or effects. It focused either on the *process* of teaching (how the teacher was behaving in the classroom) or on the *products* of teaching (that is, student outcomes). Through the 1990s, the research on teaching has been examining the multifaceted nature and context of teaching, including the relationship of teaching and learning, the subject-matter knowledge of the teacher, how knowledge is taught, and how knowledge relates to pedagogy.

The new emphasis on teaching goes beyond what the teacher is doing and explores teacher thinking from the perspective of teachers themselves. The teacher is depicted as one who copes with a complex environment and simplifies it, mainly through experience, by attending to a small number of important tasks, and synthesizing various kinds of information that continually evolve. The impact of professional knowledge (that is, knowing *what* you know, and how well you know it) is now considered important for defining how teachers and students construct meaning for their respective academic roles and perform tasks related to those roles.

An alternative for understanding the nature of teaching has evolved—one that combines teaching and learning processes, incorporates holistic practices, and goes beyond what teachers and students appear to be doing and inquires about what they are thinking. This model relies on language and dialogue, not on mathematical or statistical symbols, to provide the conceptual categories and organize the data. It uses the approaches that reformers, reconceptualists, and postliberal theoreticians have advocated: metaphors, stories, biographies and autobiographies, conversations (with experts), and voices (or narratives). Such research, which has surfaced within the last ten years, looks at teaching "from the inside." It focuses on the personal and practical knowledge of teachers, the culture of teaching, and the language and thoughts of teachers.

Metaphors

Teachers' knowledge, including the way they speak about teaching, exists not only in prepositional form but also includes figurative language or metaphors. The thinking of teachers consists of personal experiences, images, and jargon, and therefore figurative language is central to the expression and understanding of teachers' knowledge of pedagogy.

Metaphors of space and time figure in teachers' descriptions of their work ("pacing a lesson," "covering the content," "moving on to the next part of the lesson"). The studies on teacher style, examined earlier in this chapter, represent concepts and beliefs about teachers that can be considered as metaphors: the teacher as a "boss," "coach," "comedian," or "maverick." The notions of a "master" teacher, "lead" teacher, "star" teacher, or "expert" teacher are also metaphors, or descriptors, used by current researchers to describe outstanding or effective teachers.

Metaphors are used by a person to explain or interpret reality. In traditional literature, this process of understanding evolves through experience and study—without the influence of researchers' personal or cultural biases. But the use of metaphors can also be conceptualized in the literature of sociology to include ideas, values, and behaviors that derive in part from a person's position within the political and economic order. Similarly, critical pedagogists and liberal theorists such as Banks (1993) and Giroux (1992) argue that personal and cultural factors such as gender, class, and caste influence the formation of knowledge, especially metaphors as well as behavior.

Stories

Increasingly, researchers are telling stories about teachers—their work and how they teach—and teachers are telling stories about their own teaching experiences. Most stories are narrative and descriptive, and their language is rich. Stories about teachers make a point about teaching that would otherwise be difficult to convey with traditional research methods. The stories told reflect the belief that there is much to learn from "authentic" teachers who tell their stories about experiences they might otherwise keep to themselves or fail to convey to others (Elbaz, 1991).

Stories have an important social and psychological meaning. Stories of teachers allow us to see connections between the practice of teaching and the human side of teaching. The stories of individual teachers allow us to see their knowledge and skills enacted in the real world of classrooms, and lead us to appreciate their emotional and moral encounters with the lives of the people they teach.

Stories by teachers such as Bel Kaufman, Herbert Kohl, Jonathan Kozol, and Sylvia Ashton-Warner have become bestsellers because of their rich descriptions of the very stuff of teaching and personal narratives. These stories are aesthetic and emotional landscapes of teaching and learning that would be missed by clinically based process-product research studies of teacher effectiveness. Still, others criticize such personal teacher stories for lacking scholarly reliability and accuracy—flaws they see as grounded in egoism or exaggeration (Ornstein, 1995a, b).

Stories of teachers by researchers are less descriptive, less emotional, and less well known. Nevertheless, they are still personal and rich encounters of teachers. They provide us with a view of teachers' knowledge and experiences, not quite in their own terms, but in a deep way that helps us understand what teaching is all about. These stories provide unusual opportunities to get to know and respect teachers as persons, on an emotional as well as intellectual level. Most important, these stories represent an important shift in the way researchers are willing to convey teachers' pedagogy and understanding of teaching. However, some researchers point out that observers and authors construct different realities, so that different storytellers could write very different versions of the same teacher. But the author is only one variable. Subject matter, students, and school settings could lead to striking contrast in portrayal and interpretation of the same teacher.

Biographies and Autobiographies

Stories written by researchers about teachers tend to be biographical, and stories written by teachers about themselves tend to autobiographical. Both biography and autobiography encompass a "whole story" and represent the full depth and breadth of a person's experience to make present action meaningful—that is, knowledge of a person's past experiences helps us to understand his or her present experiences.

The essence of an autobiography is that it provides an opportunity for people to convey what they know and have been doing for years, and what is inside their heads, unshaped by others. Whereas the biography is ultimately filtered and interpreted by a second party, the autobiography permits the author (in this case the teacher) to present the information in a personal way in his or her own terms.

As human beings, we all have stories to tell. Each person has a distinctive biography or autobiography, which is shaped by a host of experiences and practices and a particular standpoint or way of looking at the world. For teachers, this suggests a particular set of teaching experiences and practices, as well as a particular style of teaching and pedagogy.

Researchers (Grant, 1991; Solas, 1992) inform us that biographies and autobiographies of teachers may be described as the life story of one teacher who is the central character based in a particular classroom or school, and of the classroom dynamics and school drama that unfold around the individual. These types of stories are concerned with longitudinal aspects of personal and professional experiences that can bring much detailed and insightful information to the reader. They help us reconstruct teachers' and students' experiences that would not be available to us by reading typical professional literature on teaching.

The accounts in biographies and autobiographies suggest that the author is in a position of "authority" with respect to the particular segment of the life being described—hence the thoughts and experiences of the author take on a sense of reality and objectivity not always assumed in other stories. However, when teachers write an autobiography (as opposed to someone else writing the story in biography form), they risk being considered partial or writing self-serving descriptions of their teaching prowess.

Thus Grumet (1987) suggests that researchers publish multiple accounts of teachers' knowledge and pedagogy, instead of a single narrative. The problem is that this approach suggests taking stories out of the hand of the teachers. Joint publication between teachers and researchers may be appropriate in some situations and a method for resolving this problem.

The Expert Teacher

The expert-teacher concept involves new research procedures—such as simulations, videotapes, and case studies—and a new language to describe the work, prestige, and authority of teachers (Welker, 1992). The research usually consists of small samples and in-depth studies (the notion of complete lessons and analysis of what transpired), in which expert (sometimes experienced) teachers are distinguished from novice (sometimes beginning) teachers. Experts usually are identified through administrator nominations, student achievement scores, or teacher awards (like Teacher of the Year). Novices commonly are selected from groups of student teachers or first-year teachers.

Dreyfus and Dreyfus (1986) delineate five stages from novice to expert across fields of study. In stage one, the novice is inflexible and follows principles and procedures the way they were learned; the advanced beginner, stage two, begins to combine theory with on-the-job experiences. By the third stage, the competent performer becomes more flexible and modifies principles and procedures to fit reality. At the next stage, the proficient performer recognizes patterns and relationships and has a holistic understanding of the processes involved. Experts, stage five, have the same big picture in mind but respond effortlessly and fluidly in various situations. Cushing, Sabers, and Berliner (1992) point out that "expert teachers make classroom management and instruction look easy," although we know that teaching is a complex act, requiring the teacher "to do many things at the same time" (p. 109).

Data derived from recent studies suggest that expert and novice teachers teach as well as perceive and analyze information about teaching in different ways. Whereas experts are able to explain and interpret classroom events, novices provide detailed descriptions of what they did or saw and refrain from making interpretations. Experts recall or see multiple interactions, and explain interactions in terms of prior information and events, whereas novices recall specific facts about students or what happened in the classroom. What experts (or experienced teachers) say or do about teaching is now considered important for building a science of teaching. Studies of expert and novice teachers show they differ in many specific areas of teaching and instruction.

1. Experts are likely to refrain from making quick judgments about their students and tend to rely on their own experiences and gut feelings, whereas novices tend to lack confidence in their own judgments and are not sure where to start when they begin teaching.
2. Experts tend to analyze student cues in terms of instruction, whereas novices analyze them in terms of classroom management.
3. Experts make the classroom their own, often changing the instructional focus and methods of the previous teacher. Novices tend to follow the previous teachers' footsteps. Experts talk about starting over and breaking old routines; they tell us about how to get students going and how to determine where the students are in understanding content. Novices, on the other hand, tend to begin where the previous teacher left off. They have trouble assessing where the students are, what their capabilities are, and how and where they are going.
4. Experts engage in a good deal of intuitive and improvisational teaching. Novices spend much more time planning, stay glued to the content, and are less inclined to deviate or respond to students' needs or interests while the lesson is in progress.
5. Experts seem to have a clear understanding of the types of students they are teaching and how to teach them. Novices do not have a well-developed idea of the students they are teaching. Whereas novices have trouble beginning the new term, experts routinely find out just what it is the students already know and proceed accordingly.
6. Expert teachers are less egocentric and more confident about their teaching. Novices pay more attention to themselves, worrying about their effectiveness as teachers and about potential discipline problems (Borko and Livingston, 1989; Carter, 1993; Sabers, Cushing, and Berliner, 1991).

Voice

The notion of voice sums up the new linguistic tools for describing what teachers do, how they do it, and what they think when they are teaching. Voice corresponds with such terms as the "teacher's perspective," "teacher's frame of reference," or "getting into the teacher's head." The concern with voice permeates the teacher-empowerment movement and the work of researchers who collaborate with teachers in field-based projects. The idea of voice should be considered against the backdrop of previous teacher silence and impotence in deciding on issues and practices that affect their lives as teachers. As Elbaz (1991) asserts, researchers' willingness to give credibility to teachers' knowledge, teachers' practices, and teachers' experiences helps redress an imbalance that in the past gave little recognition to teachers. Now teachers have a right and a role in speaking for themselves and about teaching.

Although there are some serious attempts to include teachers' voices, the key issue is to what extent these new methods permit the "authentic" expression of teachers to influence the field of teacher-effectiveness research and teacher-preparation programs. In the past, it has been difficult for teachers to establish a voice, especially one that commanded respect and authority, in the professional literature. The reason is simple: the researchers and theoreticians have dominated the field of inquiry and decided on what should be published.

With the exception of autobiographies and stories written by teachers, teachers' voices generally are filtered through and categorized by researchers' writings and publications. For decades, first-hand expressions of teacher experiences and wisdom (sometimes conveyed in the form of advice or recommendations) were considered nothing more than "recipes" or lists of "dos and don'ts"—irrelevant to the world of research on teaching. Recently, however, under umbrella terms such as "teacher thinking," "teacher processes," "teacher cognition," "teacher practices," and "practical knowledge," it has become acceptable and even fashionable to take what teachers have to say, adapt it, and turn it into "professional knowledge," "pedagogical knowledge," or "teacher knowledge." Yet, although researchers are now collaborating with practitioners, taking teacher views seriously, and accepting teachers on equal terms as part of teacher-training programs, teachers still do not always receive credit where it is due. Whereas researchers are named as co-authors in scholarly publications, practitioners may be acknowledged only by pseudonyms such as "Nancy" or "Thomas." The culture of schools and universities, and of teachers and professors, should be compatible enough to bridge this gap in the near future.

HOW BEGINNING TEACHERS (NOVICES) TEACH AND IMPROVE

The personal styles and images of beginning teachers, commonly called *novices*, tend to remain inflexible throughout their preservice training. Candidates are likely to use the information provided in course work to confirm rather than reconstruct their views about teaching. Further compounding the problem of adjusting to future classroom life, according to Kagan (1992), candidates are often presented with contradictory and inconsistent views of teaching and learning in their course work and while student teaching. As a result, novices come to their first job with an inadequate and oversimplified notion of classroom practice (what is commonly called *pedagogy*) and are unprepared to adjust their approach in response to varied problems of classroom management, instruction, and student learning. As beginning teachers acquire knowledge on the job, they must begin to use it to modify, adapt, and reconstruct their view as a teacher and their teaching methods. Eventually, for those who are successful, they move from focusing on their own behaviors to those of their students; they move from emphasizing classroom management to instructional techniques, and finally, to the matter of how students learn.

Two separate research studies (Mumby and Russell, 1994; Reynolds, 1992) draw similar conclusions: many teacher educators oversimplify the reality of student teaching and ignore complex teaching and learning variables that affect a teacher's classroom decisions. Both student teachers and beginning teachers are expected to function on levels beyond their capacity; in fact, many possess minimal survival skills. At issue is the failure of teacher educators to provide student teachers with sufficient procedural knowledge. Lacking sufficient methodology when thrust into the classroom as beginning teachers, novices tend to rely on their own recent experiences as a student—an approach that is inappropriate and insufficient for teaching.

While mastering procedural knowledge or generic teaching methods is important, another group of teacher educators contends that novices must be concerned with learning how to teach content and helping students learn it (Grossman, 1992). This position stresses the importance of subject matter and subject matter pedagogy: if there are any methods to learn, they are methods related to subject matter delivery. This school of thought is rooted in the post-Sputnik era and in the old schism between professors of arts and science and those of education over the centrality of disciplinary knowledge versus knowledge of pedagogy. Arts and science faculty today, as in the past, continue to advocate the necessity of subject matter pedagogy and are likely to remain skeptical of education pedagogy.

Recently, L. Schulman (1986, 1991) introduced the phrase "pedagogical content knowledge," and sparked a whole new wave of scholarly articles on teachers' knowledge of their subject matter and the importance of this knowledge for successful teaching. For the most part, content knowledge was ignored by researchers on teaching in the 1970s and 1980s because generic methods and principles of effective teaching were emphasized. In the 1990s, the shift in interest is toward specialized or content-based methods and the modification of teaching programs.

In Schulman's theoretical framework, teachers need to master two types of knowledge: (1) content, also known as "deep" knowledge of the subject itself, and (2) knowledge of curricular development. Content knowledge encompasses what Jerome Bruner would call the "structure of knowledge"—the theories, principles, and concepts of a particular discipline. Especially important is content knowledge that deals with the teaching process, including the most useful forms of representing and communicating content and how students best learn the specific concepts and topics of a subject.

In short, the teachers' orientation to their subject matter influences their method of planning, their choice of content, the way they use textbooks, the supplementary materials they use, their pedagogical strategies, and their perceptions of students' instructional needs. Likewise, it determines the way the teacher formulates, demonstrates, and explains the subject so that it is comprehensible to learners. All this suggests that beginning teachers need to integrate subject matter content and pedagogy.

Attitudes toward the relative importance of content and method will impact how educators believe novice teachers should learn to teach. Kagan's theories, which coincide with evolving research at the University of Arizona (David Berliner, Walter Doyle, and Gary Griffin) and Michigan State University (Jere Brophy, Chris Clark, and Penelope Peterson), suggest that once teachers learn generic methodology they can turn their attention to content and then learning. Schulman's approach, stemming from Stanford University's research program (and work of doctoral students such as Grace Grant, Pamela Grossman, and Sigrun Gudmundsdottir) contend that issues of subject matter and methodology are dependent. If beginning teachers are to be successful, they must wrestle simultaneously with issues of pedagogical content (or knowledge) and professional pedagogy (or generic teaching methods). Only by integrating both forms of pedagogy can a teacher personally define and understand the purpose of teaching, understand students' learning, and develop realistic curricular and instructional strategies.

Support from Colleagues and Peer Evaluation

In general, having to learn by trial and error without support and supervision has been the most common problem faced by new teachers. Expecting teachers to function without support is based on the false assumptions that (1) teachers are well prepared for their initial classroom and school experiences, (2) teachers can develop professional expertise on their own, and (3) teaching can be mastered in a relatively short period of time. Researchers find that there is little attempt to lighten the class load and limit extra-class assignments to make the beginning teacher's job easier. In the few schools that do limit these activities, teachers have reported that they have had the opportunity to "learn to teach" (Carter, 1990; Duke, 1993).

Unquestionably, new teachers need the feedback and encouragement experienced teachers can provide. The exchange of ideas can take place in school and out (sharing a ride to a local meeting). Most important, experienced teachers must be willing to open their classrooms to new teachers. Because of the desire for autonomy in the classroom, there is seldom as much communication or visitation between teachers as there should be. In some case studies, as many as 45 percent of the teachers report no contact with other teachers during the school day, and another 32 percent report having infrequent contact with other teachers (Heck and Williams, 1984). No matter how successful individuals

Analyzing and Improving Teaching

are as student teachers and how good their preservice training is, they can benefit from the advice and assistance of experienced colleagues. Talking to other teachers gives novices the chance to sound out ideas and pick up information.

Studies of elementary and secondary schools have shown that teachers expect to learn from one another when the school provides opportunities for teachers (1) to talk routinely to one another about teaching, (2) to be observed regularly in the classroom, and (3) to participate in planning and preparation (Clift, Houston, and Pugach, 1990). Teachers feel more confident in their individual and collective ability to perform their work when they are given the opportunity to (1) develop and implement curriculum ideas, (2) join study groups about implementing classroom practices, or (3) experiment in new skills and training (Gordon and Moles, 1994; Pultorak, 1994).

Peer coaching or mentoring takes place when classroom teachers observe one another, provide feedback concerning their teaching, and together develop instructional plans. Whether observing other teachers is done on an informal or formal basis, permission should be granted by the teacher to be observed and by the supervisor or administrator in charge of the new teacher's professional development. The new teachers should look for techniques of teaching and lesson planning that are unfamiliar to them, that coincide with their teaching style, and that are an improvement over what they are doing. A short follow-up conference with the experienced teacher to go over specific points should be scheduled either the same day or the next day while the observation is fresh.

According to Joyce and Showers (1995), an experienced teacher who acts as a peer coach or mentor teacher for an inexperienced teacher performs five functions: (1) *companionship*, discussing ideas, problems, and successes; (2) *technical feedback*, especially related to lesson planning and classroom observations; (3) *analysis of application*, integrating what happens or what works as part of the beginning teacher's repertoire; (4) *adaptation*, helping the beginning teacher adapt to particular situations; and (5) *personal facilitation*, helping the teacher feel good about her- or himself after trying new strategies.

Data have been reported by Neubert and Bratton (1987) involving visiting mentor teachers in Maryland school districts who, rather than observe classroom teachers, teach alongside them. They describe five characteristics of the mentor or resource teachers that promote an effective coaching relationship: (1) *knowledge*—more knowledge about teaching methods than the classroom teacher; (2) *credibility*—demonstrated success in the classroom; (3) *support*—mix of honest praise and constructive criticism; (4) *facilitation*—recommending and encouraging rather than dominating in the classroom; and (5) *availability*—accessible to the classroom teacher for planning, team teaching, and conferences.

In one Pennsylvania school district, a "buddy system" has been developed for beginning and experienced teachers who need additional assistance. Continual peer support is provided with teachers teamed together from the same subject or grade level. The teacher "coaches" who are selected work full time (and often after school) helping their less experienced colleagues become better teachers. Four characteristics help define this program: (1) *collegiality and teamwork*—such as coaches covering classes so that their colleagues can observe other teachers and gather ideas to adapt to their own teaching style, or coaches engaging in direct peer coaching; (2) *instructional support*—coaches introducing new instructional strategies that enhance student learning; (3) *professional growth*—coaches taking an active role in presenting in-service sessions so that new teachers are helped to better understand the school philosophy and policies; and (4) *special services*—coaches providing special education services and programs that can be used by all teachers in the school (visiting authors, artists in residence, environmental projects, computer competitions [Witmer, 1993]).

Data show, however, that beginning teachers are selective in who they ask for help. They seek help from experienced teachers they perceive as "knowledgeable," "friendly," and "supportive," independent of whether the teachers are formally recognized as their mentors or coaches. In a study of 128 teachers in 90 different schools, 75 percent (n=96) sought help from teachers who were not their mentors; moreover, only 53 percent were generally satisfied with their mentors (Tellez, 1995).

Although mentors are usually comfortable offering help to their inexperienced colleagues, the success of any mentoring program hinges on whether the inexperienced teacher is comfortable seeking help from the experienced counterpart. The decision for adults to seek help, then to accept it, is influenced by numerous variables. Basically, two tensions impact: the embarrassment of continued failure versus the embarrassment of asking for help in solving a problem. Indeed, the staggering

Analyzing and Improving Teaching

number of teachers who leave the profession after only a few years of service (Colbert and Wolff, 1992; Ornstein, 1995b) suggests the need to be sensitive to the concerns of beginning teachers and the need to improve mentoring programs. Table 1-4 provides ways to improve support for novice teachers.

Self-Evaluation

Teaching presents ample opportunities for self-evaluation. The teacher who does a good job, and knows it, has the satisfaction of seeing students grow, feeling their respect and affection, and obtaining the recognition of colleagues, parents, and the community.

Self-evaluation by the teacher can contribute to professional growth. This idea is a logical outgrowth of the modern belief in the value of teacher-supervisor cooperation. If teacher evaluations are accepted as an integral part of an effective supervisory situation for professional development, then teachers should be involved in the clarification and continual appraisal of their goals and effectiveness.

According to Good and Brophy (1991), teachers "seek opportunities to evaluate and improve their teaching, if acceptable and useful methods are available." The trouble is, these researchers continue, teachers have not been encouraged or taught to engage in self-criticism, to recognize weaknesses, and to link criticisms with constructive plans designed to improve skills. Tuckman (1995b) concludes that teachers are willing to engage in and even welcome self-evaluation as long as it is conducted in an appropriate manner, they participate in the planning stages, and they have some assurance of how the results will be used.

Research (Kottkamp, Provenzo and Cohn, 1986) also indicates that teachers favor self-evaluation over evaluation by students, peers, and supervisors. Teachers rated as "good" by supervisors picked self-evaluation as their first choice among methods for judging teacher effectiveness (selected by 37 percent of more than 2,700 teachers surveyed). Objective evaluations by students and reactions of other teachers familiar with their work were second (19 percent) and alternative choices for assessing personal performance ranked third (16 percent). Furthermore, as many as 52 percent of teachers assert that it is *relatively easy* to know when one is teaching effectively.

There are good reasons for self-evaluation. A U.S. government survey of 10,000 secondary teachers and 400 schools re-

Table 1-4
Guidelines for Improving Support for Beginning Teachers

- Schedule beginning teacher orientation in addition to regular teacher orientation. Beginning teachers need to attend both sessions.
- Appoint someone to help beginning teachers set up their rooms.
- Provide beginning teachers with a proper mix of courses, students, and facilities (not all leftovers). If possible, lighten their load for the first year.
- Assign extra-class duties of moderate difficulty and requiring moderate amounts of time, duties that will not become too demanding for the beginning teacher.
- Pair beginning teachers with master teachers to meet regularly to identify general problems before they become serious.
- Provide coaching groups, tutor groups, or collaborative problem-solving groups for all beginning teachers to attend. Encourage beginning teachers to teach each other.
- Provide for joint planning, team teaching, committee assignments, and other cooperative arrangements between new and experienced teachers.
- Issue newsletters that report on accomplishments of all teachers, especially beginning teachers.
- Schedule reinforcing events, involving beginning and experienced teachers, such as tutor-tutoree luncheons, parties, and awards.
- Provide regular (say, twice monthly) meetings between the beginning teacher and supervisor to identify problems as soon as possible and to make recommendations for improvement.
- Plan special and continuing in-service with topics directly related to the needs and interests of beginning teachers. Eventually, integrate beginning teacher development activities with regular teacher activities.
- Carry on regular evaluation of beginning teachers; evaluate strengths and weaknesses, present new information, demonstrate new skills, and provide opportunities for practice and feedback.

vealed that one-fourth (26 percent) of the respondents indicated they were "never" evaluated by their building principal or supervisor the previous year and another 27 percent indicated only one visit. When teachers were asked how many times they visited other teachers to observe or discuss teaching techniques, 70 percent said "never" (*High School and Beyond*, 1985). In other words, teacher evaluation and feedback from administrators, supervisors, or colleagues is infrequent and in many cases nonexistent.

Since most teachers operate with virtual autonomy in the classroom and receive minimal assistance from supervisors or colleagues, it follows that self-evaluation may be more useful than we might initially think and possibly be less biased than an outside evaluation based on one or two visits from a person who is rushed or going through motions to satisfy some school policy.

There are basically two forms of self-evaluations. First, teachers can rate themselves on their *teaching methods* at the classroom level. This type of evaluation form can be developed by the teacher, a group of teachers, the school district, or researchers. The main consideration is for teachers to have input in devising the instrument (to build acceptance of the process), or they can agree on an instrument already developed or in use in another school district, and modify it according to their purposes. The point is, teachers should feel comfortable with the evaluation instrument, and they should make decisions about what to do with the results.

Second, the teachers can rate themselves on their *professional responsibilities* at the school and community level. According to administrators, this form might include (1) classroom climate, (2) student learning, (3) contractual responsibilities, (4) service to school, and (5) professional development (Dwyer, 1993; Wood, 1992). To this list might be added (6) relations with students, (7) relations with colleagues, (8) service to the community, and (9) membership in professional associations.

Reflection

The terms *reflection* and *reflective practice* are partly based on the works of Rogers (1980) and Schon (1983, 1991), who studied the actions and thoughts of workers in a variety of fields as they learn to analyze and interpret events in ways that guide their own development and day-to-day practice. According to these authors, each person is capable of examining questions and answers needed to improve their professional performance. Through open-mindedness and maturity, and with the help of colleagues, individuals can discover new ideas and illuminate what they already understand and know how to do. Such reflection, in effect, combines the essentials of self-evaluation and peer evaluation.

Reflection can help beginning and experienced teachers alike, and can be incorporated into preservice, internship, and in-service or staff-development programs. Most participants are resistant at the beginning, and usually express ambivalence or confusion about what is required, especially as unsettling questions about their own teaching are examined. But more often than not, reflection results in more questions and clearer perceptions of themselves and in better plans for solving individual problems.

One of the sophisticated tools for analyzing teachers' reflective thoughts was developed by Ross (1989), who contends that reflection becomes increasingly complex depending on the individual's maturity and perception of safety in expressing one's views. Ross identifies three levels of complexity in the reflection process: (1) describing a teacher's practice with little detailed analysis and little insight into the reasons behind teacher or student behaviors; (2) providing a cogent critique of a practice from one perspective but failing to consider multiple factors; (3) analyzing teaching and learning from multiple perspectives and recognizing that teachers' actions have a pervasive impact beyond the moment of instruction.

In the later stages, individuals come to realize that behaviors (and feeling) are contextually based. Rather than dealing in absolutes or so-called objectivity, they begin to deal in relative truths and points of view. In the third stage, people are open to more change and willing to admit that they don't always know the answer. However, the third stage suggests considerable experience and maturity. Most beginning teachers operate at the lower levels of reflection, and therefore are more close-minded and unwilling to accept other viewpoints about their teaching. Ross's data suggest that only 22 percent of preservice teachers function at or above level 2 and then only for particular topics.

It is through reflection that teachers focus on concerns, come to better understand their own teacher behavior, and help themselves or colleagues improve as teachers. Through reflective practices in a group setting, or forums, teachers learn to listen carefully to each other, which also provides insight into one's own work. In turn, as researchers hear teachers reflect on their practices, what they do in the classroom, and the basis for those actions, they are in the position to translate the teachers' practice knowledge and particular point of view into theoretical knowledge and integrate it with other viewpoints.

Thus, as teachers probe and further examine specific teaching situations, a language of practice can emerge that allows us to better understand how teachers cope with the complexity of their work. Here the key is to make sense of what teachers have to say, to clarify and elaborate on particular scripts or situations, and delineate what meaning these reflections have for the teachers themselves and other professionals.

REFERENCES

Azumi, J. E., and Lerman, J. L. (1987). Selecting and rewarding master teachers. *Elementary School Journal, 88*, 197.

Banks, J. A. (1993). The canon debate, knowledge construction and multicultural education. *Educational Researcher, 22*, 4–14.

Barr, A. S. (1958). Characteristics of successful teachers. *Phi Delta Kappan, 39*, 282–284.

Bellack, A. A., et al. (1966). *The language of the classroom.* New York: Teachers College Press.

Biddle, B. J., and Ellena, W. J. (1964). The integration of teacher effectiveness. In B. J. Biddle and W. J. Ellena (eds.), *Contemporary research on teacher effectiveness* (p. 3). New York: Holt, Rinehart and Winston.

Borko, H., and Livingston, C. (1989). Cognition and improvisation: Differences in mathematics instruction by expert and novice teachers. *American Educational Research Journal, 26*, 473–498.

Brophy, J. E. (1986). Classroom management techniques. *Education and Urban Society, 18*, 182–194.

Carter, K. (1990). Teacher's knowledge and learning to teach. In W. R. Houston (ed.), *Handbook of research on teacher education* (pp. 291–310). New York: Macmillan.

Carter, K. (1993). The place of story in research on teaching. *Educational Researcher, 22*, 5–12.

Clark, K. B. (1965). *Dark Ghetto.* New York: Harper and Row.

Clift, R. T.; Houston, W. R.; and Pugach, M. (1990). *Encouraging reflective practice.* New York: Teachers College Press.

Colbert, J. A., and Wolff, D. E. (1992). Surviving in urban schools: A collaborative model for a beginning teacher support system. *Journal of Teacher Education, 43*, 193–199.

Cooper, H. M. (1979). Pygmalion grows up: A model for teacher expectation communication and performance influence. *Review of Educational Research, 49*, 389–410.

Cooper, H. M., and Good, T. L. (1983). *Pygmalion grows up.* New York: Longman.

Cushing, K. S.; Sabers, D. S.; and Berliner, D. C. (1992). Investigations of expertise in teaching. *Educational Horizons, 70*, 109.

Doyle, W. (1985). Effective teaching and the concept of master teacher. *Elementary School Journal, 86*, 30.

Doyle, W. (1992). Curriculum and pedagogy. In P. W. Jackson (ed.), *Handbook of research on curriculum* (pp. 486–516). New York: Macmillan.

Dreyfus, H. L., and Dreyfus, S. E. (1986). *Mind over machine.* New York: Free Press.

Duke, D. L. (1993). How a staff development program can rescue at-risk students. *Educational Leadership, 50*, 28–30.

Dwyer, C. A. (1993). Teaching and diversity: Meeting the challenges for innovative teacher assessment. *Journal of Teacher Education, 44,* 119–129.

Eisner, E. W. (1994). *Cognition and curriculum* (2nd ed.). New York: Teachers College Press.

Elbaz, F. (1991). Research on teacher's knowledge: The evolution of a discourse. *Journal of Curriculum Studies, 23,* 1–19.

Emmer, E. T., and Evertson, C. M. (1994). *Classroom management for secondary schools* (3rd ed.). Englewood Cliffs, N.J.: Prentice Hall.

Flanders, N. A. (1965). *Teacher influence, pupil attitudes, and achievement.* Washington, D.C.: Government Printing Office.

Flanders, N. A. (1970). *Analyzing teaching behavior.* Reading, Mass.: Addison-Wesley.

Gage, N. L. (1978). *The scientific basis of the art of teaching.* New York: Teachers College Press, Columbia University.

Gage, N. L., and Needels, M. C. (1989). Process-product research on teaching. *Elementary School Journal, 89,* 253–300.

Galloway, C. M. (1968). Nonverbal communication. *Theory into Practice,* 172–175.

Galloway, C. M. (1984). Nonverbal behavior and teacher student relationships: An intercultural perspective. In A. Wolfgang (ed.), *Nonverbal behavior: Perspectives, applications, intercultural insights* (pp. 411–430). Toronto: Hogrefe.

Giroux, H. A. (1992). Curriculum, multiculturalism, and the politics of identity. *NASSP Bulletin, 76,* 1–11.

Good, T. L., and Brophy, J. E. (1986). Teacher behavior and student achievement. In M. C. Wittrock (ed.), *Handbook of research on teaching* (3rd ed., pp. 328–375). New York: Macmillan.

Good, T. L., and Brophy, J. E. (1991). *Looking in classrooms* (5th ed.). New York: Harper and Collins.

Gordon, D., and Moles, M. (1994). Mentoring becomes staff development. *NASSP Bulletin, 78,* 62–65.

Grant, G. E. (1991). Ways of constructing classroom meaning: Two stories about knowing and seeing. *Journal of Curriculum Studies, 23,* 397–408.

Greene, M. (1986). Philosophy and teaching. In M. C. Wittrock (ed.), *Handbook of research on teaching* (3rd ed., pp. 479–500). New York: Macmillan.

Greene, M. (1988). *The dialectic of teaching.* New York: Teachers College Press.

Grossman, P. (1992). Why models matter: An alternative view on professional growth in teaching. *Review of Educational Research, 62,* 171–179.

Grumet, M. R. (1987). The politics of personal knowledge. *Curriculum Inquiry, 17,* 319–329.

Haberman, M. (1992). The ideology of star teachers of children of poverty. *Educational Horizons, 70,* 125–129.

Haberman, M. (1995). The dimensions of excellence. *Peabody Journal of Education, 70,* 24–43.

Heck, S. F., and Williams, C. R. (1984). *The complex roles of the teacher.* New York: Teachers College Press.

High school and beyond: Teacher and administrator survey. (1985). Washington, D.C.: National Institute for Education.

Jackson, P. W. (1968). Life in classrooms. New York: Holt, Rinehart & Winston.

Joyce, B., and Showers, B. (1995). *Student achievement through staff development* (2nd ed.). New York: Longman.

Kagan, D. M. (1990). How schools alienate students at risk. *Educational Psychologist, 25,* 105–125.

Kagan, D. M. (1992). Professional growth among preservice and beginning teachers. *Review of Educational Research, 62,* 129–170.

Knapp, M. S., and Shields, P. M. (1990). Reconceiving academic instruction for the children of poverty. *Phi Delta Kappan, 71,* 753–758.

Kottkamp, R. B.; Provenzo, E. F.; and Cohn, M. M. (1986). Stability and change in a profession: Two decades of teacher attitudes, 1964–1984. *Phi Delta Kappan, 67,* 559–566.

Lippitt, R., and White, R. K. (1943). The social climate of children's groups. In R. G. Barker, J. S. Kounin, and H. F. Wright (eds.), *Child behavior and development* (pp. 485–508). New York: McGraw-Hill.

Lytle, S. L., and Cochran-Smith, M. (1992). Teacher research as a way of knowing. *Harvard Educational Review, 62,* 447–474.

McDiarmid, G. W. (1992). What to do about differences? A study of multicultural education for teacher trainees. *Journal of Teacher Education, 43,* 83–93.

Munby, H., and Russell, T. (1994). The authority of experience in learning to teach. *Journal of Teacher Education, 45,* 86–95.

Neubert, G. A., and Bratton, E. C. (1987). Team coaching: Staff development side by side. *Educational Leadership, 44,* 29–32.

Ogbu, J. U. (1994). Racial stratification and education in the United States: Why inequality persists. *Teachers College Record, 96,* 264–299.

Ogbu, J. U. (1995). Understanding cultural diversity and learning. In A. C. Ornstein and L. Behar (eds.), *Curriculum issues* (pp. 349–366). Needham Heights, Mass.: Allyn and Bacon.

Ornstein, A. C. (1985). Research on teaching issues and trends. *Journal of Teacher Education, 36,* 27–31.

Ornstein, A. C. (1990). A look at teacher effectiveness research: Theory and practice. *NASSP Bulletin, 74,* 78–88.

Ornstein, A. C. (1991). Teacher effectiveness research: Theoretical considerations. In H. C. Waxman and H. J. Walberg (eds.), *Effective teaching* (pp. 63–80). Berkeley, Calif.: McCutchan.

Ornstein, A. C. (1993). Successful teachers: Who are they? *American School Board Journal, 180,* 24–27.

Ornstein, A. C. (1995a). Beyond effective teaching. *Peabody Journal of Education, 70,* 2–23.

Ornstein, A. C. (1995b). Research for improving teachers. In A. C. Ornstein and L. Behar (eds.), *Curriculum issues* (pp. 77–89). Needham Heights, Mass.: Allyn and Bacon.

Patterson, M. L. (1983). *Nonverbal behavior: A functional perspective.* New York: Springer.

Peterson, P. L. (1979). Direct instruction reconsidered. In P. L. Peterson and H. J. Walberg (eds.), *Research on teaching: Concepts, findings, and implications* (pp. 57–69). Berkeley, Calif.: McCutchan.

Prawat, R. S. (1992). Teacher beliefs about teaching and learning. *American Journal of Education, 100,* 354–395.

Pultorak, E. G. (1994). Facilitating reflective thought in novice teachers. *Journal of Teacher Education, 44,* 288–295.

Reynolds, A. (1992). What is competent beginning teaching? *Review of Educational Research, 62,* 1–36.
Rogers, C. A. (1980). *A way of being.* Boston: Houghton Mifflin.
Rosenshine, B. V. (1979). Content, time and direct instruction. In P. L. Peterson and H. J. Walberg (eds.), *Research on teaching: Concepts, findings, and implications* (pp. 28–56). Berkeley, Calif.: McCutchan.
Rosenshine, B. V., and Furst, N. F. (1971). Research in teacher performance criteria. In B. O. Smith (ed.), *Research on teacher education* (pp. 37–42). Englewood Cliffs, N.J.: Prentice-Hall.
Rosenshine, B. V., and Furst, N. F. (1973). The use of direct observation to study teaching. In R. M. Travers (ed.), *Second handbook of research on teaching* (pp. 122–183). Chicago: Rand McNally.
Rosenthal, R., and Jacobson, L. (1968). *Pygmalion in the classroom.* New York: Holt, Rinehart and Winston.
Ross, D. D. (1989). First steps in developing a reflective approach. *Journal of Teacher Education, 40,* 22–30.
Ryans, D. G. (1960). *Characteristics of teachers.* Washington, D.C.: American Council of Education.
Sabers, D. S.; Cushing, K. S.; and Berliner, D. C. (1991). Differences among teachers in a task characterized by simultaneity, multidimensionality, and immediacy. *American Educational Research Journal, 28,* 63–88.
Schon, D. A. (1983). *The reflective practitioner: How professionals think in action.* New York: Basic Books.
Schon, D. A. (1991). *The Reflective turn: Case studies in and on educational practice.* New York: Teachers College Press.
Schulman, L. S. (1986). Those who understand: Knowledge growth in teaching. *Educational Researcher, 15,* 4–14.
Schulman, L. S. (1991). Ways of seeing, ways of knowing: Ways of teaching, ways of learning about teaching. *Journal of Curriculum Studies, 23,* 393–396.
Siegman, A. W., and Feldstein, S. (eds.). (1978). *Nonverbal behavior and communication.* Hillsdale: N.J.: Erlbaum.
Smith, O., and Meux, M. (1970). *A study of the logic of teaching* (2nd ed.). Urbana, Ill.: University of Illinois Press.
Solas, J. (1992). Investigating teacher and student thinking about the process of teaching and learning using autobiography and repertory grid. *Review of Educational Research, 62,* 205–225.
Stephens, P., and Valentine, J. (1986). Assessing principal nonverbal communication. *Educational Research Quarterly, 11,* 60–68.
Tellez, K. (1995). Mentors by choice, not design. *Journal of Teacher Education, 43,* 214–221.
Thorndike, R. (1968). Review of pygmalion in the classroom. *American Educational Research Journal, 5,* 708–711.
Tuckman, B. W. (1991). An interpersonal construct model of teaching. Paper presented at the annual meeting of the American Educational Research Association, Chicago, April.
Tuckman, B. W. (1995a). The interpersonal teacher model. *Educational Forum, 59,* 177–185.
Tuckman, B. W. (1995b). Assessing effective teaching. *Peabody Journal of Education, 70,* 127–174.

Wang, M. C.; Reynolds, M. C.; and Walberg, H. J. (1995). Serving students at the margins. *Educational Leadership, 52,* 12–17.

Wehlage, G. C., and Rutter, R. A. (1986). Dropping out: How much do schools contribute to the problem? *Teachers College Record, 87,* 374–392.

Welker, R. (1992). Reversing the claim of professional status. *Educational Horizons, 70,* 115–119.

Witmer, J. T. (1993). Mentoring: One district's success story. *NASSP Bulletin, 77,* 71–78.

Wood, C. J. (1992). Toward more effective teacher evaluation. *NASSP Bulletin, 76,* 52–59.

2
Toward a Knowledge Base for School Learning

Margaret C. Wang, Geneva D. Haertel, and Herbert J. Walberg

Changes in education should be grounded in a knowledge base derived from research, and such a base is now beginning to take shape. By analyzing the content of 179 handbook chapters and reviews, compiling 91 research syntheses, and surveying 61 educational researchers, we created a knowledge base comprising 11,000 statistical findings that shows reasonable consensus on the most significant influences on learning (Wang, Haertel, and Walberg, 1990; Reynolds, Wang, and Walberg, 1992).[1]

In general, we found that direct influences have a greater impact on learning than do indirect influences. Direct influences include the amount of time a teacher spends on a topic and the quality of the social interactions teachers have with their students. Indirect influences include policies adopted by a school, district, or state, and organizational features such as site-based management.

---

[1] This research was supported by the Temple University Center for Research in Human Development and Education and by the Office of Educational Research and Improvement of the U.S. Department of Education. The opinions expressed here do not necessarily reflect the position of the supporting agencies. For complete details on the methods and results of the syntheses, see M. C. Wang, G. D. Haertel, and H. J. Walberg (1993).

Reprinted from M.C. Wang, G.D. Haertel, and H.J. Walberg, "What Helps Students Learn?" *Educational Leadership 51*, 4 (December 1993/January 1994): 74-79. Reprinted with permission of the Association for Supervision and Curriculum Development. Copyright © 1993 by ASCD. All rights reserved.

ACCUMULATING THE DATA

We summarized the results of our analysis, using a twenty-eight category conceptual framework based on models of schooling that posited influences on learning.[2] The earlier models included variables such as student ability, motivation, prior knowledge, and background. Classroom instructional variables such as enthusiasm, clarity, feedback, and correctives were also key elements. Increasingly, models of schooling have been extended to include out-of-school variables, social-psychological influences, instructional delivery systems, program design, and implementation. Figure 2-1 lists the twenty-eight categories of the conceptual framework we employed and a representative variable for each category.[3]

By combining the results from the content analysis, the research synthesis, and the survey of experts, we obtained an average score for each of the twenty-eight categories.[4] Figure 2-2 presents the twenty-eight categories of influence from most to least influential. Classroom management, metacognitive processes, cognitive processes, home environment/parental support, and student and teacher social interactions had the greatest influence on school learning. Program demographics, school demographics, state-level policies, school policies and organization, and district demographics had the least influence on learning.

This method of statistically aggregating the findings of many studies varying in sample size, rigor, and characteristics is called *meta-analysis*. Meta-analysis yields estimates of the effect of all studies

---

[2] Models reviewed included those by S. N. Bennett, B. S. Bloom, J. S. Bruner, J. B. Carroll, R. Glaser, and A. Harnischfeger and D. E. Wiley. See Haertel, Walberg, and Weinstein (1983); Wang and Lindvall (1984); and Wang and Walberg (1985).

[3] The variables listed as part of the conceptual framework were transformed into a 228-item rating form and used to code results from the narrative reviews and research syntheses. Based on the proportions of the confirmatory studies reported, the size of the correlations, or qualitative indicators, we rated the data culled from the narrative reviews and the research syntheses on a three-point scale. A "1" indicated a weak relationship between a given strategy and student learning while a "3" indicated a strong relationship.

[4] To make the results comparable, the data from the three sources were transformed into T scores, standard scores with a mean of 50 and a standard deviation of 10. The relative influences on the variables were calculated by weighing composites of effect sizes and ratings obtained from experts and content analyses of authoritative literature.

Figure 2-1
Twenty-Eight Categories of Influence on School Learning

Categories	Examples of One Variable in Category

Student Aptitude includes gender; academic history; and a variety of social, behavioral, motivational, cognitive, and affective characteristics.

1. Metacognitive Processes	*Comprehension monitoring (planning; monitoring effectiveness of attempted actions and outcomes of actions; testing, revising, and evaluating learning strategies)*
2. Cognitive Processes	*Level of specific academic knowledge in subject area*
3. Social and Behavioral Attributes	*Positive, nondisruptive behavior*
4. Motivational and Affective Attributes	*Attitude toward subject matter instructed*
5. Psychomotor Skills	*Psychomotor skills specific to area instructed*
6. Student Demographics	*Gender and socioeconomic status*

Classroom Instruction and Climate includes classroom routines and practices, characteristics of instruction as delivered, classroom management, monitoring of student progress, quality and quantity of instruction provided, student-teacher interactions, and classroom atmosphere.

7. Classroom Management	*Group alerting (teacher uses questioning/recitation strategies that maintain active participation by all students)*
8. Student and Teacher Social Interactions	*Positive student response to questions from teacher and other students*
9. Quantity of Instruction	*Active engagement in learning*
10. Classroom Climate	*Cohesiveness (class members share common interests and values and emphasize cooperative goals)*
11. Classroom Instruction	*Clear and organized direct instruction*
12. Academic Interactions	*Frequent calls for substantive oral and written response*
13. Classroom Assessment	*Assessment used as a frequent, integral component of instruction*
14. Classroom Implementation and Support	*Establishing efficient classroom routines and communicating rules and procedures*

Context includes community demographics, peer culture, parental support and involvement, and amount of time students spend out of class on such activities as television viewing, leisure reading, and homework.

15. Home Environment/Parental Support	*Parental involvement in ensuring completion of homework*
16. Peer Group	*Level of peers' academic aspirations*
17. Community Influences	*Socioeconomic level of community*
18. Out-of-Class Time	*Student participation in clubs and extracurricular school activities*

Program Design refers to the physical and organizational arrangements for instructional delivery and includes strategies specified by the curriculum and characteristics of instructional materials.

19. Curriculum Design	*Instructional materials employ advance organizers*
20. Curriculum and Instruction	*Alignment among goals, content, instructions, students' assignments, and evaluation*
21. Program Demographics	*Size of instructional group (whole class, small group, one-on-one instruction)*

School Organization refers to culture, climate, policies, and practices; includes demographics of the student body, whether the school is public or private, funding for categorical programs, school-level decision-making variables, and school-level policies and practices.

22. School Culture	*Schoolwide emphasis on and recognition of academic achievement*
23. Teacher/Administrator Decision Making	*Principal actively concerned with instructional program*
24. Parental Involvement Policy	*Parental involvement in improvement and operation of instructional program*
25. School Demographics	*Size of school*
26. School Policies	*Explicit schoolwide discipline policy*

State and District Characteristics refers to governance and administration, state curriculum and textbook policies, testing and graduation requirement, teacher licensure, provisions in teacher contracts, and district-level administrative and fiscal variables.

27. State-Level Policies	*Teacher licensure requirements*
28. District Demographics	*School district size*

Figure 2-2
Relative Influences on Learning

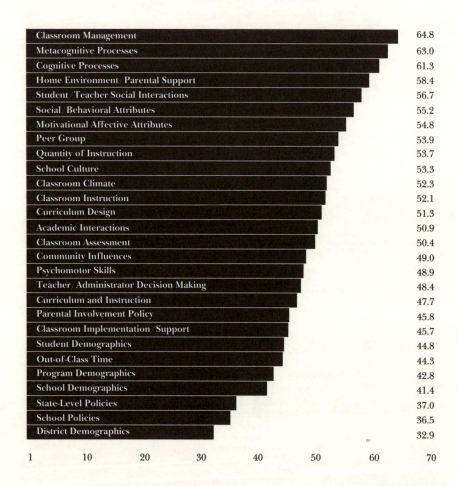

Influence	Value
Classroom Management	64.8
Metacognitive Processes	63.0
Cognitive Processes	61.3
Home Environment/Parental Support	58.4
Student/Teacher Social Interactions	56.7
Social/Behavioral Attributes	55.2
Motivational Affective Attributes	54.8
Peer Group	53.9
Quantity of Instruction	53.7
School Culture	53.3
Classroom Climate	52.3
Classroom Instruction	52.1
Curriculum Design	51.3
Academic Interactions	50.9
Classroom Assessment	50.4
Community Influences	49.0
Psychomotor Skills	48.9
Teacher/Administrator Decision Making	48.4
Curriculum and Instruction	47.7
Parental Involvement Policy	45.8
Classroom Implementation/Support	45.7
Student Demographics	44.8
Out-of-Class Time	44.3
Program Demographics	42.8
School Demographics	41.4
State-Level Policies	37.0
School Policies	36.5
District Demographics	32.9

that can be found for a given method or condition. Thus, the estimates we obtained represent an average or mean effect.

It should be noted that many of the meta-analyses were based only on standardized tests, essay examinations, and other traditional measures of learning outcomes. Few studies employed portfolio ratings, exhibitions, laboratory exercises, and other newly recommended measures, largely because little research has been done on such measures. Nonetheless, the many scholars who participated in our survey showed a high level of consistency in weighing the possible effects of some of the methods and conditions on the new outcome measures. The collective judgment of these experts then served as one of the indexes of the effectiveness of each method.

To better understand which influences were most important, we grouped the twenty-eight categories into six broad types of influences: student aptitude, classroom instruction and climate, context, program design, school organization, and state and district characteristics (see Figure 2-1). Figure 2-3 lists the six broad categories and their average rating of influence. These averages again confirmed the significant effect of direct influences.

STUDENT APTITUDES

Our research indicated that student aptitude was the most influential of the six broad types of influences. Among the categories of student aptitude, a student's *metacognitive processes*—that is, a student's capacity to plan, monitor, and, if necessary, replan learning strategies—had the most powerful effect on his or her learning. Research on metacognitive processes has generated new curriculums and new instructional techniques such as reciprocal teaching and cognitive skills instruction.

Cognitive processes were also identified as highly influential. Cognitive processes include not only variables such as general intelligence, but also prior knowledge, competency in reading and mathematics, and verbal knowledge.

Given the social nature of schooling, *social and behavioral attributes* constitute an important category. Children who frequently engage in disruptive behaviors, such as talking out of turn or hitting other children, often perform poorly in school, while children who engage in constructive behaviors are more likely to perform well.

The category *motivational and affective attributes* has received increased attention in the past decade. Student motivation determines effort and perseverance. Long acknowledged as significant by classroom teachers, effort and perseverance are now regarded by educational researchers as key attributes necessary for developing self-controlled, self-regulated learners.

Two remaining influences, *psychomotor skills* and *student demographics* (for example, gender and socioeconomic status) were minimally influential.

Figure 2-3
Average Influence of Six Categories of Influence on Student Learning

Types of Influence	Average Influence
Student Aptitude	54.7
Classroom Instruction and Climate	53.3
Context	51.4
Program Design	47.3
School Organization	45.1
State and District Characteristics	35.0

CLASSROOM INSTRUCTION AND CLIMATE

When averaged together, the different kinds of classroom instruction and climate had nearly as much impact on learning as the student aptitude categories. The most influential category, *classroom management*, includes group alerting, learner accountability, smooth transitions, and teacher "with-it-ness."[5] Effective classroom management increases student engagement, decreases disruptive behaviors, and makes good use of instructional time.

Constructive *student and teacher social interactions* also have a documented effect on school learning. The frequency and quality of these interactions contribute to students' sense of self-esteem and foster a sense of membership in the class and school.

The extensive research on *quantity of instruction* indicates that students need to be fully engaged in their academic pursuits and teachers need to make wise use of instructional time. Other things being equal, the more time spent in instruction, the better (within limits, of course).

Classroom climate refers to the socio-psychological dimensions of classroom life, including cooperation among teachers and students, common interests and values, the pursuit of common goals, a clear academic focus, well-organized and well-planned lessons, explicit learning objectives, an appropriate level of task difficulty

---

[5] The relationship between well-managed classrooms and student achievement is documented in Brophy and Evertson (1976), and in Good (1979). Some of the earliest and most informative research on classroom management resulted in the new terminology described in Kounin (1970).

for students, and an appropriate instructional pace (Haertel, Walberg, and Haertel, 1981).

Classroom instruction includes the techniques for ensuring that students understand both the goals of instruction and the content being presented. One example of these techniques is direct instruction, which emphasizes systematic sequencing of lessons, including the use of review, the presentation of new content and skills, guided student practice, the use of feedback and correctives, and independent student practice.

Both *academic interactions* and *classroom assessment* were moderately influential. Academic interactions include teachers' styles for questions, praise, reinforcement, and use of correctives. Classroom assessment, perhaps more than other methods, depends heavily on the nature and implementation of the assessment for its effectiveness. Many studies indicated that frequent assessment and feedback effectively promoted learning. Some researchers, however, were concerned about national and state assessments and outcome-based education driving educational reform. The mixture of these good results and grave concerns probably accounted for the moderate rating for assessment.

Classroom implementation and support deals with the delivery of instructional services, and staff development and the adequate training of teachers. This category was the least influential of the classroom instruction and climate categories. As with other categories that have been perceived by educators as important but which showed a weak influence on student learning, this category's weak showing may reflect the lack of implementation of its variables more than its relative influence. Although teachers may receive training on how to implement a particular practice or innovation, they may not be successful at putting these practices into action. This can be due to lack of resources, such as time or materials, or a lack of fit between existing classroom and school routines, instructional goals, and the new innovation.

Even though classroom implementation and support variables did not appear to be strong determinants of student performance in the present knowledge base analysis, they can have large effects if they are well implemented and well aligned with school and district goals. However, implementation not geared toward the targeted student outcomes may do little to enhance student learning.

CONTEXT

The four out-of-school contexts influenced school learning to nearly the same degree as student aptitude and classroom instruction and climate. The category *home environment/parental support* was among the most influential of the twenty-eight categories. The benefits of family involvement in improving students' academic performance have been well documented, as have its effects on improving school attendance and on reducing delinquency, pregnancies, and dropping out (Epstein, 1984; Moles, 1982; Peterson, 1989; Walberg, 1984). According to the data reported in the current research, the *peer group* category also had a strong influence on school learning.

The *community influences* category had less effect on school learning than either the home environment/parental support or the peer group categories. Only recently has the influence of the community on school learning been examined through empirical studies, and the evidence is not yet sufficient to suggest strong effects.

Out-of-class time includes student extracurricular activities and social clubs. These activities had considerably less influence on school learning than did the other contextual influences. The lack of measurement of the degree or validity of implementation limits research on student activities. Nevertheless, if well designed and well executed, such activities can contribute much to academic accomplishments. Out-of-class time spent on nonconstructive or nontargeted educationally related activities would not likely yield the expected student outcomes.

PROGRAM DESIGN

As a set, the three program design categories had a moderate influence on learning. Well-designed textbooks, appropriate organization of instructional groups, and effective alignment of goals and classroom activities yielded moderate benefits. The degree of program implementation is one likely determinant of the impact of program design variables on student learning.

SCHOOL ORGANIZATION

On average, school organization yielded moderate influence. Of its five categories, *school culture* was the most influential. School culture is an ethos conducive to teaching and learning. For example, a school might convey its academic atmosphere through participation in intramural academic competitions or through the use of incentives to reward student scholarship.

The category *teacher/administrator decision making* focuses on the role of the principal as an instructional leader. Although much attention has been paid to the importance of the principal's role, the research showed no strong link between principal leadership and student performance. The influence of an outstanding principal may be mitigated by many factors such as a high teacher turnover rate, an inexperienced team of teachers, or a high concentration of students in at-risk circumstances.

Parental involvement policy refers to parent involvement in the improvement and operation of the instructional program. A school may adopt a parental involvement policy, but successful implementation of a policy closely related to student development has a greater impact on student learning.

The last two categories, *school demographics* and *school policies*, had little influence on school learning compared to the other twenty-six categories. School demographics include the size of the school, the number of classrooms, and the number of teachers and aides. Examples of school-level policies include assertive discipline and telephoning the home when a child is tardy or absent.

STATE AND DISTRICT CHARACTERISTICS

Of the twenty-eight categories we examined, *state-level policies* and *district demographics* were among the least influential in improving student learning. Most of the variables included in these two categories are associated with school governance and administration. Examples of state-level policies include requirements for teacher licensure and evaluation and guidelines for the development and selection of curriculums and textbooks. Examples of district demographics include per-pupil expenditure, contractual limits on class size, and the degree of school district bureaucracy. Given that state and district influences are many steps removed from day-to-day classroom life, their impact on student learning is understandably limited.

CONCLUSIONS AND IMPLICATIONS

Although our three independent sources of evidence generally agreed on the impact of the twenty-eight categories on school learning, discrepancies existed, indicating areas for additional research. We hope that future studies and syntheses will yield greater consistency, but obtaining precise results has limitations. Due to varying circumstances and implementation, educators should not expect results identical to what others have attained. Practices that work well in some settings and with some students may not work well in others (although evidence for such exceptionality is easier to hypothesize than to show consistently).

The estimates obtained on the effectiveness of various educational strategies for improving student learning provide a set of considerations for formulating educational policies and practices as well as a way of identifying school improvement priorities. Overall, our findings support renewed emphasis on psychological, instructional, and contextual influences.

Paradoxically, the state, district, and school policies that have received the most attention recently appear to have the least influence on learning. Fifty years of research contradict educators' current reliance on school restructuring and organizational variables as key components of school reform. Because indirect influences may only affect direct influences, they appear to be weaker and less consistent in their results. For example, implementing a districtwide policy for teacher evaluation does not guarantee that students in any given classroom will have a competent teacher.

Unless reorganization and restructuring strongly affect the direct determinants of learning, they offer little hope of substantial improvement. Changing policies is unlikely to change practices in classrooms and homes, where learning actually takes place. Better alignment of remote policies and direct practices and more direct intervention in the psychological determinants of learning promise the most effective avenues of reform.

REFERENCES

Brophy, J., and Evertson, C. M. (1976). Learning. In *Teaching: A developmental perspective*. Boston: Allyn and Bacon.

Epstein, J. (1984). Effects of parent involvement on change in student achievement in reading and math. Paper presented at the annual meeting of the American Educational Research Association, New Orleans, La.

Good, T. (1979). Teacher effectiveness in the elementary school: What we know about it now. *Journal of Teacher Education, 30,* 52–64.

Haertel, G. D.; Walberg, H. J;. and Haertel, E. H. (1981). Social-psychological environments and learning: A quantitative synthesis. *British Educational Research Journal 7*: 27–36.

Haertel G. D.; Walberg, H. J.; and Weinstein, T. (1983). Psychological models of educational performance: A theoretical synthesis constructs. *Review of Educational Research, 53:* 75–91.

Kounin, J. (1970). *Discipline and group management in classrooms.* New York: Holt, Rinehart and Winston.

Moles, O. C. (1982). Syntheses of recent research on parent participation in children's education. *Educational Leadership 40*: 44–47.

Peterson, D. (1989). *Parent involvement in the educational process.* Urbana, Ill.: ERIC Clearinghouse on Educational Management, University of Illinois.

Reynolds, M. C.; Wang, M. C.; and Walberg, H. J. (1992). The knowledge bases for special and general education. *Remedial and Special Education 13*: 6–10, 33.

Walberg, H. J. (1984). Families as partners in educational productivity. *Phi Delta Kappan 65*: 397–400.

Wang, M. C.; Haertel, G. D.; and Walberg, H. J. (1990). What influences learning? A content analysis of review literature. *Journal of Educational Research 84*: 30–43.

Wang, M. C.; Haertel, G. D.; and H. J. Walberg. (1993). Toward a Knowledge Base for School Learning. *Review of Educational Research, 63*: 3.

Wang, M. C.; and Lindvall, C. M. (1984). Individual differences and school learning environments. In E.W. Gordon (ed.), *Review of research in education, vol 11* (pp. 161–225). Washington, D.C.: American Education Research Association.

Wang, M. C., and Walberg, H. J. (1985). Classroom climate as mediator of educational inputs and outputs. In B. J. Fraser (ed.), *The study of learning environments, 1985* (pp. 47–58). Salem, Ore.: Assessment Research.

3
Productive Teaching

Herbert J. Walberg

Twenty years ago several psychologists wrote an article entitled "The Quiet Revolution in Educational Research," in which they described the small, but growing, number of studies in education (Walberg, Schiller, and Haertel, 1979). Just five years later, the results of nearly 3,000 studies could be analyzed and reported (Walberg, 1984). In 1987, an Australian-United States team assessed 134 reviews of 7,827 field studies and several large-scale United States and international surveys of learning (Fraser, Walberg, Welch, and Hattie, 1987). This chapter provides a compact summary of the findings of approximately 8,000 studies on elementary and secondary school students and also assesses still more recent and definitive reviews of research on teaching and instruction.

I begin with the effects of the psychological elements of teaching and then discuss methods and patterns of teaching—all of which can be accomplished by a single teacher without unusual arrangements and equipment. Then I turn to the effects of systems of instruction that require special planning, student grouping, and materials. Next described are effects that are unique to reading, writing, science, and mathematics. The remaining results concern special students and techniques, and the effects of training on teachers.

The tables in this chapter summarize the results for each of fifteen categories of effects. Each table shows the number of studies reviewed and the size of the effect (expressed as the difference

---

Copyright 1990 Herbert J. Walberg. A previous version of this chapter was published in *Phi Delta Kappan* (vol. 71, February 1990, pp. 470–478).

between experimental and control groups in units of standard deviation), and also gives a graphic representation of the size of the effect. (For further details and references as to the procedures followed, see Walberg [1986] and Fraser et al. [1987].)

The compilation of effects allows us to compare educational methods with one another—including some effective ones that are no longer popular. We can see that some techniques have enormous effects, while others confer only trivial advantages or even harm learning. To plan and evaluate programs, we can examine the findings in the light of our own experience. In practice, however, we might attain results half or twice as good as the average estimates reported here. Our success will depend on our care in implementing our purposes. The best saw swung as a hammer may do little good.

PSYCHOLOGICAL ELEMENTS OF TEACHING

A little history will help us understand the evolution of psychological research on teaching. Psychologists have often emphasized either thought, feeling, or behavior at the expense of the other two, even though educators require a balance of the three. Today, thinking or cognition is sovereign in psychology, but a half-century ago behaviorists insisted on specific operational definitions—a standard still required.

In particular, Yale psychologists Neal Miller and John Dollard (1941), stimulated by E. L. Thorndike and B. F. Skinner, wrote about cues, response, and positive reinforcement, especially in psychotherapy. Later Dollard and Miller (1950) emphasized three components of teaching—cues, engagement, and reinforcement—similar to input, process, and output in physiology. Their influential conception stimulated research on what teachers do rather than on their age, experience, certification, college degrees, and other characteristics unconnected with what their students learn.

The behavioral model emphasized the quality of instructional cues impinging on the learner, the learner's active engagement in the process, and reinforcement or rewards that encourage continuing effort over time. Benjamin Bloom (1976) recognized, however, that learners may fail the first time or even repeatedly in cycles of cues and effort; if they make no progress, they may practice incorrect behaviors, and they must not be reinforced.

Table 3-1
Effects of Psychological Elements of Teaching

Elements	Number of Studies	Effect Size*	Graphic Representation of Effect Size
Cues	17	1.25	.xxxxxxxxxxxxx
Engagement	22	0.88	.xxxxxxxxx
Corrective feedback	20	0.94	.xxxxxxxxx
Reinforcement	39	1.17	.xxxxxxxxxxxx

* In all tables in this chapter, effect size is expressed as the difference between experimental and control groups in units of standard deviation.

Therefore, he introduced the ideas of feedback to correct errors and frequent testing to check progress. Inspired by John Carroll's (1963) model of school learning, Bloom emphasized learning time, and he also pointed out that some learners require much more time than others.

Table 3-1 shows the effects of certain psychological elements of teaching. Since an effect of 0.2 or 0.3 is worthwhile, the effects of cues, engagement, corrective feedback, and reinforcement that range from 0.88 to 1.25 are huge—they are among the largest estimates in this compilation. The underlying research has been unusually rigorous and well controlled. Even though it was conducted in school classes, the investigators helped to ensure precise timing and deployment of the elements in short-term studies lasting usually less than a month. Similar effects are difficult to sustain for long time periods.

Cues, as operationalized, show what is to be learned and explain how to learn it. Their quality can be seen in the clarity, salience, and meaningfulness of explanations and directions provided by teacher, instructional materials, or both. Ideally, as the learners gain confidence, the salience and numbers of cues can be reduced.

Engagement is the extent to which learners actively and persistently participate until appropriate responses are firmly entrenched in their repertoires. Such participation can be indexed by the extent to which the teacher engages students in overt or covert activity—indicated by absence of irrelevant behavior, concentration on tasks, enthusiastic contributions to group discussion, and lengthy study.

Corrective feedback remedies errors in oral or written responses. Ideally, students waste little time on incorrect responses, and teachers rapidly detect and remedy difficulties by reteaching or using alternate methods. When necessary, teachers also provide additional time for practice.

Reinforcement. The immense effort elicited by athletics, games, and other cooperative and competitive activities illustrates the power of immediate and direct reinforcement, and how some activities are intrinsically rewarding. By comparison, reinforcement in the classroom may seem crass or jejune.

The usual classroom reinforcers are acknowledgement of correctness and social approval in the form of, say, a smile or praise. More unusual reinforcers include contingent activity—allowing, for example, a music lesson or some other enjoyable activity for 90 percent correctness on a math test. Other reinforcers are tokens or check marks accumulated for steps accomplished and later exchanged for tangible reinforcers such as cookies, trinkets, or toys.

In special education programs, students have been reinforced not only for achievement but also for minutes of reading, attempts to learn, and accuracy of performance on tasks in special programs. When the environment can be rigorously controlled, and when teachers are able to gear reinforcement to performance accurately, as in programs for unruly or emotionally disturbed students, the results have been impressive (Mastropieri and Scruggs, 1987). Improved behavior and achievement, however, often fail to extend past the period of reinforcement or beyond the special environment.

Educators ordinarily confine reinforcement to marks, grades, and awards because they must assume that students work for intangible, long-term goals such as pleasing parents, further education, and adult success, and also (we hope) for an ultimate aim of education—the reward of learning itself. Even so, when corrective feedback and reinforcement are clear, rapid, and appropriate, they can powerfully affect learning by signaling what to do next without wasting time. In ordinary classrooms, then, the chief value of reinforcement is in providing information rather than incentive.

METHODS OF TEACHING

The psychological elements undergird many teaching methods and the design of instructional media. When the affective or informational content of cues, engagement, correctives, and reinforcement is improved, these methods have shown a range of effects from small to enormous, although generally not as big as short-term, highly controlled studies of the pure elements. (See Table 3-2.)

Cues

Cues can take many forms, of which the following are examples.

Advance organizers are brief overviews that abstractly relate new concepts or terms to previous learning. They are effective if they bridge new to old learning. Those spoken by the teacher or graphically illustrated in texts work best.

Adjunct questions alert students about key questions to answer—particularly in texts. They work best on questions repeated on posttests, and moderately well on questions related to the adjuncts. As we might expect, however, adjunct questions distract attention away from incidental material that might otherwise be learned.

Goal setting sets forth objectives, guidelines, methods, or standards for learning. Like adjunct questions, goal setting sacrifices incidental for intended learning.

Learning hierarchies assume that instruction can be made efficient if facts, skills, or ideas that logically or psychologically precede others are presented first. Teaching and instructional media sequenced in this way appear slightly more effective. Learners, however, may adapt themselves to apparently ill-sequenced material; and it may be advantageous to learn to do so, since human life, as Franz Kafka showed, may depart from logical progression.

Pretests are benchmarks for determining how much students learn under various methods of teaching. Psychologists have found, however, that pretests can have positive cuing effects if they show students what will be emphasized by instruction and on posttests.

Several principles follow from these results. To concentrate learning on essential points and to save time, as in training, remove elaborations and extraneous oral and written prose. To focus learners on selected questions or to teach them to find answers in elaborated prose such as in textbooks, use adjunct questions and goal setting. To encourage acquisition of as much undifferentiated material as possible, as in college lecture courses, assign big blocks of text and test students on randomly selected points. Although the means may seem clear, consensus about educational purposes may be difficult.

Table 3-2
Effects of Methods of Teaching

Method	Number of Studies	Effect Size	Graphic Representation of Effect Size
Advance organizers			
Overall effect	29	0.45	.xxxxx
Bridging			
from previous knowledge	a	0.75	.xxxxxxxx
from previous material	a	0.71	.xxxxxxx
unspecified bridging	a	−0.02	
Presentation mode			
spoken	a	0.68	.xxxxxxx
written and illustrated	a	0.40	.xxxx
written only	a	0.34	.xxx
Advance organizers in science	16	0.24	.xx
Adjunct questions			
repeated	61	0.96	.xxxxxxxxxx
related	61	0.50	.xxxxx
unrelated	61	−0.13	x.
Goal setting			
on intended outcomes	21	0.40	.xxxx
on unintended outcomes	20	−0.20	xx.
Focusing in science	25	0.48	.xxxxx
Learning hierarchies	15	0.18	.xx
Pretests			
outcome			
cognitive	a	0.43	.xxxx
attitude	a	0.29	.xxx
pretest-posttest			
same	a	0.25	.xxx
different	a	0.11	.x
Behavioral objectives	111	0.12	.x
High expectations	77	0.32	.xxx
Frequent testing			
on quizzes	4	0.49	.xxxxx
on final examinations	30	0.19	.xx
on attitudes	5	0.50	.xxxxx
Increased testing in science	33	0.37	.xxxx
Questioning	14	0.26	.xxx
Questioning in science	11	0.56	.xxxxxx

Productive Teaching

Wait time in science	2	0.53	.xxxxx
Homework			
with teacher comments	2	0.83	.xxxxxxxx
graded	5	0.78	.xxxxxxxx
assigned	47	0.28	.xxx
Remediation/Feedback			
in science	28	0.54	.xxxxx
Feedback	15	0.45	.xxxxx
Praise	14	0.16	.xx

[a] The reviews examined did not include information on the number of studies involved in these comparisons.

Clarity at the start saves time and helps learners to see things the teacher's way; but it deters autonomy and deep, personal insights. For example, at one extreme, Zen masters ask novitiates about the sound of one hand clapping and wait a decade or two for an answer. Hiroshi Azuma and Robert Hess find that Japanese mothers use indirection and vagueness in teaching their young children more than do assertive American mothers; and I have observed Japanese science teachers asking questions and leaving them long unresolved. Does such vagueness cultivate initiative and perseverance?

Engagement

A variety of means can help to increase students' engagement.

High expectations transmit teachers' standards of learning and performance. These may function as both cues and incentives for students to engage actively with extended effort and perseverance.

Frequent tests increase learning by demanding increased effort and feedback. Their effects are larger, however, on performance on quizzes than on final examinations.

Questioning also appears to work by increasing students' engagement and may encourage deeper thinking, as in Plato's accounts of Socrates. Questioning has bigger effects in science than in other subjects. Mary Budd Rowe and Ken Tobin have shown that *wait time*, that is, allowing students several seconds to reflect rather than the usual 0.9 second, leads to longer and better answers.

Correctives and Reinforcement

Corrective feedback remedies errors by reteaching, using the same or a different method. It has moderate effects that are somewhat higher in science than in other subjects—perhaps because science requires more conceptual thinking than memorization.

Homework by itself constructively extends engagement or learning time. Correctives and reinforcement in the form of grades and comments on homework raise its effects dramatically.

Praise has a small, positive effect. For young or disturbed children, praise may lack the power of tangible and token reinforcers used in psychological experiments. For students able to see ahead, grades and personal standards may be more powerful reinforcers than momentary encouragement. Praise may be under- or oversupplied; it may appear demeaning or sardonic; and it may pale in comparison with the incentives of U.S. youth culture, such as cars, clothes, dating, and athletics.

None of this is to say that encouragement, incentives, and good classroom morale should be abandoned; honey may be better than vinegar. As cognitive psychologists point out, moreover, the main classroom value of reinforcement may lie in its information for the student about his or her progress rather than in its power to reward.

PATTERNS OF TEACHING

As explained above, methods of teaching enact or combine more fundamental psychological elements. By further extension, patterns of teaching integrate elements and methods of teaching. These more inclusive formulations follow the evolution of psychological research on education. Behavioral research moved in the 1950s from psychological laboratories to classrooms, where short-term, controlled experiments were conducted on one element at a time. And in the 1970s, educational researchers tried to find patterns of effective practices from observations of ordinary teaching.

Thus, behaviorists traded educational realism for theoretical parsimony and scientific rigor; later psychologists preferred realism until their insights were experimentally confirmed. Fortunately, the results from both approaches appear to converge. It seems possi-

Productive Teaching

Table 3-3
Effects of Patterns of Teaching

Patterns	Number of Studies	Effect Size	Graphic Representation of Effect Size
Explicit or direct teaching	13	0.55	.xxxxxx
Comprehension teaching	20	0.71	.xxxxxxx

ble, moreover, to incorporate the work of cognitive psychologists that took place during the 1980s into an enlarged understanding of teaching.

Table 3-3 summarizes results of studies of two patterns of teaching—explicit teaching and comprehension teaching.

Explicit Teaching

Explicit teaching can be viewed as traditional or conventional whole-group teaching done well. Since most teaching has changed little in the last three-quarters of a century (Hoetker and Ahlbrand, 1969) and may not change substantially in the near future, it is worthwhile knowing how the usual practice can excel. Since it has evolved from ordinary practice, explicit teaching is easy to carry out and does not disrupt conventional institutions and expectations. it can, moreover, incorporate many previously discussed elements and methods.

Systematic research was initiated about 1960 by N. L. Gage, Donald Medley, and others who employed "process-product" investigations of the association between what teachers do and how much their students learn. Jere Brophy, Carolyn Evertson, Thomas Good, and Jane Stallings later contributed substantially to this effort. Walter Doyle, Penelope Peterson, and Lee Shulman put the results in a psychological, particularly cognitive, context. Barak Rosenshine has periodically reviewed the research; Gage and Margaret Needels measured the results and sharply pointed out their implications.

These various contributors do not completely agree about the essential components of explicit teaching; and they refer to it by different names, such as explicit, process-product, direct, active, and effective teaching. The researchers, moreover, weigh their own results heavily; but Rosenshine, a long-standing and comprehensive reviewer, has given us an eagle's eye view of the results (see Wittrock, 1986).

In his early reviews of correlation studies, Rosenshine discussed the traits of effective teachers, which include clarity, task orientation, enthusiasm, and flexibility, as well as their tendencies to structure their presentations and occasionally use student ideas. From later observational and control-group research, Rosenshine identified six phased functions of explicit teaching: (1) daily review, homework check, and, if necessary, reteaching; (2) rapid presentation of new content and skills in small steps; (3) guided student practice with close monitoring by teachers; (4) corrective feedback and instructional reinforcement; (5) independent practice in seatwork and homework with a high, more than 90 percent, success rate; and (6) weekly and monthly review.

Comprehension Teaching

The descendants of Aristotle and the Anglo-American tradition of Bacon, Locke, Thorndike, and Skinner objected to philosophical "armchair" opinions—mid-century behaviorists, particularly John Watson, constructively insisted on hard empirical facts about learning. But they also saw the child's mind as a blank tablet, and seemed to encourage active teaching and passive acquisition of isolated facts. Around 1980, cognitive psychologists reacted to such atomism and William James's "bucket" metaphor by reviving research on student-centered learning and "higher mental processes," in the tradition of Plato, Socrates, Kant, Rousseau, Dewey, Freud, and Piaget. At times, however, contemporary interpretation of this tradition has led to vacuity and permissiveness, as in the extremes of the "progressive education" movement of the 1930s.

The Russian psychologist Lev Vygotsky (1978) developed an influential compromise. Emphasizing the two-way nature of teaching, he identified a "zone of proximal development" extending from what learners can do independently to the maximum they can do with the teacher's help. Accordingly, teachers should set up "scaffolding" for building knowledge but remove it when it becomes unnecessary. In mathematics, for example, the teacher can give hints and examples, foster independent use, and then remove support. This approach is similar to the "prompting" and "fading" of the behavioral cues and to common sense; but it sufficed to revive interest in transferring some autonomy to students.

Productive Teaching

In the 1980s, cognitive research on teaching sought ways to encourage self-monitoring, self-teaching, and "metacognition" to foster independence. Skills were important, but the learner's monitoring and management of them had primacy, as the explicit teaching functions of planning, allocating time, and review are partly transferred to learners.

Pearson (1985), for example, outlined three phases of metacognitive teaching: (1) modeling, where the teacher exhibits the desired behavior; (2) guided practice, where students perform with help from the teacher; and (3) application, where the student performs independently of the teacher—much like explicit teaching functions. Pallincsar and Brown (1984), moreover, described a program of "reciprocal teaching" to foster comprehension. In that program, students took turns leading dialogues on pertinent features of a text. By assuming the planning and executive control ordinarily exercised by teachers, students learned planning, structuring, and self-management—which is perhaps why tutors learn from teaching, and why we say that if you want to learn something well, teach it.

Comprehension teaching encourages students to measure their progress toward explicit goals. If necessary, they can reallocate time for different activities. In this way, self-awareness, personal control, and positive self-evaluation can be enlarged.

Learner Autonomy in Science

The National Science Foundation sponsored many studies of student inquiry and autonomy that showed that giving students opportunities to manipulate science materials, to contract with teachers about what to learn, to inquire on their own, and to engage in activity-based curricula all have substantial effects, as shown in Table 3-4. Group work and self-direction, however, had smaller positive effects; and pass-fail grading and self-grading had small negative effects. Methods of providing greater learner autonomy may work well in subjects other than science, as in the more radical and general approach discussed next.

Open Education

In the late 1960s, open educators increased autonomy in primary grades by enabling students to join teachers in planning educational purposes, means, and evaluation. In contrast

Table 3-4
Effects of Learner Autonomy in Science

Method	Number of Studies	Effect Size	Graphic Representation of Effect Size
Student manipulatives	24	0.56	.xxxxxx
Contracts for learning	12	0.47	.xxxxx
Inquiry-discovery	38	0.41	.xxxx
Activity-based curricula	57	0.35	.xxxx
Self-directed study	27	0.08	.x
Pass-fail or self-grading	13	−0.13	x.

to teacher- and textbook-centered education, students were given a voice in choosing what to learn—even to the point of writing their own texts to share with one another. Open educators tried to foster cooperation, critical thinking, constructive attitudes, and self-directed life-long learning. Open educators revived the spirit of the New England town meeting—of Thoreau's self-reliance, Emerson's transcendentalism, and Dewey's progressivism. Their ideas also resonate with the late Carl Rogers's "client-centered" psychotherapy that emphasizes the "unconditional worth" of the person. The effects of open education are summarized in Table 3-5.

Giaconia and Hedges's (1982) synthesis of 153 studies showed that open education had worthwhile effects on creativity, independence, cooperation, attitudes toward teachers and schools, mental ability, psychological adjustment, and curiosity. They found that students in open programs were less motivated to grub for grades, but they differed little from other students in actual achievement, self-concept, and anxiety. They also found, however, that open programs that are more effective in producing the nonachievement outcomes—attitudes, creativity, and self-concept—sacrificed some academic achievement on standardized measures. These programs emphasized the role of the child in learning, use of diagnostic rather than norm-referenced evaluation, individualized instruction, and manipulative materials; but they neglected to emphasize three other components thought by some to be essential to open programs—multi-age grouping, open space, and team teaching.

Giaconia and Hedges speculated that children in the most extreme open programs may do somewhat less well on conventional achievement tests because they have little experience with them. At any rate, it appears that unless they are radically extreme,

Productive Teaching

Table 3-5
Effects of Open Education

Attitude/Achievement	Number of Studies	Effect Size	Graphic Representation of Effect Size
Creativity	22	0.29	.xxx
Independence	22	0.28	.xxx
Cooperativeness	8	0.23	.xx
Attitude toward teachers	17	0.20	.xx
Mental ability	16	0.18	.xx
Adjustment	9	0.17	.xx
Attitude toward school	50	0.17	.xx
Curiosity	7	0.17	.xx
Self-concept	60	0.07	.x
Locus of control	16	0.01	.
Anxiety	19	−0.01	.
Mathematics achievement	57	−0.04	.
Language achievement	33	−0.07	x.
Reading achievement	63	−0.08	x.
Achievement motivation	8	−0.26	xxx.

open classes enhance several nonstandard outcomes without detracting from academic achievement.

EFFECTS OF INSTRUCTIONAL SYSTEMS

All the techniques discussed thus far can be planned and executed by a single teacher with perhaps some extra effort, encouragement, or training but without unusual preparation and materials. In contrast, instructional systems require special arrangements and planning, and they often combine several components of instruction. Moreover, they tend to emphasize adaption of instruction to individual students rather than student adaption to a fixed pattern of teaching such as explicit whole-group instruction. The effects of instructional systems are shown in Table 3-6.

A little history will aid our understanding of current systems. *Programmed instruction*, popular in the 1950s, presents a series of "frames," each one of which conveys an item of information and requires a student response. *Linear* programs present a graduated

Table 3-6
Effects of Instructional Systems

System	Number of Studies	Effect Size	Graphic Representation of Effect Size
Programmed instruction			
in science			
branched	5	0.21	.xx
linear	47	0.17	.xx
in mathematics	153	0.10	.x
Individualization			
in science	131	0.17	.xx
in mathematics	153	0.16	.xx
in high schools	51	0.10	.x
Mastery learning			
require mastery before next unit	3	0.99	.xxxxxxxxxx
unit mastery level			
91–100	17	0.73	.xxxxxxx
81–90	15	0.51	.xxxxx
70–80	17	0.38	.xxxx
Duration of program			
up to one month	12	0.65	.xxxxxxx
17 or more weeks	6	0.30	.xxx
Level			
college	27	0.58	.xxxxxx
precollege	22	0.49	.xxxxx
Adaptive instruction	37	0.45	.xxxxx

series of frames with knowledge increments so small that learning steps may be nearly errorless and continuously reinforced by progression to the next frame; able students proceed quickly. *Branched* programs direct students back when necessary for reteaching; to the side for correctives; and ahead when they already know parts of the material. The ideas of continuous progress and branching influenced later developers who tried to optimize learning by individualization, mastery learning, and computer-assisted instruction.

Individualization adapts instruction to individual needs by varying speed or branching and by using booklets, worksheets, coaching, and the like. Perhaps because they have been vaguely defined and operationalized, individualized programs have had small effects. Other systems such as mastery learning (discussed below) appear more effective for adapting instruction to the needs of individual learners.

Mastery learning combines the psychological elements of instruction with suitable amounts of time. Formative tests are employed to allocate time and guide reinforcement and corrective feedback. In the most definitive synthesis, Kulik and Kulik (1986) reported substantial effects for mastery learning. Mastery programs that yielded larger effects established a criterion of 95 to 100 percent mastery and required repeated testing to ensure mastery before allowing students to proceed to additional units (which yielded a gigantic effect of one standard deviation). Mastery learning yielded larger effects on less able students, and reduced the disparities in performance to 82 percent of the control groups.

The success of mastery learning is attributable to several features. The Kuliks, for example, found that when control groups were provided feedback from quizzes, the mastery groups' advantage was smaller. Mastery, as Bloom pointed out, takes additional time; the Kuliks found that it required a median of 16 percent (and up to 97 percent) more time than did conventional instruction. The seven mastery studies that provided equal time for mastery and control groups showed a very small advantage for mastery learning, indicated by performance on standardized tests. The advantage, however, was moderate on experimenter-made, criterion-referenced tests for nine equal-time studies. These results illustrate the separate contribution of cues, feedback, and time components of mastery learning.

Mastery learning studies lasting less than a month's duration yielded larger effects than those lasting more than four months. Retention probably declines sharply no matter what the educational method, but the decline can be more confidently noted about mastery, since it has been more extensively investigated.

Bloom and his students have reported larger effects than has Slavin (1987), who reviewed their work. Guskey and Gates (1986), for example, reported an effect of 0.78, estimated from thirty-eight studies of elementary and secondary students. Anderson and Burns (1987), in response to Slavin, pointed out two reasons for larger effects in some studies, especially those under Bloom's supervision. Bloom has been interested more in what is possible than in what is likely; he has sought to find the limits of learning. His students, moreover, have conducted tightly controlled experiments over time periods shorter than a semester or a year.

Adaptive instruction, developed by Margaret Wang and others, combines mastery, cooperative, open, tutoring, computer, and comprehension approaches into a complex system to tailor instruction to individual and small-group needs. It includes managerial steps executed by a master teacher, including planning, time allocation, task delegation to aides and students, and quality control. It is a comprehensive program for the whole school day rather than a single method that requires simple integration into one subject or into a single teacher's repertoire. Its achievement effects are substantial, but its broader effects are probably underestimated, since adaptive instruction aims at diverse ends including student autonomy, intrinsic motivation, and teacher and student choice, which are poorly indicated by the usual outcome measures.

Computer-Assisted Instruction

Ours may be the age of computers, and they have already been shown to have substantial effects on learning. With hardware costs declining and software increasing in sophistication, we may hope that computers will have still more effects on learning as they become better integrated into school programs.

Computers show the greatest advantage for handicapped students—probably because they may be more adaptive to these students' special needs; computers may also be more patient, discreet, nonjudgmental, or even encouraging about students' progress. Perhaps for the same reasons, computers have generally bigger effects in elementary schools than in high schools and colleges. Effects of computer-assisted instruction are shown in Table 3-7.

Another explanation, however, is plausible. Elementary schools provide less tracking and differentiated courses for homogeneous groups. Computers may adapt to larger within-class differences among elementary students by allowing them to proceed at their own pace, without making invidious comparisons between students.

Simulation and games, with or without computer implementation, require active, specific learner responses and may strike a balance between the vicarious book learning and the dynamic, complicated, and competitive "real world." Their interactiveness, speed, intensity, movement, color, and sound add interest and information to academic learning. If games are not geared to an educational purpose, however, they can also waste time—as in arcade games.

Productive Teaching

Table 3-7
Effects of Computer-Assisted Instruction

Level	Number of Studies	Effect Size	Graphic Representation of Effect Size
Handicapped	26	0.66	.xxxxxxx
Elementary	28	0.47	.xxxxx
Elementary	28	0.45	.xxxxx
Japanese elementary and secondary	4	0.45	.xxxxx
Adult	24	0.42	.xxxx
Secondary, college	11	0.42	.xxxx
Elementary, secondary	33	0.42	.xxxx
Secondary	42	0.42	.xxxx
Elementary and secondary mathematics	46	0.39	.xxxx
Secondary	42	0.32	.xxx
College	101	0.26	.xxx
Simulation and games	93	0.35	.xxxx

Student Grouping

Teaching students what they already know and what they are yet incapable of learning are equally wasteful—they are perhaps even harmful to motivation. For this reason, traditional whole-class teaching of heterogeneous groups can present serious difficulties and inefficiency—often unacknowledged in our egalitarian age. Most educators recognize that it is difficult to teach arithmetic and trigonometry at the same time. (Even some English professors might balk at teaching phonics and deconstructionism simultaneously.) If we want students to learn as much as possible rather than make them all alike, we need to consider how they are grouped, and try to help the full range. Effects of various types of student grouping are shown in Table 3-8.

Acceleration programs identify talented youth (often in mathematics and science) and group them together or with older students. Such programs provide counseling, encouragement, contact with accomplished adults, grade skipping, summer school, and the compression of the standard curriculum into fewer years. The effects are huge in elementary schools, substantial in junior high schools, and moderate in senior high schools. The smaller effects at advanced levels may be attributable to the smaller advantage of acceleration over tracking and

Table 3-8
Effects of Student Grouping

Type of Grouping	Number of Studies	Effect Size	Graphic Representation of Effect Size
Acceleration of talented students			
elementary	3	1.43	.xxxxxxxxxxxxxx
junior high school	9	0.76	.xxxxxxxx
senior high school	1	0.23	.xxx
Ability grouping in high school			
talented students	14	0.33	.xxx
senior high school	18	0.20	.xx
junior high school	33	0.05	.x
average and deficient students	27	0.02	.
on subject matter attitudes	8	0.37	.xxxx
Ability grouping in elementary school			
cross-grade reading group	14	0.45	.xxxxx
within-class mathematics	5	0.32	.xxx
self-contained classes	14	0.00	.
Tutoring			
in mathematics	153	0.61	.xxxxxx
all courses	65	0.41	.xxxx

differentiated course placement practiced in high schools.

The effects of <u>acceleration</u> on educational attitudes, vocational plans, participation in school activities, popularity, psychological adjustment, and character ratings were mixed and often insignificant. These outcomes may not be systematically affected in either direction.

Ability grouping is based on achievement, intelligence tests, personal insights, and subjective opinions. In high school, ability grouping leaves deficient and average students unaffected but yields big benefits with talented students and on improving students' attitudes toward the subject matter. In elementary schools, the grouping of students with similar reading achievement but from different grades yields substantial effects. Within-class grouping in mathematics yields worthwhile effects, but generalized grouping does not.

Tutoring, because it gears instruction to individual or small-group needs, yields big effects on both tutees and tutors. It yields particularly large effects in mathematics—perhaps because of the subject's well-defined scope and organization.

In whole-group instruction, teachers may ordinarily focus on average or deficient students to ensure that they master the lessons. But when talented students are freed from repetition and slow progression, they can proceed quickly. Grouping may work best when students are accurately grouped according to their specific subject matter needs rather than IQ, demeanor, or other irrelevant characteristics.

Well-defined subject matter and student grouping may be among the chief reasons why Japanese students lead the world in achievement; their curriculum is explicit, rigorous, and nationally uniform. In primary schools, weaker students, with maternal help, study harder and longer to keep up with exacting requirements. Subject matter admission tests are used several times to screen students into lower and upper secondary schools and universities of well-known gradations of rigor and prestige. Each gradation indicates occupational, marital, and other adult prospects; future adult rewards thus reinforce educational effort.

Social Environment

The effects of various types of social environments are shown in Table 3-9. *Cooperative learning* programs delegate some control of the pacing and methods of learning to groups of two to six students who work together (and sometimes compete with other groups within classes). Their success may be attributable to (a) relief from the exclusively teacher-to-student interaction of whole-group teaching, (b) the time freed for interactive engagement of students (highest in two-person teams), and (c) the opportunities for targeted cues, engagement, correctives, and reinforcement. As in comprehension teaching, moreover, the acts of tutoring and teaching may encourage students to think about subject matter organization and productive time allocation.

Many correlational studies suggest that *classroom morale* is associated with achievement gains, greater subject matter interest, and the worthy end of voluntary participation in nonrequired subject-related activities. Morale is assessed by asking students to agree or disagree with such statements as "Most of the students know each other well" and "The class members know the purpose of the lessons."

Table 3-9
Effects of Social Environment

Type of Environment	Number of Studies	Effect Size	Graphic Representation of Effect Size
Cooperative learning	182	0.78	.xxxxxxxx
Classroom morale (correlational)			
cohesiveness	50	0.23	.xx
satisfaction	54	0.22	.xx
material environment	49	0.18	.xx
goal direction	51	0.17	.xx
democracy	50	0.17	.xx
task difficulty	50	0.13	.x
formality	57	0.06	.x
competition	35	0.06	.x
diversity	47	0.02	.
speed	48	−0.02	.
cliqueness	46	−0.12	x.
disorganization	50	−0.13	x.
apathy	48	−0.14	x.
favoritism	46	−0.16	xx.
friction	53	−0.23	xx.

Students who perceive their classroom morale as friendly, satisfying, goal-directed, and challenging and their classroom as having the required materials tend to learn more. Those who perceive student cliques, disorganization, apathy, favoritism, and friction learn less. The research, though plausible, lacks the causal confidence and specificity of control-group experiments on directly alterable methods discussed previously and in following paragraphs.

Reading Effects

Comprehension teaching, because it may extend to several subjects in elementary schools, is discussed above under patterns of teaching. Several other reading effects are substantial. (See Table 3-10.)

Adaptive speed training involves principles similar to those of comprehension training. It shows learners how to vary their pace and depth of reflection according to the difficulty of material and their purposes in reading. It yields big effects on the capacity to shift gears in reading.

Reading methods vary widely, but their largest effects seem to occur when teachers are systematically trained almost irrespec-

Productive Teaching

Table 3-10
Effects of Reading Methods

Method	Number of Studies	Effect Size	Graphic Representation of Effect Size
Adaptive speed training	28	0.95	.xxxxxxxxxx
Reading methods	97	0.61	.xxxxxx
Adjunct pictures	16	0.22	.xx
Pictures in prose			
transformative	18	1.42	.xxxxxxxxxxxxxx
interpretive	24	0.75	.xxxxxxxx
organizational	21	0.72	.xxxxxxxx
representative	79	0.54	.xxxxx
decorative	8	−0.12	x.

tive of particularities of method. *Phonics* or "word-attack" approaches, however, have moderate advantage over guessing and "whole-word" approaches in the teaching of beginning reading—perhaps because early misconceptions are avoided. Phonics may also reduce the need for excessive reteaching and correctives.

Pictures in the text can be very helpful, although they increase the cost of books, and occupy space that could otherwise be used for prose. Several types of pictures can be distinguished; in order of their effects they are:

Transformational pictures recode information into concrete memorable form, relate information in a well-organized context, and provide links for systematic retrieval.

Interpretive pictures, like advance organizers, make text comprehensible by relating abstract to concrete terms and the unfamiliar and difficult to previous knowledge.

Organizational pictures, including maps and diagrams, show the coherence of objects or events in space and time.

Representational pictures are photos or other concrete representations of what the prose relates.

Decorative pictures present information incidental to (and possibly irrelevant to or conflicting with) intended learning (researchers might concede that decoration may add interest if not information).

As Levin, Anglin, and Carney (1987) conclude, pictures can provide vivid imagery and metaphors that facilitate memorization, show what is important to learn, and intensify the effects of oral prose, as in ordinary teaching. Pictures may allow students to bypass the text; but memorable, well-written prose may obviate pictures.

Writing Effects

Well-designed studies of methods of teaching writing contrasted experimental treatments with control groups. In order of the sizes of effects on prose quality (see Table 3-11), the methods were as follows:

Inquiry requires students to find and state specific details that convey personal experience vividly; to examine sets of data to develop and support explanatory generalizations; or to analyze situations that present ethical problems and arguments.

Scales are criteria or specific questions students apply to their own and others' writing to improve it.

Sentence combining shows students how to build complex sentences from simpler ones.

Models are presentations of good pieces of writing for students to follow.

Free writing allows students to write about whatever occurs to them.

Grammar and mechanics includes sentence parsing and analysis of the parts of speech.

Science Effects

Begun about 1960 in response to the Russian space launch, the "new" science curricula, sponsored by the National Science Foundation, yielded substantial effects on learning. The curricula efficiently added value by producing superior learning on tests of their intended outcomes and general subject matter goals. The new curricula also yielded small to substantial effects on often unmeasured outcomes such as creativity, problem solving, science attitudes and skills, logical thinking, and achievement in nonscience subject matter. The effects of various science programs are shown in Table 3-12.

Perhaps these advantages were gained by a collaboration of teachers, psychologists, and scientists to ensure modern content and teaching efficacy. Scientists may have generated enthusiasm for teaching scientific methods, laboratory work, and other course reforms.

The new science curricula worked well in improving achievement and other outcomes. Ironically, they are often forgotten today despite poor U.S. mathematics and science scores by international standards. A discussion of some of these methods follows,

Table 3-11
Effects of Writing Methods

Method	Number of Studies	Effect size	Graphic Representation of Effect Size
Inquiry	6	0.57	.xxxxxx
Scales	6	0.36	.xxxx
Sentence combining	5	0.35	.xxxx
Models	7	0.22	.xx
Free writing	10	0.16	.xx
Grammar/Mechanics	5	−0.30	xxx.

Table 3-12
Effects of Science Programs

Program	Number of Studies	Effect Size	Graphic Representation of Effect Size
New curricula in general	105	0.37	.xxxx
New curricula on tests of			
new content	9	0.39	.xxxx
neutral content	11	0.41	.xxxx
old content	1	−0.13	x.
New curricula on			
creativity	5	0.71	.xxxxxxx
problem solving	4	0.71	.xxxxxxx
scientific understanding	28	0.61	.xxxxxx
spatial relations	2	0.57	.xxxxxx
subject attitude	6	0.51	.xxxxx
science attitude	25	0.50	.xxxxx
general science achievement	111	0.43	.xxxx
science method attitude	10	0.41	.xxxx
mathematics achievement	18	0.40	.xxxx
communication skills	5	0.40	.xxxx
social studies achievement	2	0.25	.xxx
critical thinking	31	0.19	.xx
scientific skills	28	0.17	.xx
logical thinking	14	0.16	.xx
reading achievement	23	0.10	.x
synthesis and analysis	11	0.05	.x
fact recall	8	0.02	.
self-concept	10	−0.08	x.

continued on page 98

Table 3-12
Continued

Program	Number of Studies	Effect Size	Graphic Representation of Effect Size
Inquiry teaching	68	0.43	.xxxx
Audio-tutorial	7	0.17	.xx
Original source papers	13	0.14	.x
Team teaching	41	0.06	.x
Departmentalized elementary programs	3	−0.09	x.
Media-based instruction television	40	0.06	.x
film	58	−0.07	x.

Inquiry teaching, often practiced in Japan, requires students to formulate hypotheses, reason about their creditability, and design experiments to test their validity. Inquiry teaching yields substantial effects—particularly on the understanding of scientific processes.

Audio-tutorials are tape-recorded instructions for using media such as laboratory equipment, manipulatives, and readings for topical lessons or whole courses. This simple approach yields somewhat better results than conventional instruction, allows independent learning, and has the further advantage of individual pacing—allowing students to pursue special topics or take courses on their own.

Original source papers derive from the "Great Books" approach of University of Chicago President Robert Maynard Hutchins and his colleague Mortimore Adler, who saw more value in reading Plato or Newton than predigested textbook accounts. Those who trade depth for breadth believe it is better to know few ideas of transcending importance than many unconnected bits of soon forgotten information. They have shown that such knowledge can be acquired by studying and discussing science papers of historical or scientific significance.

The effects of other science instruction methods are near zero, that is, close to the effects of the usual methods of teaching. They include *team teaching, departmentalized elementary programs*, and *media-based instruction*. The results for media-based instruction, however, suggest choices that can be based on cost and convenience. In particular, since live television and canned film can be broadcast, they can provide equally effective education

Productive Teaching

over wide areas (even the world by satellite); and students today, moreover, can interact "on-line" with far-away teachers and fellow students. Some precedents follow:

1. For a decade, the Chicago Community Colleges gave dozens of mainly one-way television courses to hundreds of thousands of students who studied mostly at home but also participated in discussion and testing sessions at several sites in the metropolitan area. The best lecturers, media specialists, and test constructors could be employed; and tapes of the courses could be rebroadcast indefinitely.
2. In several third-world countries gaining in student achievement and enrollments, ministries of education make efficient use of such low-cost but effective "distance education" for remote elementary and secondary schools.
3. The Oklahoma and Minnesota state departments of education apparently lead the nation in providing specialized teachers and two-way courses in advanced science, mathematics, foreign language, and other subjects by broadcasting them to small high schools in rural areas.

Mathematics Effects

In the heyday of its Education Directorate, the National Science Foundation sponsored considerable research not only on science but also on mathematics. Some worthwhile effects were found, as shown in Table 3-13.

Manipulative materials such as Cuisinnaire rods, balance beams, counting sticks, and measuring scales allow students to engage directly in learning rather than to follow passively abstract teacher presentations. Students can handle the material, see the relation of abstract ideas and concrete embodiments, and check hypothesized answers by doing quick empirical tests—without having to wait for quiz results or teacher feedback. The apparent result: enormous effects.

Problem solving in mathematics yields worthwhile effects. It requires comprehension of terms and their application to varied examples. It may motivate students by showing them the application of mathematical ideas to "real-world" questions.

The new mathematics produced beneficial results, although not as big as the new science curricula. Both reforms probably gained their learning advantages partly by testing what they taught.

Table 3-13
Effects of Mathematics Methods

Method	Number of Studies	Effect Size	Graphic Representation of Effect Size
Manipulative materials	64	1.04	.xxxxxxxxxx
Problem solving	33	0.35	.xxxx
New mathematics	134	0.24	.xx

Special Populations and Techniques

We can gain insights from programs outside the usual scope of elementary and secondary classrooms. (See Table 3-14.)

Early intervention programs include educational, psychological, and therapeutic components for handicapped, at-risk, and disadvantaged children from one month to sixty-six months of age. The immediate and large outcome advantages declined rapidly and disappeared after three years.

Preschool programs also showed initial learning effects that were unsustained. It appears that young children can learn more than is normally assumed; but, like other learners, they can also forget. The key to sustained gains may be sustained programs and effective families—not one-shot approaches.

Handicapped students classified as mentally retarded, emotionally disturbed, and learning disabled have been subjects in research that has several important implications. When they serve as *tutors* of one another and younger students, handicapped students can learn well—a finding similar to those in comprehension monitoring and tutoring studies of nonhandicapped children that show beneficial effects of teaching on tutors. "Handicapped" students, moreover, are often spuriously classified, and we may underestimate their capacities.

Mainstreaming studies show that mildly to moderately handicapped students can prosper in regular classes and thereby avoid the stereotyped, invidious "labeling" often based on misclassifications. *Psycholinguistic training* of special-needs students yields positive effects; it consists of testing and remedying specific deficits in language skills.

Patient education can affect mortality, morbidity, and lengths of illness and hospitalization. In studies of patients' learning about drug use for hypertension, diabetes, and other chronic condi-

Table 3-14
Effects of Programs for Special Populations

Program	Number of Studies	Effect Size	Graphic Representation of Effect Size
Preschool			
early intervention	326	0.50	.xxxxx
preschool programs	11	0.22	.xx
Handicapped students			
handicapped students as tutors	19	0.48	.xxxxx
psycholinguistic training	34	0.39	.xxxx
mainstreaming	11	0.33	.xxx
perceptual motor training	180	0.08	.x
Superior patient education	70	0.84	.xxxxxxxx
In-service training of M.D.s on			
physician knowledge	41	0.81	.xxxxxxxx
physician performance	41	0.74	.xxxxxxx
patient outcomes	41	0.34	.xxx

tions, one-to-one and group counseling (with or without instructional material) produced the greatest effects—in contrast to leaving instruction to bottle labels or "patient-package inserts." But labels, special containers, memory aids, and behavior modification were successful in minimizing later errors in drug use. The most efficacious educational principles were specification of intentions; relevance to learner needs; personal answers to questions; reinforcement and feedback on progress; facilitation such as unit-dose containers; and instructional and treatment regimens suited to personal convenience, such as prescribing drugs for mealtime administration.

In-service physician training shows large effects on knowledge and on classroom or laboratory performance; but only moderate effects of training can be found for patient outcomes. Knowledge and performance, even in practical training, may help but hardly guarantee successful application in practice. Can an accomplished mathematical problem solver do income tax returns?

At the request of the U.S. Army, the National Academy of Sciences evaluated exotic techniques and "*shortcuts*" for learning and performance enhancement described in popular psychology and presumably being exploited in California and the U.S.S.R.

(Druckman and Swets, 1988). Little or no evidence, however, was found for the efficacy of learning during sleep, mental practice of motor skills, "integration" of left and right brain hemispheres, parapsychological techniques, biofeedback, extrasensory perception, mental telepathy, "mind over matter" exercises, and "neurolinguistic programming" (in which instructors identify students' mode of learning and mimic the students' behavior as they teach). The Greeks found no royal road to geometry. Even kings, if they desired mastery, had to sweat over Euclid's elements. Perhaps brain research will eventually yield an elixir or panacea; but, for proof, educators should insist on hard data in scientific journals.

Effects on Teachers

Programs to help teachers in their work have had substantial effects, notwithstanding complaints about teaching practices of in-service sessions. (See Table 3-15.) Do physicians complain about the medical care they get?

Microteaching, developed at Stanford University in the 1960s, is a behavioral approach for preservice and in-service training that has substantial effects. It employs explanation and modeling of selected teaching techniques; televised practice with small groups of students; discussion, correctives, and reinforcement while watching playback; and recycling through subsequent practice and playback sessions with new groups of students.

In-service teacher education also proves to have substantial effects. Somewhat like the case of physician training, the biggest effects are on teacher knowledge; but effects on classroom behavior and student achievement are also big.

For in-service training, authoritative planning and execution seem to work best; informal coaching by itself seems ineffective. Instructor responsibility for designing and teaching the sessions works better than teacher presentations and group discussions. The best techniques are observation of classroom practices, video-audio feedback, and practice. The best combination of techniques is lecture, modeling, practice, and coaching. The size of the training group, which can range from one (in a tutoring situation) to greater than sixty, makes no detectable difference.

Some apparent effects may be attributable to participant selectivity rather than to superior efficacy: federal-, state-, and university-sponsored programs appear more effective than locally

Table 3-15
Effects on Teachers

Program	Number of Studies	Effect Size	Graphic Representation of Effect Size
Microteaching	47	0.55	.xxxxx
In-service teacher education on	91		
teacher achievement	a	0.90	.xxxxxxxxx
teacher classroom behavior	a	0.60	.xxxxxx
teacher achievement	a	0.37	.xxxx

[a] The reviews examined did not include information on the number of studies involved in these comparisons.

initiated programs. Competitive selection of participants and college credit apparently work better as incentives than extra pay, certificate renewal, and no incentives. Independent study seems to have larger effects than workshops, courses, mini-courses, and institutes.

CONCLUSION

Psychological research provides first-order estimates of the effects of instructional means on educational ends under various conditions. But some practices may be costly—not in dollars but in new or complicated arrangements that may be difficult for some teachers and districts to begin and continue. Thus, the estimates of effects are only one basis for decision making. We need to consider productivity or values of effects in relation to total costs, which include the time and energies of educators and students.

Psychology alone cannot suffice to prescribe practices, since different means bring about different ends. Educators must choose among student-, teacher-, and curriculum-direction of effort; facts and concepts; breadth and depth; short- and long-term ends; academic knowledge and real-world application; equal opportunity and equal results; and Plato's triumvirate of thinking, feeling, and acting. Once these choices, are made, the estimates of effects can provide one of the bases for choosing the most productive practices.

REFERENCES

Anderson, L.W., and Burns, R.B. (1987). Values, evidence, and mastery learning. *Review of Educational Research, 57,* 215-223

Bloom, B.S. (1976). *Human charocteristics and school learning.* New York: McGraw-Hill.

Carroll, J.B. (1963). A model of school learning. *Teachers College Record, 64,* 723-733.

Dollard, J., and Miller, N. (1950). *Personality and psychotherapy.* New York: McGraw-Hill.

Druckman, D., and Swets, J.A. (1988). *Enhancing human performance.* Washington, D.C.: National Academy Press.

Fraser, B.J.; Walberg, H.J.; Welch, W.W.; and Hattie, J.A. (1987). Syntheses of educational productivity research. *International Journal of Education Research, 11,* 73-145.

Giaconia, R.M., and Hedges, L.V. (1982). Identifying features of effective open education. *Review of Educational Research, 52,* 579-602.

Guskey, T.R., and Gates S.L. (May 1986). Synthesis of research on the effects of mastery learning in elementary and secondary classrooms. *Educational Leadership, 43,* 73-80.

Hoetker, J., and Ahlbrand, W.P. (1969). The persistence of the recitation. *American Educational Research Journal, 6,* 145-167.

Kulik, J.A., and Kulik, C-L. (1986). Mastery testing and student learning. *Journal of Educational Technological Systems, 15,* 325-345.

Levin, Joel R.; Anglin, Gary J.; and Carney, Russell N. (1987). On empirically validating functions of pictures in prose. In D.M. Willows and H.A. Houghton (eds.), *The psychology of illustration, volumes I & II.* New York: Springer-Verlag.

Mastropieri, MA., and Scruggs, T.E. (1987). *Effective instruction for special education.* Boston: Little, Brown.

Miller, N., and Dollard, J. (1941). *Social learning and imitation.* New Haven, Conn.: Yale University Press.

Pallincsar, A.M., and Brown, A. (1984). Reciprocal teaching of comprehension fostering and comprehension monitoring activities. *Cognition and Instruction, 1,* 117-176.

Pearson, D. (1985). Reading comprehension instruction: Six necessary steps. *Reading teacher, 38,* 724-738.

Slavin, R.E. (1987). Mastery learning reconsidered. *Review of educational research, 57,* 175-213.

Vygotsky, L. (1978). *Mind in society.* Cambridge, Mass.: Harvard University Press.

Walberg, H.J. (1984). Improving the productivity of America's schools. *Educational Leadership, 41,* 19-27.

Walberg, H.J. (1986). Synthesis of research on teaching. In M.C. Wittrock (ed.), *Handbook of research on teaching* (3rd ed.). New York: Macmillan.

Walberg, H.J.; Schiller, D.; and Haertel, G.D. (1979). The quiet revolution in educational research. *Phi Delta Kappan, 61,* 179-183.

Wittrock, M.C. (ed.) (1986). *Handbook of research on teaching* (3rd ed.). New York: Macmillan.

—Part II—
Research on Classroom Instruction

4

Classroom Observation Research and the Improvement of Teaching Practices

*Hersholt C. Waxman and
Shwu-Yong L. Huang*

Systematic classroom observation methods have been widely used in the past several decades to investigate effective teaching practices (Brophy and Good, 1986; Stallings and Mohlman, 1988; Waxman, 1995). The findings from these studies have led to a substantive knowledge base on effective teaching practices (Waxman and Walberg, 1982). Still, many critics have argued that this research paradigm lacks a theoretical and conceptual framework and merely focuses on discrete categories or small segments of observable teacher behaviors that can be easily measured with observation instruments (Ornstein, 1995a, 1995b). This chapter describes the use of systematic classroom observation methods to investigate instructional processes and behaviors that actually occur in classrooms. It reviews some of the ways classroom observation has contributed to the research knowledge and discusses some of the important implications for the improvement of teaching and student learning. Four specific areas where systematic classroom observation have been found especially useful for educational practice are highlighted here: (a) describing instructional practices, (b) investigating instructional inequities for different groups of students, (c) improving teacher education programs, and (d) improving teachers' classroom instruction based on feedback from individual classroom profiles. Some of the criticisms and cautions related to the use of structured observation techniques are also summarized. Finally, some new directions for observational research are reported and one specific technique, "shadowing students," is described.

Descriptions of Systematic Classroom Observation

Systematic classroom observation is a quantitative method of measuring classroom behaviors from direct observations that specifies both the events or behaviors that are to be observed and how they are to be recorded (Medley, 1982, 1992). Generally, the data that are collected from this procedure focus on the frequency with which specific behaviors or types of behavior occurred in the classroom and the amount of time they occurred. Several elements are common to most observational systems: (a) a purpose for the observation, (b) operational definitions of all the observed behaviors, (c) training procedures for observers, (d) a specific observational focus, (e) a setting, (f) a unit of time, (g) an observation schedule, (h) a method to record the data, and (i) a method to process and analyze data (Stallings and Mohlman, 1988, pp. 469–471).

Prior to the use of systematic observational methods, research on effective teaching typically consisted of subjective data from personal and anecdotal accounts of effective teaching (Nuthall and Alton-Lee, 1990). In order to develop a scientific basis for teaching, researchers began to use the more objective and reliable measures of systematic classroom observation. In the past few decades, several hundred different observational systems have been developed and used in classrooms (Anderson and Burns, 1989), and hundreds of studies have used classroom observation systems during the past three decades. While several types of observational procedures or techniques have been used to examine effective teaching (e.g., charts, rating scales, checklists, and narrative descriptions), the most widely used procedure or research method has been systematic classroom observation based on interactive coding systems. These interactive coding systems allow the observer to record nearly everything that students and teachers do during a given time interval (Stallings and Mohlman, 1988). These interaction systems are very objective and typically do not require the observer to make any high inferences or judgments about the behaviors they observe in the classroom. In other words, these low-inference observational systems provide specific and easily identifiable behaviors that observers can easily code (Stodolsky, 1990).

Some of the major strengths of classroom observation are that it (a) permits researchers to study the processes of education in natural settings, (b) provides more detailed and precise evidence than do other data sources, and (c) can be used to stimulate change and verify that the change occurred (Anderson and Burns, 1989). The descriptions of instructional events that are provided by this method have also been found to lead to improved understanding and better models for improving teaching (Copley and Williams, 1993; Good and Biddle, 1988).

A final strength of this research method is that the findings from these observational studies have provided a coherent, well-substantiated knowledge base about effective instruction. Many of the reviews and summaries of the classroom observation research have consistently found that a number of classroom behaviors significantly relate to students' academic achievement (Brophy and Good, 1986; Rosenshine, 1987; Rosenshine and Stevens, 1986; Walberg, 1986, 1991, 1995). Several aspects of classroom instruction such as (a) conducting daily reviews, (b) presenting new material, (c) conducting guided practice, (d) providing feedback and correctives, (e) conducting independent practice, and (f) conducting weekly and monthly reviews have been found to be significantly related to students' academic achievement (Rosenshine, 1987). In other words, research using classroom observation has provided us with a substantial knowledge base that has helped us understand effective teaching.

PURPOSES OF CLASSROOM OBSERVATION

Classroom observation has many valid and important educational purposes. This section summarizes four of the most important purposes or areas where systematic classroom observation has been widely used. These major purposes are (a) describing instructional practices, (b) investigating instructional inequities for different groups of students, (c) improving teacher education programs, and (d) improving teachers' classroom instruction based on feedback from individual classroom or school profiles.

Describing Instructional Processes

One of the fundamental purposes of classroom observation research is to describe the current status of instructional practices and identify instructional problems (Good, 1988; Waxman, 1995). As Good (1988) puts it, "one role of observational research is to describe what takes place in classrooms in order to delineate the complex practical issues that confront practitioners" (p. 337). Many observational studies have been specifically designed to describe specific educational phenomena. Large-scale observational studies such as those conducted by Sirotnik (1983) and Waxman, Huang, and Padrón (1995) have examined instructional practices in elementary and secondary schools. Sirotnik (1983) examined one thousand elementary and secondary classrooms and found very little variety in teaching practices across subjects and grades—most of the class time was spent with either the teacher lecturing to the class or students working on written assignments. Waxman, Huang, and Padrón (1995) observed ninety sixth- and eighth-grade classrooms from sixteen inner-city middle-level schools and found results similar to Sirotnik's (1983). Students were typically involved in whole-class instruction and did not interact with either their teacher or other students. Students rarely selected their own instructional activities. They were generally very passive in the classroom, often just watching or listening to the teacher, even though they were on task about 94 percent of the time. The teacher observation results revealed that teachers typically focused on the content of the task or assignment, responded to students' signals, communicated the task's procedures, and checked students' work. Teachers spent very little time interacting with students regarding personal issues, encouraging students to succeed, showing personal regard for students, and showing interest in students' work.

Another example of descriptive, observational studies involves the extent to which technology is used in the classroom. Although a large number of studies have examined technology use in schools, most of these studies have relied on self-report data from administrators, teachers, or students. These types of data, however, are often unreliable and tend to be upwardly biased in the direction of overreporting the actual amount of technology use. Therefore, it is important to observe the actual extent to which technology is used in classrooms and to look specifically at the technology used in the classroom and that used by individual students. In one such study, Waxman and Huang (1995) used systematic classroom observation to examine the extent to which computer technology was integrated into the curriculum of two hundred classrooms in elementary and secondary inner-city schools. They found that there was no integration (i.e., use) of computer technology in the elementary school classrooms, and students were observed working with computers only 2 percent of the time in middle-school classrooms. Huang and Waxman (1996) also conducted systematic observations of 1,315 middle-school students from 220 mathematics classrooms in order to examine the amount of technology used. The descriptive results revealed that students used calculators about 25 percent of the time and computers less than 1 percent of the time in their mathematics classes.

Our work in this area has also focused on observing how technology use affects instructional behaviors and students' motivation, anxiety, and perceptions of their classroom learning environment (Waxman and Huang, 1996, 1996–97). In a study involving classroom observations of over two thousand middle-school students, Waxman and Huang (1996) found that there are significant differences in classroom instruction, depending on the amount of technology used by the teacher. Instruction in classroom settings where technology was not often used tended to be whole-class approaches where students generally listened or watched the teacher. Instruction in classroom settings where technology was moderately used had much less whole-class instruction and much more independent work. These findings are quite similar to previous research that supports the notion that technology use may change teaching from the traditional teacher-centered model to a more student-centered instructional approach. Another important finding from the study was that students in classrooms where technology was moderately used were also on task significantly more than were students in settings where technology was not widely used.

Some other uses of descriptive observational studies have been to (a) evaluate programs and, more specifically, evaluate the fidelity or degree of implementation of programs (Stallings and Freiberg, 1991), (b) examine the extent to which higher-level thought processes are emphasized in schools (Padrón and Waxman, 1993), and (c) investigate the extent to which multicultural education is emphasized in urban classrooms (Saldana and Waxman, 1996, 1997). A final important use involves school effectiveness studies where classroom observation data has been used to investigate observable differences between effective and ineffective schools (Stringfield and Teddlie, 1991; Teddlie, Kirby, and Stringfield, 1989; Teddlie and Stringfield, 1993; Waxman and Huang, 1997; Waxman, Huang, Anderson and Weinstein, 1997). Waxman and Huang (1997), for example, observed over seven hundred students from four effective and four ineffective urban elementary schools with a predominantly African-American enrollment. They found that students from the effective schools significantly more often (a) worked in an individualized setting, (b) interacted with their teacher, and (c) worked on written assignments. On the other hand, students from the ineffective schools more often (a) were in whole-class settings, (b) did not interact with their teacher, (c) interacted with others, (d) read, and (e) worked with manipulative materials.

Identifying Instructional Inequities

Systematic classroom observation has also been useful in investigating instructional inequities for different groups of students. Classroom observation can be used to answer some important questions. Are some students being treated differently in the classroom? If so does that explain why some students learn more than others. Often this issue has been defined as differences in opportunity to learn or inequitable allocation of instruction. In other words, classroom observation can help find the extent of variation in the quality and quantity of instruction that students experience in school and if that variation explains inequality in educational outcomes.

Several studies have found that some groups or types of students are treated differently by teachers in classrooms and that these inequitable patterns of teacher-student interaction result in differential learning outcomes for students (Fennema and Peterson, 1987). Many studies, for example, have found differences in teachers' interaction patterns with boys and girls. Brophy and Good's (1974) review of the research found consistent sex-related differences in teachers' interaction patterns. For example, boys typically receive more praise and criticism in the classroom than do girls, and teachers have more behavioral, procedural, and academic interactions with boys than with girls. Boys also ask more questions in the classroom and teachers ask boys more questions. Good and his colleagues (Good, Slavings, Harel, and

Emerson, 1987; Good, Slavings, and Mason, 1988) have also conducted several observational studies that examined why low-achieving students in secondary schools ask fewer questions than do high-achieving students. They also found that students from an upper-middle-class elementary school asked more questions than did students from lower-middle-class schools.

Other studies have looked at differences in the classroom related to sex and ethnicity. Hart (1989) considered race and sex when examining the relationship between teacher-student interaction and mathematics achievement. She found that (a) white and black male students had more interactions with the teacher than did students from other groups, (b) there was a disparity between white and black students in the type of interaction, and (c) boys were involved in more public interactions with teachers than were girls. In other words, it appears that patterns of teacher-student interaction may be influenced not only by the sex of the student but also by the ethnicity of the student.

The findings from these classroom observational studies have important policy implications for schools. If teachers' interactions with their students vary by the students' sex and ethnicity, policymakers may need to specifically examine the quality and quantity of classroom instruction for some groups of students and determine if instructional interventions are needed. Future studies might also examine teachers' expectations and or the classroom behavior of teachers to see if they affect the classroom behavior of individual students.

Improving Teacher Education Programs

While there are conflicting findings in the research on the effects of teachers' early field experiences (Waxman and Walberg, 1986), there is some evidence that systematic classroom observation is an effective component of preservice teacher education programs (Freiberg and Waxman, 1988; Merkley and Hoy, 1992–93; Timm and Marchant, 1992; Waxman, Rodriguez, Padrón, and Knight, 1988). Systematic observation of classroom teachers provides prospective teachers with the opportunity to actually observe specific teaching behaviors that are emphasized in their teacher education courses. It allows prospective teachers the opportunity to integrate what they are learning in their teacher education courses with the realities of the classroom. Furthermore, such focused observations allow prospective teachers to see how classroom instruction can differentially influence student behavioral and affective outcomes.

Waxman, Rodriguez, Padrón, and Knight (1988) illustrated how the use of systematic classroom observation can be an important component of teacher education programs. Not only did the prospective teachers in the study observe some of the teaching skills that were emphasized in their teacher education courses, but they also observed how those instructional behaviors differentially affected student outcomes. Merkley and Hoy (1992–93) found observation improved preservice teachers' ability to describe selected classroom teaching behaviors and cite significantly more examples than did students in the control group that received a traditional lecture and written material about a classroom lesson. Systematic classroom observation can provide a common language for describing effective teaching. Such observations enable prospective teachers to focus on specific teaching skills that they have been learning about in their pedagogy courses. Many of the prospective teachers in the study by Waxman and colleagues (1988), for example, indicated that the systematic observations were the most beneficial aspect of the course for them. They also reported that their observations helped them become more aware of the social reality of teaching from the teacher's perspective.

Another area where systematic classroom observation can help prospective teachers is during the student-teaching phase. Freiberg, Waxman, and Houston (1987), for example, used systematic classroom observation to provide feedback to student teachers. In their experimental study, one group of student teachers received traditional supervision from a university supervisor, a second group of student teachers received the traditional supervision and systematic feedback about their classroom instruction from the Stallings Observational System (SOS), and the third group of student teachers received the systematic feedback, engaged in self-analysis, and received feedback from their peers. At the end of the student-teaching semester, student teachers who engaged in the self-analysis and collegial feedback significantly improved their classroom instruction in desired directions, while the student teachers in the other two groups did not improve their instruction. This study clearly suggests that when student teachers receive systematic feedback about their classroom instruction, engage in discussions about their instruction with their peers and supervisor, and conduct further self-analyses of their own teaching, they are likely to improve their instruction. The findings from this study also suggest that systematic feedback alone may not help student teachers to improve their instruction.

A final area where observation may be especially useful is during the induction phase or first few years of teaching. Schaffer, Stringfield, and Wolfe (1992), for example, used classroom observation data collected from a university-based, collaborative two-year teacher induction program to improve beginning teacher's classroom instruction. For each year of the project, individualized feedback on their classroom instruction was provided to these teachers near the beginning of the school year. These teachers also received a three-hour feedback/instruction session each week where their classroom profiles were discussed along with other instructional and organizational classroom issues. Classroom observation data were similarly collected for each teacher near the end of the school year. During the first year, these first-year teachers improved their classroom organizational and management skills. During the second year of the program, the improvement was in the more intellectually complex areas of teaching.

Improving Teaching Practices

Research using observational methods has yielded important information that has practical implications for the improvement of teaching practices. One of the traditional problems hindering teachers' classroom instruction has been the lack of valid and accurate information that teachers could use in order to facilitate their professional growth (Johnson, 1974). Many teachers, even experienced ones, are not always aware of the nature of their interactions with individual students (Doyle, 1979). Consequently, one of the most important purposes of systematic classroom observation is to improve teachers' classroom instruction (Stallings and Freiberg, 1991; Stallings, Needels, and Stayrook, 1979). Feedback from individual classroom profiles derived from systematic observations has been found to help teachers understand their own strengths and weaknesses and has consequently enabled them to significantly improve their instruction. Through feedback, teachers can become aware of how their classroom functions and thus bring about changes they desire (Brophy, 1979; Stallings, Needels, and Sparks, 1987). This process typically involves having trained observers systematically observe teachers and their students in their classrooms and later provide teachers with information about their instruction in clinical sessions. This approach is based on the assumption that teachers value accurate information that they can use to improve their instruction.

There is growing evidence that feedback from systematic observations can be used to improve teaching (Stallings and Freiberg, 1991). Several studies have found that teachers could positively change their attitude and behaviors toward pupils after receiving feedback from classroom observations (Ebmeier and Good, 1979; Good and Brophy, 1974; Good and Grouws, 1979; Stallings, 1980). Good and Brophy's (1974) "treatment study" exemplifies this type of research. In that study, teachers were given feedback after they were observed for forty hours in their classroom. As a result of this "one-shot" interview where feedback was given, teachers' interaction patterns changed, and their attitudes toward individual students changed, too. Stallings (1980), Ebmeier and Good (1979), and Good and Grouws (1979) have used similar strategies in other projects. In those studies, teachers were given individual feedback regarding their classroom instruction and then were found to change their behavior in desirable ways. All these studies have found that teachers can improve their classroom instruction when given appropriate feedback and suggestions for improvement.

The overall findings from these studies suggest that feedback from classroom observations is a viable and effective mechanism for providing teachers with the information they need about their classroom behavior. This feedback is intended to create an "imbalance" in teachers' perceptions of their own behaviors. This imbalance exists whenever teachers find out that their attitudes or perceptions of their teaching differ from that of trained observers. Teachers in such a state of "imbalance" are motivated to do something about their behavior in order to restore themselves to a balanced condition (Gage, 1972). A similar notion is that self-awareness increases teachers' control of their actions and the possibility that they will modify them (Feiman, 1981). More recently, Waxman, Huang, and Padrón (1995) provided schoolwide feedback to middle-school teachers that compared their school profile on classroom instructional behaviors to an overall districtwide average of these same behaviors. Feedback from these profiles was used to stimulate dialogue and discussion about instructional strengths and weaknesses in the school. The profiles also helped initiate discussion about specific instructional areas that needed to be improved in the school. It should be pointed out again that these profiles provided some guidelines for practice—they were not attempts to tell teachers what do do, but gave teachers concepts and criteria that they could use to reflect on their own teaching (Nuthall and Alton-Lee, 1990). The feedback session was not viewed as one where research findings should be turned into specific rules or guidelines for teachers to follow. Rather, the intent was that observational feedback be used as guides to allow teachers and their colleagues to reflect about their practices on their own and decide what action to take. Teachers could choose to participate in in-service training, workshops, formalized staff-development programs, and university courses if they wanted to continue to collaborate with the researchers in order to help them improve their instruction. In summary, the use of feedback from classroom observations appears to be a potent strategy that can improve instructional behaviors in specific classrooms and schools.

LIMITATIONS OF CLASSROOM OBSERVATION

While the previous sections have highlighted some of the important purposes of classroom observation, there have also been several criticisms and cautions related to the use of structured observation techniques (Delamont and Hamilton, 1986; Evertson and Green, 1986; Galton, 1988; McIntyre and Macleod, 1986). We will discuss next three general criticisms and limitations of using structured observation techniques: (a) Theoretical and epistemological criticisms, (b) methodological concerns, and (c) pragmatic concerns.

Theoretical and Epistemological Criticisms

Although observational research has produced a substantial body of important findings that can lead to improved teaching practices, there is still a lack of consensus or a lack of confidence regarding the research (Nuthall and Alton-Lee, 1990). There have been many theoretical and epistemological criticisms of classroom observational, process-product research (Doyle, 1977; Evertson and Green, 1986; Fenstermacher, 1978; Galton, 1988; Popkewitz, Tabachnick, and Zeichner, 1979; Winne and Marx, 1977; Winne, 1987). Several critics, for example, have argued that this research is devoid of theory or is atheoretical, and consequently cannot explain why some instructional behaviors impact student outcomes. Related concerns center on why some variables are selected to be observed at the exclusion of other variables. Because there is no model or theory behind the research, the critics argue that there is no justification for the selection of variables or no meaningfulness associated with the interpretation of results. They further argue that the selection of events or behaviors may not be clear to anyone except the observer or instrument developer. In other words, these critics argue that classroom observation research has not dealt with the theoretical assumptions of why a particular style of teaching or set of instructional variables influences student learning.

Popkewitz, Tabachnick, and Zeichner (1979) argue that this research approach has a behaviorist orientation that maintains "it is possible to identify, control, and manipulate specific outcomes of teaching by altering selected aspects of a teacher's overt behavior" (p. 52). They further contend that teaching is viewed, "as the sum of discrete behaviors and a change in one or several of these behaviors is assumed to affect the quality of teaching as a whole" (p. 52). Their most strenuous argument, however, concerns the notion that these teaching behaviors "are often viewed independent of the curricular context with which the techniques are associated" (p. 52). In other words, they are concerned that observers generally focus on isolated behaviors without attention to the preceding and subsequent behaviors that, these researchers feel, provide the context and meaning of the behavior. Other related criticisms focus on the fact that most observational systems are generally limited in that they can be used only to observe overt behavior that can be quantitatively measured. Furthermore, these observational systems make it difficult to record complex instructional behaviors.

Methodological Concerns

Most observational techniques have limitations. Some of these concerns or limitations are related to methodological issues that can interfere with drawing valid conclusions. One of the primary methodological concerns or sources of invalidity that needs to be addressed regarding the use of systematic observational techniques relates to the obtrusiveness of the technique. Observer effects may occur because teachers and students are aware that their behaviors are being observed. In other words, the presence of an observer may change teacher or student behaviors. This may result in reactive effects such as teacher anxiety or teachers performing less well than usual, which can interfere with drawing valid inferences about what normally occurs in the classroom. On the other hand, other evidence indicates that teachers' instruction may be slightly better than usual when they are being observed (Samph, 1976). While some researchers (e.g., Medley, Coker, and Soar [1984]) maintain that observer effects are not serious concerns, others argue that such effects can threaten the validity and reliability of data.

A number of other methodological concerns must be addressed, including whether observational systems are reliable and valid. Although many systems report interrater agreement or observer accuracy, they do not specify the reliability regarding the stability of teacher behavior or the internal consistency of the scale (Hoge, 1985; Medley, 1992). Validity is another important concern. For example, construct validity, which focuses on the "theoretical integrity" of the behaviors, is particularly important (Hoge, 1985). Criterion-related validity (the extent to which the observational measures relate to a criterion measure) is rarely reported, as is concurrent validity (the extent to which a particular instrument is related to other instruments).

Other methodological concerns are related to the actual amount of time needed to obtain a valid observation period as well as the appropriate number of observations required in order to obtain reliable and valid measures of instruction. Similarly, a number of methodological concerns are related to the analyses of data. Most of these concerns address the appropriate level of analysis (e.g., a student, the class, or students within the class) that should be used when analyzing the observation data. Students are nested within classrooms, while classrooms are nested within schools. Prior teacher effectiveness research has often aggregated data to classroom-level analyses, which may underestimate the importance of processes within classes because all the within-class variation is lost. Recent analytic developments such as hierarchical linear modeling (HLM) allow researchers to disentangle these nested effects and investigate hypotheses about the effects of within- and between-school or class factors on classroom instruction or students' perceptions of their learning environments (Bryk and Raudenbush, 1989; Raudenbush and Bryk, 1989; Raudenbush and Willms, 1991). Advanced statistical models such as HLM allow researchers to identify and separate individual effects from group effects, after statistically controlling for other explanatory variables (Morgenstein and Keeves, 1994). Such multilevel models can estimate how group-level variables (e.g., characteristics of the classroom or school) influence the way in which individual-level variables (e.g., students' classroom behavior) affect students' achievement (Stockard, 1993).

Another concern related to prior classroom observation research is that it has typically been generic (i.e., generalizing across grade levels and content areas), rather than focusing on a given grade level or subject area (Anderson and Burns, 1989; Gage, 1985; Gage and Needels, 1989; Needels and Gage, 1991). Similarly, the content of the lesson is often neglected as is the quality of the interaction that is being recorded (Anderson and Burns, 1989).

Pragmatic Concerns

Finally several pragmatic concerns are related to classroom observation. These concerns focus on the practicality of conducting observational research. One such concern is that observation research is costly to do because it requires extensive training of the observer as well as time for the observer to do the observations. Some training programs for observers, for example, require as much as seven full days of intensive training before the observations are conducted in classrooms (Stallings and Freiberg, 1991). Gaining access to schools and classrooms to conduct observations is another serious concern. Many school districts are reluctant to allow researchers to observe in their schools because they feel it would be too disruptive to the learning environment. Teachers have also been known to dramatically alter their instruction when observers are present in the classroom.

Another pragmatic concern relates to the misuse of classroom observation data. Classroom observations can be very useful as a formative evaluation procedure, but they are not useful and should not be used to provide summative decisions such as whether or not a teacher should be dismissed or rehired. Similarly, classroom observations should not be tied to summative decisions like salary increases. Unfortunately, several school districts and state departments of education have misused observational research and translated findings into specific rules or standards that they have used in developing evaluation instruments (Ornstein,

1991). These misuses are more "accidents" of the research, however, rather than problems associated with the "essence" of the research (Needels and Gage, 1991).

The previously mentioned criticisms and limitations, however, do not necessarily detract from the value and utility of the observational method. As previously discussed, many of these criticisms are "accidents" or incidental aspects of some observational research. Gage and Needels (1989), Needels and Gage (1991), and others, for example, have refuted many of these criticisms and have provided several examples of how observation research has contributed to instructional theories. Medley (1992) has also argued that the previous methodological limitations of observational research have been greatly reduced in recent years. He points out, for example, the impact that the lap-top computer will have on classroom observation research. In addition to replacing traditional clipboards and stopwatches, the lap-top computer will help researchers accurately record events as well as provide a detailed account of contextual items that occur during the observation. Nevertheless, observational research can be improved, and the next section addresses some ways the research paradigm can be strengthened.

NEW DIRECTIONS FOR OBSERVATIONAL RESEARCH

Although research on classroom observation has made significant progress over the past several decades, some areas need further investigation. In order to capture all the processes and nuances that occur in classrooms, triangulation procedures are needed to collect data from multiple perspectives (Evertson and Green, 1986). Collecting multiple measures or indicators of classroom processes may help alleviate some of the concerns and criticisms of observational research and provide us with a more comprehensive picture of what goes on in classrooms. Student and teacher self-report survey and interview data as well as more qualitative, ethnographic data (e.g., extensive field notes) could all be used to help supplement classroom observation data.

One new observational approach that combines aspects of both systematic classroom observations and ethnographic data is "shadowing." "Shadowing" is a quasi-ethnographic observation method designed to gather qualitative data on the classroom experiences of individual students during a typical class period or school day (Lounsbury and Johnston, 1988). Recent studies have developed shadowing observation schedules that systematically record "snapshots" of classroom experiences from the perspective of students. Waxman, Huang, and Wang (1997), for example, used shadowing techniques to observe a total of sixty-four fourth- and fifth-grade, resilient (i.e., educationally successful) and nonresilient (i.e., less successful) students from sixteen classrooms in four urban elementary schools. The shadowing observations consisted of narrative descriptions of (a) the physical environment of the classroom, (b) teachers' instructional approaches, behaviors, and attitudes toward students, and (c) students' observed attitudes, actions, mannerisms, and interactions. The shadowing observations were recorded on lap-top computers that were programmed to provide observers with specific time prompts that told them exactly when they were to record the information (i.e., narrative comments) about each student. An interobserver agreement of .73 was obtained on the high-inference behaviors by selecting the central descriptions recorded by one observer and then comparing them to the descriptions of the other observer in order to determine their percentage of agreement. While the primary focus of the shadowing observations was on resilient and nonresilient students, these shadowing techniques also allowed the researchers to observe the instructional contexts that were prevalent in these classrooms. The findings revealed that the overall instruction in these classrooms was whole-class instruction with students working in teacher-assigned activities, generally in a passive manner (i.e., watching or listening). There was very little small-group work observed in any of the classrooms, and when it did occur, it would typically be one student working with another student. Teachers were observed keeping students on task most of the time, focusing on the task, communicating the tasks' procedures, and checking students' work. They also spent more time explaining than questioning, cueing, or prompting students. Teachers were not frequently observed encouraging extended student responses or encouraging students to help themselves or help each other. Generally, there was little engagement in the classroom and the intellectual level of the curriculum was low, with very few authentic activities occurring that had content related to students' interests or the world outside school. The predominant culture of classrooms observed was related to "getting work done," rather than an emphasis on authentic learning situations. This example illustrates some of the "rich" information that is available from shadowing data. Future studies may want to incorporate this valuable observational method in their data-collection procedures.

Although the findings summarized by current observational research suggest several consistent relationships between classroom instruction and students' outcomes, further correlational, longitudinal, and especially experimental research is needed to verify these results. Other research questions that still need to be investigated in this area include examining (a) the ideal or optimum levels and ranges of student and teacher behaviors that should exist in various classrooms, (b) whether there are content area differences or other contextual variables that influence student or teacher behaviors, (c) whether there are different teaching practices used among student subgroups or characteristics such as sex, ethnicity, grade, and achievement level, (d) if teacher characteristics such as training and experience influence classroom instruction, and (e) what other variables or factors influence classroom teaching. More studies are also needed to examine how teaching influences students' cognitive learning strategies and higher-level thinking. Similarly, more observation instruments that emphasize inquiry-based or constructivist learning environments need to be developed and validated. Since observational research has not been able to explain how students cognitively interact with process variables (Winne, 1987), further research may need to specifically focus on students' cognitive operations and observations of students' responses. Finally, studies should attempt to replicate some of the previous studies in other settings, especially in urban schools where many students are underachieving and at risk of dropping out and not furthering their education. These and similar issues still need to be examined so that we can continue to understand and improve teaching practices.

CONCLUSION

In summary, systematic classroom observations are useful for a variety of educational purposes, including describing instructional practices, investigating instructional inequities for different groups of students, improving teacher education programs, and improving teachers' classroom instruction with feedback from individual classroom profiles. In addition, the substantive findings from this research have significantly contributed to our knowledge base about effective teaching practices. Classroom observation, however, also has some limitations. It is costly to do because it requires extensive training as well as time for someone to actually do the observations. Furthermore, there are some validity concerns related to the obtrusiveness of the technique and the actual amount of time and number of observations needed to obtain a valid measure of the classroom. Finally, there are concerns related to the instrumentation involved in classroom observations. Do the classroom observation instruments currently used in the field, for example, capture the important instructional variables that we should be looking at? There have been other theoretical and epistemological criticisms of classroom observational research, but these concerns appear to be more "accidental" or incidental features of the research rather than the true "essence" of the research.

It is important to point out again that no one data source or methodology will sufficiently answer all our critical educational questions. Multiple measures or indicators of instruction are needed to help us capture a more comprehensive picture of what goes on in classrooms. In conclusion, classroom observation is a powerful research methodology that can be used for several important educational purposes. Combined with some of the other research methods previously described, it can be used to help us improve educational processes.

REFERENCES

Anderson, L. W., and Burns, R. B. (1989). *Research in classrooms: The study of teachers, teaching, and instruction.* Oxford, England: Pergamon.

Brophy, J. E. (1979). *Using observation to improve your teaching* (Occasional Paper No. 21). East Lansing: Michigan State University, Institute for Research on Teaching.

Brophy, J. E., and Good, T. L. (1974). *Teacher-student relationships: Causes and consequences.* New York: Holt, Rinehart, and Winston.

Brophy, J. E., and Good, T. L. (1986). Teacher behavior and student achievement. In M. C. Wittrock (ed.), *Handbook of research on teaching* (3rd ed., pp. 328–375). New York: Macmillan.

Bryk, A. S., and Raudenbush, S. W. (1989). Toward a more appropriate conceptualization of research on school effects: A three-level hierarchical linear model. In R. D. Bock (ed.), *Multilevel analysis of educational data* (pp. 159–204). San Diego: Academic Press.

Copley, J. V., and Williams, S. E. (1993). Systematic classroom observations of technology use. In H. C. Waxman and G. W. Bright (eds.), *Approaches to research on teacher education and technology* (pp. 113–122). Charlottesville, Va.: Association for the Advancement of Computing in Education.

Delamont, S., and Hamilton, D. (1986). Revisiting classroom research: A cautionary tale. In M. Hammersley (ed.), *Controversies in classroom research* (pp. 25–43). Philadelphia: Open University Press.

Doyle, W. (1977). Paradigms for research on teacher effectiveness. In L. S. Shulman (ed.), *Review of research in education* (Vol. 5, pp. 163–198). Itasca, Ill.: Peacock.

Doyle, W. (1979). Making managerial decisions in classrooms. In D. L. Duke (ed.), *Classroom management* (pp. 42–74). Chicago: National Society for the Study of Education.

Ebmeier, H., and Good, T. L. (1979). The effects of instructing teachers about good teaching on the mathematics achievement of fourth-grade students. *American Educational Research Journal, 16*, 1–16.

Evertson, C., and Green, J. (1986). Observation as inquiry and method. In M. C. Wittrock (ed.), *Handbook of research on teaching* (3rd ed., pp. 162–207). New York: Macmillan.

Feiman, S. (1981). Exploring connections between different kinds of educational research and different conceptions of inservice education. *Journal of Research and Development in Education, 14*(2), 11–21.

Fennema, E., and Peterson, P. L. (1987). Effective teaching for girls and boys: The same or different? In D. C. Berliner and B. V. Rosenshine (eds.), *Talks to teachers* (pp. 111–125). New York: Random House.

Fenstermacher, G. (1978). A philosophical consideration of recent research on teacher effectiveness. In L. S. Shulman (ed.), *Review of research in education* (Vol. 6, pp. 157–185). Itasca, Ill.: Peacock.

Freiberg, H. J.; Waxman, H. C.; and Houston, W. R. (1987). Enriching feedback to student-teachers through small group discussion. *Teacher Education Quarterly, 14*(3), 71–82.

Freiberg, H. J., and Waxman, H. C. (1988). Alternative feedback approaches for improving student teachers' classroom instruction. *Journal of Teacher Education, 39*(4), 8–14.

Gage, N. L. (1972). *Teacher effectiveness and teacher education*. Palo Alto, Calif.: Pacific.

Gage, N. L. (1985). *Hard gains in the soft science: The case of pedagogy*. Bloomington, Ind.: Phi Delta Kappa.

Gage, N. L., and Needels, M. C. (1989). Process-product research on teaching? A review of criticisms. *Elementary School Journal, 89*, 253–300.

Galton, M. (1988). Structured observation techniques. In J. P. Keeves (ed.), *Educational research, methodology and measurement: An international handbook* (pp. 474–478). Oxford, England: Pergamon.

Good, T. L. (1988). Observational research . . . grounding theory in classrooms. *Educational Psychologist, 25*, 375–379.

Good, T. L., and Biddle, B. (1988). Research and the improvement of mathematics instruction: The need for observational resources. In D. Grouws and T. Cooney (eds.), *Research agenda for mathematics education: Effective mathematics teaching* (pp. 114–142). Reston, Va.: National Council of Teachers of Mathematics.

Good, T. L., and Brophy, J. E. (1974). Changing teacher and student behavior: An empirical investigation. *Journal of Educational Psychology, 66,* 390–405.

Good, T. L., and Grouws, D. (1979). The Missouri Mathematics Effectiveness Project: An experimental study in fourth-grade classrooms. *Journal of Educational Psychology, 71,* 355–362.

Good, T. L.; Slavings, R.; Harel, K.; and Emerson, H. (1987). Student passivity: A study of questioning-asking in K-12 classrooms. *Sociology of Education, 60,* 181–199.

Good, T. L.; Slavings, R. L.; and Mason, D. A. (1988). Learning to ask questions: Grade and school effects. *Teaching and Teacher Education, 4,* 363–378.

Hart, L. E. (1989). Classroom processes, sex of students, and confidence in learning mathematics. *Journal for Research in Mathematics Education, 20,* 242–260.

Hoge, R. D. (1985). The validity of direct observation measures of pupil classroom behavior. *Review of Educational Research, 55,* 469–483.

Huang, S. L., and Waxman, H. C. (1996). Classroom observations of middle school students' technology use in mathematics. *School Science and Mathematics, 96*(1), 28–34.

Johnson, D. W. (1974). Affective outcomes. In H. J. Walberg (ed.), *Evaluating educational performance* (pp. 99–112). Berkeley, Calif.: McCutchan.

Lounsbury, J. H., and Johnston, J. H. (1988). *Life in the three sixth grades.* Reston, Va.: National Association of Secondary School Principals.

McIntyre, D., and Macleod, G. (1986). The characteristics and uses of systematic classroom observation. In M. Hammersley (ed.), *Controversies in classroom research* (pp. 10–24). Philadelphia: Open University Press.

Medley, D. M. (1982). Systematic observation. In H. E. Mitzel (ed.), *Encyclopedia of educational research* (5th ed., pp. 1841–1851). New York: The Free Press.

Medley, D. M. (1992). Structured observation. In M. C. Alkin (ed.), *Encyclopedia of educational research* (6th ed., pp. 1310–1315). New York: Macmillan.

Medley, D. M.; Coker, H.; and Soar, R. S. (1984). *Measurement-based evaluation of teacher performance: An empirical approach.* New York: Longman.

Merkley, D. J., and Hoy, M. P. (1992–93). Observation as a component in teacher preparation. *National Forum of Teacher Education Journal, 2,* 15–21.

Morgenstern, C., and Keeves, J. P. (1994). Descriptive scales for measuring educational climate. In T. Husen and T. N. Postlethwaite (eds.), *International encyclopedia of education* (2nd. ed., pp. 1475–1483). Oxford, England: Pergamon.

Needels, M., and Gage, N. L. (1991). Essence and accident in process-product research on teaching. In H. C. Waxman and H. J. Walberg (eds.), *Effective teaching: Current research* (pp. 3–31). Berkeley, Calif.: McCutchan.

Nuthall, G., and Alton-Lee, A. (1990). Research on teaching and learning: Thirty years of change. *The Elementary School Journal, 90,* 546–570.

Ornstein, A. C. (1991). Teacher effectiveness research: Theoretical considerations. In H. C. Waxman and H. J. Walberg (eds.), *Effective teaching: Current research* (pp. 63–80). Berkeley, Calif.: McCutchan.

Ornstein, A. C. (1995a). Beyond effective teaching. *Peabody Journal of Education*, 70(2), 2–33.

Ornstein, A. C. (1995b). The new paradigm in research on teaching. *The Educational Forum*, 59, 124–129.

Padrón, N. Y., and Waxman, H. C. (1993). Teaching and learning risks associated with limited cognitive mastery in science and mathematics for limited-English-proficient students. In Office of Bilingual Education and Minority Language Affairs (eds.), *Proceedings of the Third National Research Symposium on Limited English Proficient Students: Focus on middle and high school issues* (Vol. 2, pp. 511–547). Washington, D.C.: National Clearinghouse for Bilingual Education.

Popkewitz, T. S.; Tabachnick, R.; and Zeichner, K. (1979). Dulling the senses: Research in teacher education. *Journal of Teacher Education*, 30, 52–60.

Raudenbush, S. W., and Bryk, A. S. (1989). Quantitative models for estimating teacher and school effectiveness. In R. D. Bock (ed.), *Multilevel analysis of educational data* (pp. 205–232). San Diego: Academic Press.

Raudenbush, S. W., and Willms, J. D. (eds.). (1991). *Schools, classrooms, and pupils: International studies of schooling from a multilevel perspective*. San Diego: Academic Press.

Rosenshine, B. V. (1987). Explicit teaching. In D. C. Berliner and B. V. Rosenshine (eds.), *Talks to teachers* (pp. 75–92). New York: Random House.

Rosenshine, B., and Stevens, R. (1986). Teaching functions. In M. C. Wittrock (ed.), *Handbook of research on teaching* (3rd, ed., pp. 376–391). New York: Macmillan.

Saldana, D. C., and Waxman, H. C. (1996). The integration of multicultural education in urban middle level schools. *Issues in Middle Level Education*, 5(2), 9–29.

Saldana, D. C., and Waxman, H. C. (1997). An observational study of multicultural teaching in urban elementary schools. *Equity and Excellence in Education*, 30(1), 40–46.

Samph, T. (1976). Observer effects on teacher behavior. *Journal of Educational Psychology*, 68, 736–741.

Schaffer, E.; Stringfield, S.; and Wolfe, D. (1992). An innovative beginning teacher induction program: A two-year analysis of classroom interactions. *Journal of Teacher Education*, 43, 181–192.

Sirotnik, K. A. (1983). What you see is what you get—Consistency, persistency, and mediocrity in classrooms. *Harvard Educational Review*, 53, 16–31.

Stallings, J. A. (1980). Allocated academic learning time revisited, or beyond time on task. *Educational Researcher*, 9(11), 11–16.

Stallings, J. A., and Freiberg, H. J. (1991). Observation for the improvement of teaching. In H. C. Waxman and H. J. Walberg (eds.), *Effective teaching: Current research* (pp. 107–133). Berkeley, Calif.: McCutchan.

Stallings, J. A., and Mohlman, G. G. (1988). Classroom observation techniques. In J. P. Keeves (ed.), *Educational research, methodology, and measurement: An International handbook* (pp. 469–474). Oxford, England: Pergamon.

Stallings, J. A.; Needels, M. C.; and Sparks, G. M. (1987). Observation for the improvement of student learning. In D. C. Berliner and B. V. Rosenshine (eds.), *Talks to teachers* (pp. 129–158). New York: Random House.

Stallings, J. A.; Needels, M. C.; and Stayrook, N. (1979). *How to change the process of teaching basic reading skills at the secondary school level.* Menlo Park, Calif.: SRI International.

Stodolsky, S. S. (1990). Classroom observation. In J. Millman and L. Darling-Hammond (eds.), *The New handbook of teacher evaluation: Assessing elementary and secondary school teachers* (pp. 175–190). Newbury Park, Calif.: Sage.

Stringfield, S., and Teddlie, C. (1991). Observers as predictors of schools' effectiveness status. *Elementary School Journal, 91,* 357–376.

Stockard, J. (1993). Methodological issues in the multi-level analysis of school environments. In S. B. Bacharach and R. T. Ogawa (eds.), *Advances in research and theories of school management and educational policy* (Vol. 2, pp. 217–240). Greenwich, Conn.: JAI.

Teddlie, C.; Kirby, P. C.; and Stringfield, S. (1989). Effective versus ineffective schools: Observable differences in the classroom. *American Journal of Education, 97,* 221–236.

Teddlie, C., and Stringfield, S. (1993). *Schools make a difference: Lessons learned from a 10-year study of school effects.* New York: Teachers College Press.

Timm, J. T., and Marchant, G. J. (1992). Using a structured observational instrument in observational settings in teacher education. *Teaching Education, 5,* 65–70.

Walberg, H. J. (1986). Synthesis of research on teaching. In M. C. Wittrock (ed.), *Handbook of research on teaching* (3rd ed., pp. 214–229). New York: Macmillan.

Walberg, H. J. (1991). Productive teaching and instruction: Assessing the knowledge base. In H. C. Waxman and H. J. Walberg (eds.), *Effective teaching: Current research* (pp. 33–62). Berkeley, Calif.: McCutchan.

Walberg, H. J. (1995). Generic practices. In G. Cawelti (ed.), *Handbook of research on improving student achievement* (pp. 7–19). Arlington, Va.: Educational Research Services.

Waxman, H. C. (1995). Classroom observations of effective teaching. In A. C. Ornstein (ed.), *Teaching: Theory into practice* (pp. 76–93). Needham Heights, Mass.: Allyn and Bacon.

Waxman, H. C., and Huang, S. L. (1995). An observational study of technology integration in urban elementary and middle schools. *International Journal of Instructional Media, 22,* 329–339.

Waxman, H. C., and Huang, S. L. (1996). Classroom instruction differences by level of technology use in middle school mathematics. *Journal of Educational Computing Research, 14,* 147–159.

Waxman, H. C., and Huang, S. L. (1996–97). Differences by level of technology use on students' motivation, anxiety, and classroom learning environment in mathematics. *Journal of Educational Technology Systems, 25*(1), 67–77.

Waxman, H. C., and Huang, S. L. (1997). Classroom instruction and learning environment differences between effective and ineffective urban elementary schools for African American students. *Urban Education, 32*(1), 7–44.

Waxman, H. C.; Huang, S. L.; Anderson, L.; and Weinstein, T. (1997). Investigating classroom processes in effective/efficient and ineffective/inefficient urban elementary schools. *Journal of Educational Research, 91,* 49–59.

Waxman, H. C.; Huang, S. L.; and Padrón, Y. N. (1995). Investigating the pedagogy of poverty in inner-city middle level schools. *Research in Middle Level Education, 18*(2), 1–22.

Waxman, H. C.; Huang, S. L.; and Wang, M. C. (1997). Investigating the multilevel classroom learning environment of resilient and nonresilient students from inner-city elementary schools. *International Journal of Educational Research, 27,* 343–353.

Waxman, H. C.; Rodriguez, J.; Padrón, Y. N.; and Knight, S. L. (1988). The use of systematic classroom observations during field experience components of teacher education programs. *The College Student Journal, 22,* 199–202.

Waxman, H. C., and Walberg, H. J. (1982). The relation of teaching and learning: A review of reviews of process-product research. *Contemporary Education Review, 1,* 103–120.

Waxman, H. C., and Walberg, H. J. (1986). Effects of early field experiences. In J. D. Raths and L. G. Katz (eds.), *Advances in teacher education* (Vol. 2, pp. 165–184). Norwood, N. J.: Ablex.

Winne, P. H. (1987). Why process-product research cannot explain process-product findings and a proposed remedy: The cognitive mediational paradigm. *Teaching and Teacher Education, 3,* 333–356.

Winne, P. H., and Marx, R. W. (1977). Reconceptualizing research on teaching. *Journal of Educational Psychology, 69,* 668–678.

5
Effective Instruction in Effective Schools

Bert P. M. Creemers

When the school effectiveness movement started, it was assumed that a restricted set of factors, such as strong educational leadership, high expectations of student achievement, emphasis on basic skills, a safe and orderly climate, and frequent evaluation of pupils' progress, made a distinction between effective and ineffective schools. Initially, no distinction was made between the different levels within schools, such as departments and classrooms, in order to make the point as strong as possible: schools matter. The factors connected with educational effectiveness were in fact a combination of all kinds of elements, as can be seen in an analysis of the five-factor model and other models (Creemers and Scheerens, 1991; Scheerens, 1992). Later, the loose theoretical framework of school effectiveness was criticized, and as a result more emphasis was given to the development of a conceptual framework that contains levels—including the classroom level within the school and the school level—in addition to the student level. There are also the departmental level in the school organization and levels immediately above the school, such as the school board.

In the effectiveness models developed later on (Creemers, 1991; Scheerens, 1989; Slater and Teddlie, 1992; Stringfield and Slavin, 1992), a relationship between the classroom and the school level can be found. The educational processes—instruction and learning—take place at the classroom level, and the other levels are supposed to provide the conditions for instruction at the classroom level. This conceptual framework, however, did not stop the search for all kinds of correlates of effectiveness, and the list of possible correlates for effectiveness continued to grow. As a result of the methodology used, these correlates can be found at all levels—the classroom, the school, the school board, the district, and the national levels. One of the criticisms against the correlates is that it is not clear what the relationships between these correlates and what goes on at the classroom level might be. Research of the school level and the classroom level showed that the classroom level was important, quite often even more so than the school level (see, for example, Scheerens, Vermeulen, and Pelgrum, 1989). Also, theory-oriented publications stressed the predominance of the classroom level. This implies that in school effectiveness research, attention for the school level is diminishing while the classroom level gets more attention than before. In fact, we could be back at the stage before the school effectiveness movement began: teachers and classrooms make a difference, albeit quite small.

However, even when learning and teaching take place primarily at the classroom level, educational effectiveness means more than outcomes in just *one* class. Educational effectiveness has to do with outcomes and effectiveness in successive classes in a school and in the educational system as a whole. The classroom level alone cannot guarantee adequate transitions between different classes. Effectiveness of education therefore is more than effectiveness at the classroom level.

I begin this chapter by discussing the correlates of effective instruction. Due to the complexity of teaching and learning, it is unrealistic to expect that just one factor or characteristic can explain that small amount of variance (between 4 percent and 8 percent). Probably a combination of characteristics and variables contributes to the effectiveness. In this section, a theory on effective instruction will be outlined based on the empirical evidence of research on learning and instruction. In the next section, the conditions at the school level and above the school level will be formulated. In developing a theory on effective education, a list of correlates, even when they start within a common scheme or framework, is not sufficient. Therefore, in the last section of this chapter more formal criteria for effective education will be presented. These formal criteria for effectiveness at the different levels of education, together with the correlates and conditions, contribute to a conceptual framework that can serve as a start for an educational theory, or in terms of practical knowledge, a mission statement for schools that intend to become more effective.

CORRELATES OF EFFECTIVENESS AT THE CLASSROOM LEVEL

After 1985, the second generation of school effectiveness studies was carried out. These were rooted in the school effectiveness research and school improvement experiences and projects, but they took advantage of the criticism of earlier school effectiveness research and the availability of new techniques for statistical analysis such as hierarchical linear modeling (HLM). Quite a lot of research projects still used outlier or survey designs. The survey studies were carried out with more adequate techniques like observations, but experimental studies are still hardly available.

Major studies carried out or published after 1985 were the studies by Mortimore and colleagues (1988) in the United Kingdom and by Teddlie and Stringfield (1993) in the United States. In the same period, school effectiveness studies also began in other countries, including the Netherlands, Australia, Hong Kong, and Norway (for an overview, see Reynolds et al., 1994).

There are communalities in the findings of the British and the American studies, and in the past studies and the major studies of the late eighties. Differences were also found. For example, the nature of effective leadership in the United States seems to be somewhat different from that in the United Kingdom. The United States research emphasizes strong educational leadership by the principal, but in the United Kingdom effectiveness is related to leadership by the head *and* the deputy head, and also to the involvement of teachers in decision making. In the Netherlands, after 1985, quite a lot of research was started. The studies mostly used the same designs as well as the translated versions of instruments that had previously been used in British and American studies. Surprisingly, quite often results found in British and American studies could not be replicated.

The research projects carried out in the second half of the eighties had better research designs than had the earlier studies and made use of more sophisticated techniques for data analysis. In some countries, including the United States and the United Kingdom, the techniques for data collection also included observation. In other countries, like the Netherlands, quite a lot of surveys were used to collect data. In the case of survey research, we have to be cautious about the results. For example, the somewhat disappointing research results in the evaluation of the Dutch Educational Priority Programme might have been caused by the fact that teachers knew how to fill in surveys about teaching. That could explain why only a few differences between effective and ineffective schools were found.

Some studies, such as the Louisiana School Effectiveness studies, already made a distinction between school and classroom levels, whereas other studies showed a mix of classroom and school factors. This holds in particular for most of the reviews of the research literature. Although research was improved, the result was still a long list of correlates for effectiveness that needed regrouping and rethinking in order to generate better understanding. As Stringfield and colleagues (1992) concluded in their presentation of the follow-up study in Louisiana: "We need to be developing sophisticated, practical, contextually sensitive models of effective schooling" (p. 412).

Recently, in response to a plea for a theoretical foundation of school effectiveness research, several theoretical models were developed that take into account the difference between the classroom level, where instruction and learning take place, and the levels above the classroom level, where the conditions that contribute to effectiveness at the classroom level should be provided (Creemers, 1994; Scheerens, 1992; Slater and Teddlie, 1992; Stringfield and Slavin, 1992). The models are mostly based on learning theories, as far as the classroom-level processes are concerned. These theories explain how learning can take place and include instructional factors. The most important elements of learning theories, however, are student-level factors like social background, aptitudes, and motivation. The instructional factors included in the theories are, next to school effectiveness, based on instructional theories related to research on teaching, curriculum research, and research on grouping.

Instructional Theories as the Basis for School Effectiveness Models

Theories about effective education that start at the classroom level focus on the instructional elements of learning theories. In fact, these theories, while taking into account students' background characteristics, try to explain how the instructional factors can contribute to the outcomes of education, or more precisely how differences in educational outcomes can be explained by differences in instruction at the classroom level. These theories emphasize instructional factors that may be changed. In addition to considering students' background characteristics, instructional theories take elements or components of instruction at the classroom level into account, like the methods and other learning materials used at the classroom level, the learning environment, and especially the teacher. From the differences among components of instruction at the classroom level, one can discover correlates for effectiveness in research, and in fact the correlates for effectiveness from past research can be rearranged into a conceptual framework. When theories about learning are taken as a point of departure, it is possible to rearrange these correlates with respect to learning outcomes and to develop a theory and a program for educational research accordingly.

In various instructional theories developed in the past (Bloom, 1976; Carroll, 1963; Cooley and Lohnes, 1976; Glaser, 1976; Harnischfeger and Wiley, 1976; for an overview see Walberg, 1986; Warries and Pieters, 1992), the theoretical constructs are almost the same. The theories and the theoretical frameworks often make a distinction between quality of instruction, time on task, and opportunity to learn. Like Carroll's (1963) research, these studies take time and opportunity together. However, one could argue that time itself is somewhat different from what happens within the time framework. This is especially stressed by research on the curriculum and on the implementation of curricula and textbooks by the teacher. For that reason, we would like to make a distinction between the time on task on the one hand and the opportunity to learn on the other.

Time and opportunity can be discerned in several categories. Harnischfeger and Wiley (1976), for example, distinguish seven categories of time. The same holds even more for quality of instruction, which can be outlined in quite a lot of different elements, especially when quality is distinguished for the different components within the instructional process like curricula, grouping procedures, and teacher behavior. Each of these three components of instruction can contribute to the quality of instruction and can have, to put it differently, characteristics that are all connected with the effectiveness of education at the classroom level. These components can have a direct influence on learning outcomes, but they can also influence time and opportunity: the quality of instruction can influence learning outcomes directly and have an indirect influence as well by generating time for learning and enlarging the opportunity to learn.

When we make a distinction between instruction and learning, then it is obvious that there is a difference between what is offered to students and the actual use students make of that offer. That holds for time and for opportunity. The quality of instruction can influence the use that students make of time and opportunity as well as the amount they need before they master the objectives of education. With respect to time, this distinction between offered time and used time is obvious in terms of allocated and engaged time. With respect to opportunities, it is more rare to make a distinction between the opportunities, for example, the possibility for learning experiences offered, and the use students make of these opportunities, but this distinction can provide a good instrument to explain differences in student outcomes. Related directly to student outcomes and in connection with time and opportunity for quality of instruction, and based on a vast amount of research, meta-analyses, and theoretical analyses, a set of correlates can be formulated (Creemers, 1994). An overview of correlates, based on empirical evidence ranging from plausible to strong, can be given for these components: curriculum (including textbooks), grouping procedures, and teacher behavior.

With respect to the curriculum, the effective correlates are the following:

- Explicitness and ordering of goals and content
- Structure and clarity of content
- Use of advance organizers
- Use of material for evaluation of student outcomes, feedback, and corrective instruction

With respect to grouping procedures:

- Mastery learning
- Ability grouping
- Cooperative learning, which is highly dependent on
  - Differentiated material
  - Material for evaluation, feedback, and corrective instruction

With respect to teacher behavior:

- Management, an orderly and quiet atmosphere
- Homework
- High expectations
- Clear goal setting
  - Restricted set of goals
  - Emphasis on basic skills
  - Emphasis on cognitive learning and transfer
- Structuring the curriculum content
  - Ordering of goals and content
  - Advance organizers
  - Making use of students' prior knowledge
- Clarity of presentation
- Questioning
- Immediate exercise after presentation of new content
- Evaluation, feedback, and corrective instruction

It is obvious that teachers are the central component in instruction at the classroom level. They make use of curricular materials and they actually carry out grouping procedures in their classrooms. Teachers need curricular materials that should be consistent with the grouping procedure used.

CONDITIONS FOR EFFECTIVENESS AT THE SCHOOL LEVEL

The Conditional Role of the School Level

We take as a point of departure that learning and especially differences in learning outcomes have to be explained by the primary processes at the classroom level. The primary processes directly influence time on task and opportunities to learn used by students and indirectly influence student achievement. It cannot be expected that the school level directly contributes to time on task and opportunities used by students or to student achievement, but the school, as said before, can provide conditions for quality of instruction, time for learning, and opportunity to learn at the classroom level. We have to keep in mind, though, that in the empirical process with respect to the influence of the school-level conditions, these conditions can be absorbed by the classroom level. It is postulated that at the school level the conditional factors can be related to the overarching categories mentioned earlier: quality, time, and opportunity.

Quality, Time, and Opportunity at the School Level

School-level factors are supposed to influence directly the quality of instruction, time for learning, and opportunity to learn at the classroom level. Their influence on student achievement is mediated by time on task and opportunities used at the student level. School-level factors are categorized within the same conceptual notions of quality, time, and opportunity as are the classroom-level factors. All specific school-level factors are supposed to be related to either quality or time or opportunity.

The school level includes the organization of the school (teachers, students, parents), but also the educational system above the classroom level, which relates to the curriculum of the school, such as the textbooks and the time schedule. This suggests a distinction in the school level as an organizational and an educational system. Both systems are related to each other, but the first can create and sustain the situation in which education takes place to some extent, comparable with what management of the classroom "does" for instruction. The factors at the school level are conditions for what goes on at the classroom level. Conditions can be clear, such as the curriculum, or less apparent, like the structure of the organization, but they can affect the instructional process by, for example, influencing what happens between principals and teachers (see, for example, Rosenholz, 1989; Stoll, 1992; Teddlie and Stringfield, 1993).

A distinction has been made between educational and organizational aspects of the *quality of instruction*, although both are interrelated. With respect to the *educational* aspects, the rules and agreements in the school concerning the instructional process at the classroom level are of utmost importance, especially those related to curricular materials, grouping procedures, and teacher behavior. It is important to choose curricular materials for specific grade levels that are also used in other grade levels, or at least to ensure that they have the same structure. There should be a policy at the school level that defines educational goals that have to be achieved in classrooms. This does not imply a wide range of goals that may be impossible to achieve by schools and teachers, but realistic goals that can actually be achieved in education and that can give guidance to teacher behavior. When a specific grouping procedure is chosen, it is important to implement the same grouping procedure in several grade levels because effectiveness is also enhanced by constancy. There should be a policy at the school level to guide the continuity of grouping procedures across grade levels. Schools should have an evaluation policy that directs activities at classroom and student level by means of a student monitoring system. Schools can promote the testing of students and stimulate teachers to give information about test results to students, to take corrective measures, to monitor student progress, and to act as necessary based on the student progress, providing opportunities for rehearsal, corrective materials, and remedial teaching.

The *organizational* aspects of quality at the school level deal with the intervision (mutual supervision) of teachers and the professionalization of teachers and principals. These aspects refer not only to the structure of the organization but also to the way teachers and principals cooperate to promote the effectiveness of instruction at the classroom level and of the school as a whole. In this respect, the school principal as an "instructional leader," who takes responsibility for the conditions mentioned above can be an important conditional variable (Smith and Andrews, 1989). Team consensus about the mission of the school and the way to fulfill this mission through shared values will clearly support the activities of individual teachers and result in continuity (see Sashkin and Walberg, 1993). This can create a school culture, with principals, teachers, students, and parents, that promotes and supports effectiveness (Cheng, 1993). In this respect, the influence of the school board can also be mentioned. School boards, like principals, can support school effectiveness and the effectiveness of classroom instruction. When they confirm school curriculum documents, they should attend to the elements mentioned above. They should strive for effective education when deciding about personnel, for example, when they recruit new teachers or make decisions about career planning. School boards that are more attentive in this respect can increase effectiveness at the classroom level in the end, through school principals, school teams, and individual teachers (Hofman, 1993).

Conditions for *time* at the school level are connected with the time schedule. For all grade levels, this schedule spells out how much time should be devoted to different subjects. Above that, it is important to keep track of the time schedule. In less effective schools, a lot of scheduled time is wasted, because there is no system to control classrooms in this matter. The time available for learning can be expanded by a homework policy. In this respect, good relations with the home environment can contribute to effectiveness. When homework assignments are well controlled and structured, and adequate feedback is given, such assignments can expand effective learning time outside the school. Good contacts between schools and parents and agreements about school policies and activities may lead to effective use of time spent on homework. When parents expect their children to achieve goals set by the school, the effectiveness of education increases.

Measures at the school level can maintain an orderly atmosphere that facilitates teaching and learning at the classroom level. Learning time is increased by an orderly and quiet classroom climate. At the school level, such a climate can be fostered; therefore, it is necessary to establish order, a quiet atmosphere, and regularity, and to support teachers trying to achieve an orderly climate in their classes.

At the school level, conditions can be created that contribute to the *opportunity to learn* at the classroom level. This is especially important, at the school level, between classes and grade levels within the school. At the school level, the opportunity to learn is provided by the development and availability of documents such as a formal curriculum, a school working plan, and an activity plan on what has to be done to pursue the goals of the curriculum and the working plan. In this document, the school management team can explain its vision about education and make clear how effectiveness will be pursued in the school. Schools should have a policy that increases effectiveness. Schools should feel responsible for student achievement: it is their "mission" to contribute to achievement. A school policy based on these principles can yield important effects. It has already been mentioned that school working plans are not very effective, but their effects might be improved by a stronger relationship to instructional effectiveness at the classroom level. But not only the document is important; it is also important to use the document and to "control" what happens in the schools and classrooms with respect to the school curriculum. This is especially important for transitions between classes and grades. Therefore, there should be rules and agreements about how to implement the curriculum at the school level.

In summary, the following conditions at the school level can be described for *quality of instruction* with respect to the *educational* aspects:

- Rules and agreements about all aspects of classroom instruction, especially curricular materials, grouping procedures, and teacher behavior, and the consistency between them
- An evaluation policy and a system at school level to check on pupil achievement, to prevent learning problems, or to correct problems at an early stage. This includes regular testing, remedial testing, student counseling, and homework assistance

With respect to the *organizational* aspects at the school level, important conditions for *quality of instruction* are

- A school policy on intervision and supervision of teachers, heads of departments, and school principals by higher-ranking persons, and a school policy to correct and further professionalize teachers who do not live up to the school standards
- A school culture inducing and supporting effectiveness

Conditions for *time* at the school level are

- The development and provision of a time schedule for subjects and topics
- Rules and agreements about time use, including the school policy on homework, pupil absenteeism, and cancellation of lessons
- The maintenance of an orderly and quite atmosphere in the school

Conditions for the *opportunity to learn* at the school level are

- The development and availability of a curriculum, school working plan, or activity plan

- Consensus about the mission of the school
- Rules and agreements about how to proceed and how to follow the curriculum, especially with respect to transition from one class to another or from one grade to another (Creemers, Reezigt, and van der Werf, 1992)

It is not our purpose to give an overview of all kinds of school factors. This has been done before (Levine and Lezotte, 1990). For the International School Effectiveness Research Programme, Reynolds (1993) provided a list of possible factors. Most of the factors in these lists are comparable with the ones mentioned above, which were derived according to the conceptual notions of quality, time, and opportunity. Resources are not regarded as a separate category of school factors. It is not expected that just providing additional finance and resources to schools is likely to improve them (Cohn and Geske, 1990; Walberg, 1992). Resources should be defined in such a way that their relationship to effectiveness is clarified, that is, by describing their influence on curricular materials, teacher behavior, and other factors that support education.

FORMAL CRITERIA FOR EFFECTIVENESS: A FRAMEWORK FOR EFFECTIVE SCHOOLING

Research on effective education at the classroom level shows that isolated components or effective elements of individual components do not result in strong effects on student achievement. Good curricula need teachers who can make adequate use of them and will show effective instructional behavior. The same holds for grouping procedures. Integration of components is necessary to achieve substantial effects. An integrated approach for education at the classroom level with an even higher level of integration than direct instruction or mastery learning is necessary. In this integrated approach, the educational components of curricula, grouping procedures, and teacher behavior are adapted to each other. To achieve time and opportunity to learn, the three components in general should have the same effective characteristics. This is called consistency of the effective characteristics, which can cause synergistic effects that positively influence the effects of instruction at the classroom level.

Like consistency at the classroom level, there are formal criteria for effectiveness at the school level, especially when the longitudinal aspect of effectiveness is at stake. Students move from one grade level to another one, from one class to another, and from one school subject to another. Formal criteria cannot be seen immediately in schools, but we can conclude that they exist, because the same factors are seen across instructional components, subjects, grades, and classes. They are important conditions for effectiveness and continuing instructional settings within the school. These formal criteria are consistency, cohesion, constancy, and control (Creemers, 1991, 1994; Reynolds, 1993; Reynolds and Creemers, 1992; Stringfield and Slavin, 1992), defined as follows:

Consistency. At the school level, conditions for effective instruction related to curricular materials, grouping procedures, and teacher behavior should be in line with each other.

Cohesion. All members of the school team show consistency of effectiveness characteristics. In this way, effective instruction between classes can be guaranteed.

Constancy. Effective instruction is provided during the total school career of students. Too often students are confronted with differences in instruction between teachers and grade levels. Constancy means that consistency and cohesion are guaranteed over longer periods of time.

Control. Control refers not only to the evaluation of student achievement and teacher behavior, but also to an orderly and quiet school climate, which is necessary to achieve results. Control also refers to teachers' holding each other responsible for effective instruction.

Although we restrict ourselves to the classroom and school levels, the theory about educational effectiveness can be expanded above the school level to the contextual level, taking into account the same elements of quality, time, and opportunity, and the formal criteria for effectiveness.

Such a comprehensive theory (as presented in Figure 5-1) can serve as a framework or point of departure for future research on effectiveness, but it also provides the elements for school improvement. The theory emphasizes, as does the research evidence, the importance of the classroom level as well as the conditions created at the school and contextual levels. Furthermore,

Figure 5-1
A Comprehensive Model of Educational Effectiveness

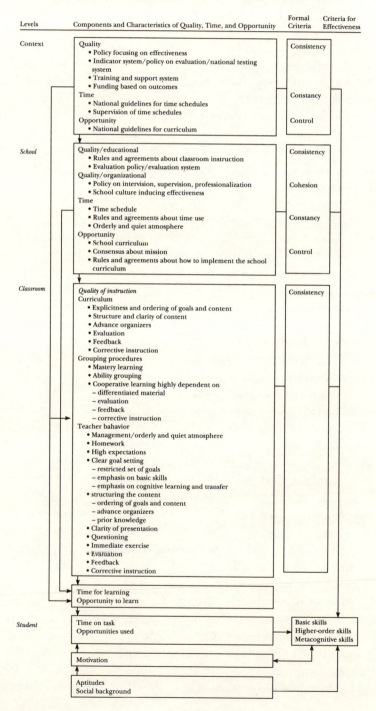

it stresses that effectiveness is something more than correlates: there is a relationship between components, correlates, and variables in the educational system. In the conceptual framework presented, these are the formal criteria, but these criteria probably refer to "ideas or vision" on schooling and education.

FURTHER RESEARCH IN THE FIELD OF EDUCATIONAL EFFECTIVENESS

Compared to the start of the school effectiveness movement, recently there have been many accomplishments in empirical research as well as in theory development. However, many essential questions still remain unanswered. These questions mainly concern the empirical validity of the theories and theoretical models on school effectiveness, which were developed fairly recently. Finally, it is important to note that it is not enough merely to start a lot of research. Instead, different types of research should be pursued at the same time.

Links with Theories on Educational Effectiveness

Effectiveness research has yielded some empirical support for some characteristics of effectiveness at different levels in the educational system. The comprehensive model for educational effectiveness described in this chapter is partly based on these research findings. For example, empirical evidence was one of the criteria for the selection of characteristics for this model. The model has gone one step further by putting the characteristics in an explanatory perspective, by describing relationships between and across levels, and by introducing the concept of formal criteria. The development of this model and of several other models should lead to new practices in research. In the past, effectiveness research has mostly been focusing on finding characteristics at the classroom and the school level that are effective. Research was hardly ever theory-driven. Effectiveness researchers have often been attacked for their lack of attention to educational theories. This situation should change, and the developments in the field of theories on educational effectiveness also justify changes in research practices.

Instead of searching for new characteristics, research should start testing the hypotheses that are put forward by theories on effectiveness. For example, the comprehensive model in this chapter tries to explain why certain sets of characteristics are effective and in what way they are effective in combination with each other. The next step is to find out whether the hypothesized relationships within levels and across levels can be validated by future research. Also, the additional value of the formal criteria has to be studied in educational practice. In short, the model should be tested to find out its explanatory power.

The comprehensive model assumes similar effects of characteristics on different types of student outcomes and on different types of students. However, differential effects on types of outcomes or on types of students may in fact occur in educational practice. Therefore, differential effects form an extra topic for future research on educational effectiveness.

The comprehensive model also assumes similar effects of characteristics in different countries. However, the role of the educational context may differ from one country to another, thereby possibly creating different effects of the school and the classroom levels. The role of the context level should be studied explicitly to find out whether national differences exist.

Research topics that can be derived from the model are

- The combinations of effective characteristics within the classroom and school levels
- The relationships between characteristics across levels, especially characteristics that represent time, opportunity, and quality of instruction at different levels
- The relationship between the organizational and the educational characteristics at the school level
- The role and the strength of the formal criteria for educational effectiveness and their relationships with effective characteristics
- Differential effects of characteristics
- The role of the context level

Types of Research

It would be untrue to say that there has been a lack of effectiveness studies. In fact, the number of studies in several countries is rather abundant and the techniques that are used to analyze the data are becoming more sophisticated. The problem in effectiveness research is not so much the number of studies, but the overrepresentation of certain types of studies, the lack of attention to the operationalization of variables, the lack of studies that include more than one level, the lack of experimental designs, the lack of internationally comparative studies, and, finally, the lack of adequate reviews of studies.

Effectiveness research studies have very often been limited to outlier research and case studies. Studies have mostly been focusing on only one dependent variable, the measurement of student achievement in the basic skills. Due to this, it is hard to generalize effectiveness findings to the full spectrum of schools and to various types of student outcomes (higher-order skills, metacognitive skills, and so on).

Effectiveness studies—in particular, surveys that use questionnaires—often use rather crude operationalizations of variables. This holds for both the independent and the dependent variables. This feature adds to the problem of generalizibility of results. Moreover, the lack of refinement in effectiveness characteristics hinders the interpretation of findings. For example, time for learning and opportunity to learn are generally considered very important factors for student achievement. The way in which these concepts are actually measured most of the time, such as with teachers' ratings of time spent during their own lessons or teachers' ratings of content and curriculum covered in their lessons during a school year, makes it hard to draw clear conclusions about the real size and meaning of effects of time and opportunity.

Effectiveness studies have often focused on independent variables on only one level of the educational system, mostly the school level. There are very few comprehensive studies, that is, those that involve more than one level. This may partly be due to financial constraints. Studies with a multilevel design are much more costly in general.

Experimental studies are very rare in the field of educational effectiveness, maybe because of the lack of theory-driven studies. The only studies that come near experimental situations are school improvement studies that pay explicit attention to a research design. In fact, school improvement settings can be used very well for effectiveness experiments in a natural setting. Unfortunately, these kinds of studies are also very rare. Most improvement studies do not meet the criteria for adequate research.

Stronger links between effectiveness researchers and school improvers therefore are necessary.

Although there is a certain tradition in international comparative research, most studies such as the IEA studies (Burstein, 1992; Elley, 1994) or studies on indicator systems (OECD, 1995), are of limited importance with respect to the independent variables of educational effectiveness. Most studies pay rather extensive attention to achievement measures, but only include some global proxies of classroom and school characteristics. The International School Effectiveness Research Programme study, Creemers, Reynolds, and Swint, 1995; Reynolds, Teddlie, and ISERP team, 1995) is a first step to internationally comparative studies that include a more elaborated set of variables on the classroom and school levels.

School effectiveness research has yielded many reviews of studies. However, many reviews focus on a limited number of studies or on only one level of research, and they also often concern fairly similar selections of studies. It sometimes seems that reviewers keep repeating themselves, a small group of researchers, and other reviewers. There are currently no reviews or meta-analyses in the field of school effectiveness that have used very strict methodological criteria for the selection of studies.

To sum up, educational effectiveness research needs the following:

- A variety of types of research (survey, case studies, outliers, representative samples, observational studies)
- A more refined operationalization of variables, in particular those variables that seem of essential importance for effectiveness (time, opportunity, and quality)
- Studies that include more than one level of the educational system, and when this is not possible, studies that pay more attention to the limitations of studying only one level
- Experimental designs, possibly in improvement settings, to find out in a more adequate way which characteristics are actually effective
- Internationally comparative research on the independent variables of educational effectiveness
- Methodologically sound reviews of effectiveness studies and meta-analyses

REFERENCES

Bloom, B. S. (1976). *Human characteristics and school learning*. New York: McGraw Hill.
Burstein, L. (ed.). (1992). *The IEA study of mathematics III: Student growth and classroom processes*. Oxford: Pergamon.
Carroll, J. B. (1963). A model of school learning. *Teachers College Record, 64*(8), 723–733.
Cheng, Y. C. (1993). Profiles of organizational culture and effective schools. *School Effectiveness and School Improvement, 4*(2), 85–110.
Cohn, E., and Geske, T. G. (1990). *The economics of education*. Oxford: Pergamon.
Cooley, W. W., and Lohnes, P. R. (1976). *Evaluation research in education*. New York: Wiley.
Creemers, B. P. M. (1991). *Effectieve instructie* [Effective instruction]. Den Haag: SVO.
Creemers, B. P. M. (1994). *The effective classroom*. London: Cassell.
Creemers, B. P. M.; Reynolds, D.; and Swint, F. E. (1995). *The International School Effectiveness Research Programme: Results of the quantitative study*. Paper for the European Conference on Educational Research, Bath, 14–17 September.
Creemers, B. P. M., and Scheerens, J. (1991). School- en instructie-effectiviteit [School and instructional effectiveness]. *Tijdschrift voor Onderwijsresearch, 16*(4).
Creemers, B. P. M.; Reezigt, G. J.; and van der Werf, M. P. C. (1992). *Development and testing of a model for school learning*. Groningen: RION.
Elley, W. B. (ed.). (1994). *The IEA study of reading achievement and instruction in thirty-two school systems*. Oxford: Pergamon.
Glaser, R. (1976). Components of a psychology of instruction: Toward a science of design. *Review of Educational Research, 46*, 1–24.
Harnischfeger, A., and Wiley, D. E. (1976). The teaching/learning process in elementary schools: A synoptic view. *Curriculum Inquiry, 6*, 5–43.
Hofman, R. H. (1993). *Effectief schoolbestuur* [Effective schoolboards]. Groningen: RION.
Levine, D. U., and Lezotte, L. W. (1990). *Unusually effective schools*. Madison, Wisc.: National Center for Effective Schools Research and Development.
Mortimore, P.; Sammons, P.; Stoll, L.; Lewis, D.; and Ecob, R. (1988). *School matters*. Somerset: Open Books.
OECD, Organisation for Economic Cooperation and Development (1995). *Education at a glance: OECD Indicators*. Paris: OECD.
Reynolds, D. (1993). *Conceptualising and measuring the school level*. Paper presented at the Annual Meeting of the American Educational Research Association, Atlanta.
Reynolds, D., and Creemers, B. P. M. (1992). *The International School Effectiveness Research Program: An outline*. Cardiff: University of Wales.
Reynolds, D.; Creemers, B. P. M.; Nesselrodt, P. S.; Schaffer, E. C.; Stringfield, S.; and Teddlie, C. (eds.). (1994). *Advances in school effectiveness research and practice*. Oxford: Pergamon Press.
Reynolds, D.; Teddlie, C.; and ISERP team (1995). *World-class schools: A pre-*

liminary analysis of data from the International School Effectiveness Research Programme. Paper for the European Conference on Educational Research, Bath, 14–17 September.

Rosenholz, S. J. (1989). *Teachers' workplace: The social organization of schools.* New York: Longman.

Sashkin, M., and Walberg, H. J. (1993). *Educational leadership and school culture.* Berkeley: McCutchan.

Scheerens, J. (1989). *Wat maakt scholen effectief* [What makes schools effective]. Den Haag: SVO.

Scheerens, J. (1992). *Effective schooling: Theory, research and practice.* London: Cassell.

Scheerens, J.; Vermeulen, C. J.; and Pelgrum, W. J. (1989). Generalizability of instructional and school effectiveness indicators across nations. *International Journal of Educational Research, 13*(7), 789–799.

Slater, R. O., and Teddlie, C. (1992). Toward a theory of school effectiveness and leadership. *School Effectiveness and School Improvement, 3*(4), 247–257.

Smith, W. F., and Andrews, R. L. (1989). *Instructional leadership: How principals make a difference.* Alexandria, Va.: Association for Supervision and Curriculum Development.

Stoll, L. (1992). Teacher growth in the effective school. In M. Fullan and A. Hargreaves (eds.), *Teacher development and educational change* (pp. 104–122). London: Falmer.

Stringfield, S. C., and Slavin, R. E. (1992). A hierarchical longitudinal model for elementary school effects. In B. P. M. Creemers and G. J. Reezigt (eds.), *Evaluation of educational effectiveness* (pp. 35–69). Groningen: ICO.

Stringfield, S.; Teddlie, C.; Wimpleberg, R. K.; and Kirby, P. (1992). A five-year follow-up of schools in the Louisiana School Effectiveness Study. In J. Bashi and Z. Sass (eds.), *School effectiveness and school improvement: Proceedings of the Third International Congress, Jerusalem.* Jerusalem: The Magness Press.

Teddlie, C., and Stringfield, S. C. (1993). *Schools make a difference: Lessons learned from a 10-year study of school effects.* New York: Teachers College Press.

Walberg, H. J. (1986). Syntheses of research on teaching. In M. C. Wittrock (ed.), *Handbook of research on teaching* (pp. 214–229). New York: MacMillan.

Walberg, H. J. (1992). Educational indicators for educational progress. In B. P. M. Creemers and W. Th. J. G. Hoeben (eds.), *Indicatoren van onderwijseffectiviteit* [Indicators of educational effectiveness (pp. 7–27)]. Groningen: ICO.

Warries, E., and Pieters, J. M. (1992). *Inleiding instructietheorie* [An introduction in instructional theory]. Amsterdam: Swets & Zeitlinger.

6

Interpersonal Relationships Between Teachers and Students in the Classroom

*Theo Wubbels, Mieke Brekelmans,
Jan van Tartwijk, and Wilfried Admiraal*

The search for the "effective teacher" has been conducted for more than a century (Borich, 1988). In the 1800s, effective teachers were usually thought of as individuals who were good persons, honorable citizens, well-educated, and hardworking. They had high morale and were respected for their knowledge, friendliness, and dedication. No special skills other than being well-organized, disciplined, authoritative, and dedicated to children were thought necessary. In the first half of this century, literally thousands of studies were conducted to find that special personality trait that would predict teaching effectiveness (Getzels and Jackson, 1963). It was, for example, claimed that teachers were mild in their judgment of others and very interested in culture and art, loved to interact with children, and were flexible, independent, and not aggressive. Although the research designs and lack of recommendations for improving the field were properly criticized, these analyses probably produced some commonsense truths.

Attitudes, measured by questionnaires, appeared to be slightly better predictors of teacher effectiveness than did personality traits.

For example, good and bad teachers divide over the amount of empathy and caring they showed. Teaching style became an important focus of the effectiveness research. Studies documented authoritarian, democratic, and *laissez faire* leadership, and direct and indirect teaching styles.

In the 1960s and 1970s, process-product research revealed teacher competencies and strategies that contributed to student achievement. These investigations demonstrated how some teachers excel in asking questions, monitoring student progress, organizing and managing the classroom, and building appropriate lesson structures. The process-product studies primarily analyzed teaching from what we call the *methods* or *pedagogical and management perspective*. This perspective refers to the plethora of technical strategies such as choice and organization of teaching materials and instructional methods, motivational strategies, and assessment. We distinguish the methods perspective from two other perspectives. The *content perspective* focuses on the meaning of the behavior of the teacher (usually the language) as far as it concerns the topic taught. This chapter will analyze effective teaching from a third perspective. This *interpersonal perspective* refers to the way the students and the teacher perceive the relationship with the teacher. This has mainly to do with the actions the teacher uses to create and maintain a working climate in the classroom.

The three perspectives can be applied to study every instance of teacher behavior. If a teacher lectures for an hour, one can analyze if the content she or he presents is correct from the point of view of the structure of the subject matter. One also can study the result of this behavior for the relationship between teacher and students: are the students getting impressed by the teacher or are they getting annoyed about him or her? From the methods point of view, one may wonder if this is the best way to stimulate students' active construction of knowledge. In some situations, it will be more important to study the behavior from one perspective than from another. The interpersonal perspective is especially important for beginning teachers, but this chapter will show the importance of this affective dimension of the learning environment for learning in every classroom. The interpersonal relationships of teachers with their students not only predict student achievement but are also related to teachers' satisfaction with their job and burnout (Nias, 1981). Appropriate teacher-student relationships are important to prevent discipline problems and to foster professional development.

This chapter will first introduce the systems approach to analyze teacher-student relationships and then describe a theoretical and measurement paradigm for investigating teacher behavior from an interpersonal perspective. For the sake of brevity, we will sometimes refer to the teacher behavior studied from an interpersonal perspective as *teacher interpersonal behavior*. An important part of interpersonal communication is its nonverbal aspect. We will describe the important nonverbal behaviors involved. Then we follow up with what instructional behavior will contribute to the perception of particular relationships. Having thus set the stage for a description of teacher behaviors, we analyze what good and effective teachers do. Finally, we look at professional development issues and teacher education.

A SYSTEMS APPROACH TO COMMUNICATION

The teacher-student relationship in class is based on the ongoing communication between teacher and students. The systems approach to communication (Watzlawick, Beavin, and Jackson, 1967) distinguishes two levels of extensiveness of interactions. *Short-term interactions* are the exchanges of messages of a few seconds each, consisting of one question, one assignment, one response, one gesture, and the like. In these interactions, redundancy and repeating patterns can evolve over time. Then, interactions on the second level, *relatively stable interaction patterns*, or interpersonal styles, are seen.

Teacher and student behavior in class influence each other. Teacher behavior is produced by teacher-student interaction and is shaped by the demands of securing student cooperation. Since teacher behavior also influences teacher-student interactions, the process is circular. Circularity continues over the life of the communication. People who are communicating continually exchange messages in response to earlier messages, even if there is an interruption of minutes, hours, or days. If we have not seen each other in some time, we simply "pick up where we left off." Since communication consists of series of consecutive messages, the teacher's behavior not only is *caused* by that of students, but also *confirms* their behavior (see Wubbels, Créton, and Holvast, 1988).

We consider every behavior that someone displays in the presence of someone else as communication, and therefore we assume that in the presence of someone else one can not *not* communicate (Watzlawick, Beavin, and Jackson, 1967). Whatever someone's intentions are, the other persons in the communication will infer meaning from that someone's behavior. If, for example, teachers ignore students' questions, perhaps because they do not hear them, then students may not only get this inattention but also infer that the teacher is too busy or thinks that the students are too dull to understand or that the questions are impertinent. The message that students take from the teacher's negation can be different from the teacher's intention, because they do not share an agreed-upon system to attach meaning.

When teachers meet the students in a new class, the students will be relatively open for any impression that the teacher can make. We say relatively because the context of a classroom will raise certain expectations among students of the teacher's behavior. Students will expect every new teacher to take the lead. After the first lesson, the students will have expectations of the patterns in the relationship with this particular teacher based on their experiences during the first lesson. The teacher behavior will have been interpreted in such terms as "seems a nice fellow," "will be tough but fair," "what a terrible person," "seems too uncertain," and so on. In the second lesson, the teacher may behave differently from the first, and students may consequently adjust their ideas about the teacher. After a few lessons, these rough ideas about the teacher have stabilized, and students can tell what kind of teacher someone "is." Worse, they are no longer very open to adjusting their perceptions. This stability of their conceptions applies equally to the teachers' ideas about their students. The first day or few lessons set the trend for the rest of the year. Once the pattern is set, it is difficult to modify. This stability is seen in stereotyped reactions of students to certain behaviors of a teacher and similarly of the teacher to the students'. Questions from one teacher may evoke answers from students all the time, whereas in another class with another teacher the same questions are interpreted as rhetoric and are followed by silence from the students. Similarly, the teacher may always answer in a friendly manner questions from some students, whereas she or he reacts angrily when other students ask the same questions.

The type of relationship teachers have with their students varies with the teacher (Wubbels and Levy, 1993). Some teachers prefer tight control, whereas others are more lenient; some teachers are seen as gloomy by their students, whereas others

Interpersonal Relationships Between Teachers and Students 155

are seen as friendly, and so on. Now that we have sketched the development of these rather stable patterns in interpersonal relationships in the classroom, we turn to the question of what teachers actually do if they have a particular relationship with their students and what kind of relationships teachers should strive for. In order to be able to answer these questions, we need a language for discussing interpersonal relationships in class. We use for that purpose a theory that was developed by Timothy Leary in the 1950s and adapted for analyses of classroom relationships by Wubbels and co-workers (see Leary, 1957; Wubbels and Levy, 1993, chapter 2).

A LANGUAGE FOR INTERPERSONAL RELATIONSHIPS

Theory

Leary and his co-workers analyzed hundreds of patient-therapist dialogues and group discussions in clinical and other situations. They then divided the discourse into short statements representing different kinds of interpersonal behavior. These were coded and arranged into sixteen categories that, over time, were reduced to eight. These eight can be presented in a two-dimensional plane. We have labeled the two dimensions *Proximity (Cooperation-Opposition)* and *Influence (Dominance-Submission)*. The Proximity dimension designates the degree of cooperation or closeness between those who are communicating. The Influence dimension indicates who is directing or controlling the communication, and how often.

We have refined the two-dimensional chart by drawing two extra lines to get the eight equal sections, as shown in Figure 6-1. The sections are labeled *DC*, *CD*, and so on according to their position in the coordinate system (much like the directions on a compass). For example, the two sectors DC and CD are both characterized by Dominance and Cooperation. In the DC sector, the Dominance aspect prevails over the Cooperation aspect. Thus, a teacher displaying DC behavior might be seen by students as enthusiastic, motivating, and the like. The adjacent CD sector, however, includes behaviors of a more cooperative and less dominant character; the teacher might be seen assisting, friendly, or considerate. The sections of the model describe eight different

Figure 6-1
The Model for Interpersonal Teacher Behavior

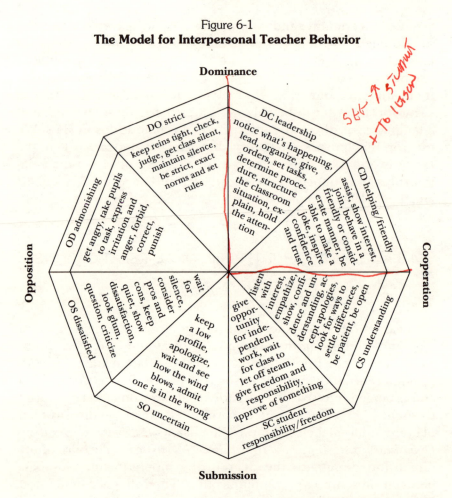

behavior aspects: Leadership (DC), Helpful/Friendly (CD), Understanding (CS), Student Responsibility/Freedom (SC), Uncertain (SO), Dissatisfied (OS), Admonishing (OD), and Strict (DO). Figure 6-1 provides examples of the eight different types of interpersonal behaviors displayed by teachers.

Measurement Instruments

Helpful instruments for teachers to use to explore their own perceptions and their students' perceptions of the interpersonal relationships are learning environment questionnaires. One dimension of a learning environment questionnaire is the relationship dimension (Moos, 1974), and questionnaire scales that address this dimension include formality, teacher support, and independence (see Fraser, 1986). From the model presented in Figure 6-1, we have developed a questionnaire to gather data on teacher-student relationships both for research and for teacher feedback purposes. This *Questionnaire on Teacher Interaction* (QTI) is divided into eight scales that conform to the eight sectors of the model. The items in the Dutch and American versions are answered on a five-point Likert scale. To make the QTI more accessible to teachers, a short (forty-eight-item) version was developed in Australia with a hand-scoring procedure. A version for primary education with a simpler reading level and a three-point response scale was developed in Singapore. Several studies have shown that the QTI has good reliability and validity (Wubbels and Levy, 1993). Versions are available in the following languages, among others: English, Dutch, Hebrew, Russian, Slovenian, Swedish, and Finnish.

The QTI has been quite successful in providing feedback to teachers. The instrument cannot be administered at the beginning of the school year, since students and teachers need a few weeks to get to know each other. After this honeymoon period, however, teachers are normally asked to select two classes that vary in age, learning ability, or some other characteristic in order to receive feedback from the widest range of student groups. Ironically, QTI scores from these two different types of classes do not generally vary much, verifying the relative stability of teacher behavior. Comparison of the students' perceptions with teacher perceptions gathered with the QTI of these teachers' own behavior and their ideal provides useful result.

Data on the patterns in the relationship between teacher and students are collected with the QTI. The model for interpersonal teacher behavior, however, also applies to the short-term interactions in class. At every moment, the behavior of teacher (and students) can be recorded on the chart according to how cooperative they are, who is controlling the discussion, and to what degree. Let us imagine a dialogue between a teacher and a student on the subject of Newton's law. As the teacher explains the relation between force, mass, and acceleration, she is engaging in Dominant behavior, since she is controlling the communication. If her explanation is presented in a patient, comfortable manner, her behavior would also be highly Cooperative. Thus, she would be displaying high Dominant-high Cooperative behavior. This behavior can be indicated on the two rating scales presented in Figure 6-2; for the example, she would be rated 5 on the

Figure 6-2
The DS and CO rating scales

Dominance (D) In this fragment the teacher determines the students' activities	5-4-3-2-1	Submission (S) In this fragment the students can determine their own activities
Cooperation (C) In this fragment the teacher shows approval of the students and their behavior	5-4-3-2-1	Opposition (O) In this fragment the teacher shows disapproval of the students and their behavior

submission-dominance scale and 4 on the opposition-cooperation scale. If, however, the student has just made the twentieth mistake in solving a "simple" problem, the teacher may be agitated and possibly angry. Her communication in this case would still be Dominant but also slightly Oppositional, changing the score on the opposition-cooperation scale from 4 to 2.

CHARACTERISTICS OF INTERPERSONAL RELATIONSHIPS

Many research studies using the QTI and the observation rating scales have been conducted in Israel, the United States, the Netherlands, Australia, Sweden, the United Kingdom, and Singapore. Some investigate the interpersonal significance of teacher nonverbal behavior. Others study all kinds of connections: for example, between the teacher behavior described from the interpersonal perspective and the same behavior analyzed from the methods or pedagogical and management perspective, or between the interpersonal behavior and other educational factors such as student cognitive achievement. In this section, we look at the nonverbal and instructional behaviors.

Interpersonal Significance of Nonverbal Teacher Behavior

Short-term behaviors of teachers (or messages) communicate information about the interpersonal relationship with their students, and students consciously or unconsciously infer an interpersonal significance from this behavior. Besides spoken words, the interpersonal significance manifests itself nonverbally through

Interpersonal Relationships Between Teachers and Students

bearing, gesture, facial expression, intonation, sound level, articulation, and context, among other indicators. The significance of nonverbal behaviors is often ambiguous. Students therefore might react in a way that is different from the teacher's intentions, as in the example of the teacher who was trying to restrain a student disturbance. With a cracking voice and flushed face he yelled, "Anyone who says another damn thing has to copy twenty-five pages from the book and will report to the principal." One student responded with, "I thought you weren't allowed to curse," which was followed by an outburst of laughing from the other students. With his words, the teacher indicated that the students ought to be afraid of him because of his power to punish them. However, the students probably interpreted his cracking voice as a sign of impotence. His words were powerful and terror-inspiring. Nonverbally, however, he communicated the opposite: that he was in danger of losing his grip on the situation. The students' reaction was therefore understandable.

Students derive the interpersonal significance of teacher behavior from both verbal and nonverbal signals. Spoken and written language are well equipped for the communication of content, but the communication of interpersonal relationships is particularly the domain of nonverbal behavior. Even though the school is very much a verbally oriented institution in which one of the main activities is the verbal transfer of information, it is important to study nonverbal teacher behavior to be able to better understand communication processes in the classroom. Results of such a study are particularly important for teacher education programs because they give clues for specific behaviors to be trained.

In a study of teacher behaviors during approximately 950 eight-second videotaped lesson fragments, we identified the characteristics of the nonverbal aspects of teacher behavior that are most important for the interpersonal significance of the teacher behavior along the dimensions of the Model for Interpersonal Teacher Behavior (van Tartwick, 1993). The behaviors were scored in nonverbal behavior categories and on the two rating scales for the two dimensions of the model. We classify nonverbal behavior into five channels:

1. Space (the teacher's use of the space in the classroom)
2. Body (position and movement of the trunk, the arms, and the head)

3. Face (various expressions)
4. Visual Behavior (duration of the teacher looking at the students)
5. Voice (the noncontent aspects of speech)

All channels appeared important for explaining variance in the DS ratings, whereas for explaining variance in the CO ratings, only the Face and Voice channels were important.

To be perceived as being at the dominant side of the model, teachers best have a body orientation frontal to the majority of the students. With regard to the body position and movement, an upright head position and moving the head around—for instance, when scanning the class—are perceived as dominant. This also implies that the face is visible to students and that it is important that the teacher looks uninterruptedly at the students. The strongest sign of dominance is speaking uninterruptedly for a rather long time while using a lecturing volume.

Teachers are perceived as being at the submissive extreme of the model when they do not look at their classroom students, when they are relatively near to them (able to touch students), and when they do not speak at all or speak in such a way that they cannot be heard clearly by students in the back of the room. With regard to their body movement and position, teachers are perceived as submissive when they bend their head downwards so that they are not looking at the students and their face is not visible.

Teachers are considered cooperative when they are laughing. Oppositional interpersonal messages are inferred especially from an angry facial expression and from raising the volume of speech.

We get still some more information about the contribution of nonverbal behaviors to the interpersonal significance of behavior if we look at frequent combinations of nonverbal behaviors. The combinations with high dominant significance imply that a teacher "holds the floor" (he or she speaks at performance level) while scanning the class (moving his or her upright head around and continuously looking at the students with a frontal body orientation). The less the teacher holds the floor or scans the class, the less the teacher behavior is perceived as dominant. One of the combinations of categories with the strongest submissive significance pictures a teacher who turns his or her back to the students and is not able to touch a student, who moves his or her head and during these movements bends it forward at an angle of more than 45 degrees, does not look at or speak to students and whose face is not visible. This combination of behaviors would be scored when, for example, a teacher is copying something from a book onto the blackboard.

Kounin (1970) found that teachers' success at management—meaning, for instance, freedom from deviancy—correlates with withitness (the teacher demonstrates that he or she knows what is going on) and overlapping (the teacher is able to attend to two issues simultaneously). The major relation between the categories of the channels Space, Body, Face, and Visual Behavior can be interpreted with these concepts. The more the teacher combines from the various channels those behaviors facilitating visual contact with the class, the more his or her behavior is perceived as dominant.

Instructional and Interpersonal Significance

It is well known that teaching behaviors and teaching styles are related to student learning (e.g., Brophy and Good, 1986). These relationships are usually described in terms of teacher instructional strategies and management behavior. When we use instructional strategies to describe teacher effectiveness, we analyze teacher behavior from what we called the methods or pedagogical and management perspective. As stated at the beginning of the chapter, the same teacher behavior can be analyzed from different perspectives. The relation between instructional behavior and student performance raises the question of the extent of overlap between teacher interpersonal behavior and instructional strategies and management techniques. Do particular interpersonal behaviors coincide with particular instructional behaviors or can a teacher applying one particular instructional strategy still have many different types of interpersonal relationships with her or his students? Two studies were conducted that shed light on this question, one by Levy, Rodriquez, and Wubbels (Wubbels and Levy, 1993) and one by Admiraal, Wubbels, and Korthagen (1996).

In the study by Levy and colleagues, the amount of overlap between the instructional and management and interpersonal behaviors appeared to be about 30 percent. While behavior analyzed from the interpersonal perspective can therefore be seen as a partial measure of instructional and management behavior, the remaining 70 percent of overlap indicates that the instructional strategy of a teacher does not predict the kind of teacher-student relationship.

The influence dimension is related to the two instructional categories of Organization and Management. The more students perceive that teachers behave in dominant ways, the more teachers display effective organizational and management techniques. Further, a teacher who, from students' perceptions, displays uncertain behavior, allows students a lot of freedom in class, or often gets angry, is seen by observers as unclear in giving directions and explaining skills and as disorganized. In addition, teachers who appeared more uncertain to students did not often display productive class management techniques.

In the study by Admiraal and colleagues about student teachers' reactions in (moderately) stressful classroom situations (such as mistakes in instruction, student off-task behavior, insufficient student achievement), the student teachers' reactions were analyzed from both the interpersonal and the methods or pedagogical and management perspectives. It appeared again that there was no one-to-one relationship between instructional or management behaviors and interpersonal behaviors. In addition, it was found that in different types of classroom situations the connections between interpersonal and instructional behaviors slightly varies. Overall, however, it appeared that certain interpersonal behaviors are observed more often together with certain instructional and management behaviors than with others.

The results of the study show that if teachers explain subject matter to students or organize their work, the students usually see the intention of the teacher to do that for the benefit of the students. On the cooperative side of the Model for Interpersonal Teacher Behavior we find such behaviors as arranging materials (looking in the book for a correct answer; putting together lab materials; distributing papers), presenting content, giving guidance, and organizing student work (such as directing their attention to the blackboard). Of these cooperative instructional categories, the first has a slightly submissive character and the last three are usually seen as slightly dominant. The results of the study of nonverbal behavior make this difference on the dominance-submission dimension plausible. Explanation of content and giving guidance are usually tied to teacher behaviors such as talking to and looking at students and are therefore perceived as rather dominant. When teachers do this with a friendly smile, they are perceived as cooperative. When teachers are arranging their materials, this is again seen as cooperative, but also slightly submissive. In this case, there may be less eye contact with students, which will lead to a more submissive perception in addition to the cooperative character, because the teacher is busy doing something for the benefit of the students.

On the very oppositional side of the model, only one management category is found: disciplining students (warning, banning). This behavior also has a highly dominant character. At the extreme dominant side of the model, we find, along with disciplining, instructional categories such as controlling and checking, criticizing students' work (such as pointing to mistakes), and also probing and inviting students' contributions. Here the dominant character probably will be a result of the teacher's behavior, which includes speaking that is clearly directed at the students and clear eye contact. On the extremely submissive side of the model, we find instructional categories where the teacher takes a passive role, such as when saying nothing or when listening.

GOOD AND EFFECTIVE INTERPERSONAL RELATIONSHIPS

Now that we have presented data on the contribution of nonverbal behaviors and instructional strategies to a particular interpersonal significance of teacher behavior, it is time to look at the question of what interpersonal relationships teachers should strive for. We use two data sources: students' and teachers' perceptions of respectively good and ideal teachers, and the connections between interpersonal relationships and student achievement and attitudes.

Norms for Good Teaching

We have asked students to complete the QTI on their best and their worst teacher. We asked teachers to depict their ideal teacher on the QTI. From the results, we conclude that teachers and students agree on the nature of appropriate interpersonal teacher behavior. Students think that their best teachers are strong Leaders. They are more Friendly and Understanding, and less Uncertain, Dissatisfied, and Admonishing than are most teachers (measured with the QTI for a very large sample, see Wubbels and Levy, 1993). Best teachers also provide students with a little more Responsibility and Freedom. The ideal teacher as seen by teachers differs in the same way from the average teacher: they want to behave in a more Cooperative and less Oppositional manner. As might be expected, teachers' vision of ideal behaviors is more extreme than are students' perceptions of their best teachers. For worst teachers, a complementary picture emerges: they are perceived by students as being much more Oppositional and less Cooperative than are average teachers.

A closer look at the ideals of individual teachers and best teachers of individual students reveals two distinct types. The first type (which we call the Dominant Ideal or Dominant Best Teacher) shows a lot of cooperative behavior and a fair amount of Leadership and Strictness. In addition to cooperative behavior, the second type (Student-Oriented Ideal or Student-Oriented Best Teacher) reflects the teacher's orientation toward student Responsibility and Freedom. The two types characterize different teachers' opinions about the nature of an appropriate classroom atmosphere. Teachers often have distinct ideas about the best way to relate to students, and they are markedly different across the profession. The Dominant Ideal teacher might say, "Students will not initiate learning activities if teachers don't control their work and demand a lot. Students are easily distracted, and allowing them too much freedom won't help them learn." In contrast, the Student-Oriented Ideal teacher might then reply, "Students have to enjoy the class before they learn anything. If there is a pleasant, stimulating atmosphere, they'll be motivated to study, which is an important prerequisite for learning, and they'll consequently thrive. It's more important to reward students for their efforts and the things they do well than it is to correct their mistakes."

Student Achievement and Attitudes

Studies by Brekelmans, Wubbels, and Créton (1990), Goh (1994), and Fisher, Henderson, and Fraser (1995) investigated interpersonal teacher behavior and student outcomes for, respectively, ninth-grade physics, fifth-grade mathematics, and twelfth-grade biology students. The image of good interpersonal relationships in the classroom outlined in the previous section is in agreement with the one that can be derived from these studies.

The more a teacher is perceived as dominant, the more his or her students achieve. Strict, Leadership, and Helpful/Friendly behaviors are positively related to student achievement, whereas Student Responsibility and Freedom, Uncertain, and Dissatisfied behaviors are negatively related. The Cooperation scales of the model for interpersonal teacher behavior (Leadership, Helpful/Friendly, Understanding, and Student Responsibility/Freedom) are positively related to student attitudes. The more teachers behave in these ways, the more their students view the lessons positively. The Opposition scales (Strict, Admonishing, Dissatisfied, and Uncertain) are all negatively related to student attitudes. This means that students with teachers whose tendency is to show above-average behavior on the right side of the D-S axis and below-average on the left side viewed their lessons more positively.

If teachers want students to be high-achieving and supportive, they may find themselves in a quandary. This is due to the conflicting demands of the Strict and Student Responsibility/Freedom categories. To realize higher student achievement, teachers have to be somewhat strict, while positive student attitudes require greater flexibility. The other six sectors of the model do not present such conflicting demands. Consequently, there is a slight difference in emphasis for the two types of teacher ideals. The Dominant Ideal teachers emphasize a learning environment that results in greater student achievement than do their Student-Oriented counterparts, who focus on student attitudes.

While the previous paragraphs described effective teachers in terms of relatively stable patterns of behavior, we did not specify the behavioral repertoire needed to build such patterns. A successful teacher's communication style does not, for example, include a great deal of admonishing behavior. This does not imply, however, that admonishing behavior should not be part of his or her repertoire. On the contrary, we believe that teaching expertise means that a teacher can suit his or her behavior to situational requirements. She or he must be able to effectively interact in all kinds of educational settings, with students who possess a variety of personal and group characteristics. This requires a broad and flexible interpersonal repertoire (see, e.g., Brophy and Good, 1986). "Broad" implies that the teacher has many interpersonal modes, while "flexible" means the teacher can smoothly switch from one interpersonal category to another.

PROFESSIONAL DEVELOPMENT

From our ongoing data collection both in longitudinal (for thirteen years now) and in cross-sectional designs, we have strong indications of the changes that occur in the teacher-student interpersonal relationships during teachers' professional careers (Wubbels and Levy, 1993). Dominant behavior appears to increase from the student-teacher period through the time that teachers have six to ten years' experience. So in this period, teachers become better leaders and instructors and they are seen as becoming progressively less insecure by their students and themselves. After this point, there is a relative constancy in the perception on the dominance and submission scales of the model for interpersonal teacher behavior. For the opposition-cooperation dimension, the results show a small increase in cooperative behavior in the first year of the career and a moderate decline after that throughout the career, but notable after the first ten years of teaching.

We have consistently found that teacher ideals are more dominant and more cooperative than are the students' and teachers' perceptions of teachers' actual behavior. Now, we can say that in the Dominance half of the model, teachers progress toward the ideal at the beginning of their career. On the Cooperation side, however, the discrepancy between the teachers' actual behavior and the teachers' ideal seems to increase after the first year in the profession. It appears that throughout their careers, teachers demonstrate increasing Leadership and Strict behavior. In effect, they attempt to behave in accordance with their ideal. This shift does not occur for the Proximity dimension—teachers do not become more Friendly and Understanding in later stages of their careers.

Noting the empirical relationship between interpersonal teacher behavior and student outcomes, we can say that relations between teachers and their students improve in the first six to ten years of their career. This improvement helps raise both student achievement and attitudes. Soon after, however, a steady change takes place, which is both welcome and unwelcome. Teachers appear to decline in cooperative behavior and increase in oppositional behavior, a change that negatively affects student attitudes. They also increase in strictness, however, which can heighten student achievement.

There is a possible explanation for this difference between the Influence and Proximity changes. Most student teachers are about twenty to twenty-five years old and have not—to any large degree—provided leadership to other people. While they develop dominance patterns through daily classroom practice, they often begin from "ground zero." Friendly, Helping, and Understanding behavior, on the other hand, are more familiar to them. As a result, their cooperative repertoire is more established and they need less practice. As their careers progress, teachers become less cooperative and their enthusiasm seems to dwindle at the hands of routine and stress. They may gradually distance themselves from students, and their norms and values may change. They also can become increasingly tired, impatient, demanding, and dissatisfied with students.

IMPLICATIONS FOR TEACHER EDUCATION

We believe the previous sections hold clear messages for preservice and in-service teacher education. They provide strong indications for the kind of behavior that should be promoted in teacher education. Briefly, teachers should be effective instructors and lecturers, as well as friendly, helpful, and congenial. They should be able to empathize with students, understand their world, and listen to them. Good teachers are not uncertain, undecided, or confusing in the way they communicate with students. They are not grouchy, gloomy, dissatisfied, aggressive, sarcastic, or quick-tempered. They should be able to set standards and maintain control while still allowing students responsibility and freedom to learn.

The student-outcome research shows that to be an effective teacher one should be perceived as relatively dominant and cooperative. Based on the results of the nonverbal behavior characteristics, we have to sketch dominant teachers as people who are verbally emphatically present, scan the class, and are with-it all the time. This may make one think that the teacher should employ whole-class teaching all the time. This is not true. A Dutch/Australian study (van Tartwijk, Fisher, Fraser, and Wubbels, 1994) showed that the results mean only that whenever teachers use whole-class teaching, they should display these behaviors. However, during small-group work, the teacher's nonverbal behavior is hardly connected to the students' perceptions of the teacher behavior. This result is in line with the earlier work of Kounin (1970).

Studies of differences between teacher and student perceptions presented evidence that effective teachers' self-perceptions were in greater agreement with their students than were those of teachers who were less effective (Wubbels and Levy, 1993). The more teachers communicate according to the Leadership, Helpful/Friendly, and Understanding sectors, the more they agree with their students about the behavior displayed. This result highlights the importance of teachers' knowing how their students perceive them and using that feedback to improve their teaching style.

Development of cooperative behavior may require teacher-education procedures that differ from those for dominance. Skill training may be most effective in developing the influence dimension. For proximity behavior, however, pre- and in-service programs might simply help teachers uncover skills they already possess. Helping teachers understand the systems nature of classroom communication can further assist them to mine their interpersonal repertoire.

Our experiences with in-service programs have demonstrated how difficult it is, even for experienced teachers, to interact properly at the right moment (cf. Hermans, Créton, and Hooymayers, 1987). Most of the veteran teachers were able to provide guidance, manage classes, and make assignments. They appeared to have no problems in taking initiative, providing structure, lecturing, giving orders and staying on the topic. Many, however, encountered difficulties when they tried to provide responsibility and initiative to students by backing off, actively listening to students' opinions, asking about ideas, and paraphrasing students' statements. When teachers try to give responsibility to students, they often confuse their students' with their own, uncertain behavior. When a teacher encourages students to take responsibility, it is imperative that the students do not perceive the given freedom as a weakness on the part of the teacher. Uncertain and undecided behavior will often lead to disorder.

Student teachers experience other difficulties. Since they have always received guidance and prescription, it is hard for them to assume an active teaching role, to take charge, to set standards, and to assess. Their professional role does not yet seem to fit their developmental stage. Moreover, when they try to take a more dominant role, they often mistake opposition for dominance. We frequently observed that being strict in class goes hand-in-hand with a certain amount of aggression. Announcing that "there is no talking allowed here" (DO) is almost always followed by the sanction "or you'll see what happens!" (OD). The combination of strictness and aggression can easily escalate, and is disapproved of by both students and teachers.

SOME FUTURE DEVELOPMENTS

This chapter has summarized results from an ongoing international research program. Several studies are underway. One study, for example, is investigating how teacher and students develop together relatively stable patterns in their communication during the first lessons in a new class and the role of teacher cognition in this process. Another line of research investigates individual differences between students in their perceptions of the teacher behavior. First, results show, for example, that boys and girls perceive teacher behavior similarly, whereas students from different cultural backgrounds perceive the same teacher differently (Levy, Wubbels, Brekelmans, and Morganfield, 1997). Interestingly, this last study also indicates that the cultural mix of the classroom influences the interpersonal teacher behavior.

REFERENCES

Admiraal, W. F.; Wubbels, Th.; and Korthagen, F. A. J. (1996). Student teacher behavior in response to daily hassles in the classroom. *Social Psychology of Education*, 1, 25–46.

Borich, G. D. (1988). *Effective teaching methods*. Columbus, Ohio: Merill.

Brekelmans, M.; Wubbels, Th.; and Créton, H. A. (1990). A study of student perceptions of physics teacher behavior. *Journal of Research in Science Teaching*, 27, 335–350.

Brophy, J. E., and Good, T. L. (1986). Teacher behavior and student achievement. In M. C. Wittrock (ed.), *Handbook of research on teaching* (3rd ed., pp. 328–375). New York: Macmillan.

Fisher, D.; Henderson, D.; and Fraser, B. (1995) Interpersonal behavior in senior high school biology classes. *Research in Science Education*, 25(2) 125–133.

Fraser, B. J. (1986). *Classroom environment.* London: Croom Helm.
Getzels, J. W., and Jackson, P. W. (1963). The teacher's personality and characteristics. In N. I. Gage (ed.), *Handbook of research on teaching* (pp. 506–582). Chicago: Rand McNally and Company.
Goh, S. C. (1994). *Interpersonal teacher behavior, classroom climate and student outcomes in primary mathematics classes in Singapore.* Perth: Curtin University, unpublished doctoral thesis.
Hermans, J. J.; Créton H. A.; and Hooymayers, H. P. (1987). Some characteristics of teacher demotivation. In J. T. Voorbach and L. G. M. Prick (eds.). *Teacher Education, 3,* 96–107.
Kounin, J. S. (1970). *Discipline and group management in classrooms.* New York: Holt, Rinehart and Winston.
Leary, T. (1957). *An interpersonal diagnosis of personality.* New York: Ronald Press Company.
Levy, J.; Wubbels, Th.; Brekelmans, M.; and Morganfield, B. (1997). Language and cultural factors in students' perceptions of teacher communication style. *International Journal of Intercultural Relationships, 21,* 29–56.
Moos, R. H. (1974). *The social climate scales: an overview.* Palo Alto: Consulting Psychologists Press.
Nias, J. (1981). Teacher satisfaction and dissatisfaction: Herzberg's two-factor hypothesis revisited. *British Journal of Sociology of Education, 2,* 235–246.
van Tartwijk, J. (1993). *Sketches of teacher behavior.* Utrecht: WCC.
van Tartwijk, J.; Fisher, D.; Fraser, B. and Wubbels, Th. (1994). The interpersonal significance of molecular behavior of science teachers in lab lessons: A Dutch perspective. Paper presented at the 1994 NARST Annual Meeting, Anaheim, Calif. (ERIC/CSMEE, ED 368 579).
Watzlawick, P.; Beavin, J. H.; and Jackson, D. (1967). *The pragmatics of human communication.* New York: Norton.
Wubbels, Th.; Créton, H. A.; and Holvast, A. J. C. D. (1988). Undesirable classroom situations. *Interchange 19*(2), 25–40.
Wubbels, Th., and Levy, J. (1993). *Do you know what you look like? Interpersonal relationships in education.* London: The Falmer Press.

7

Effective Instructional Practices for English Language Learners

Yolanda N. Padrón
and
Hersholt C. Waxman

This chapter focuses on effective instructional practices for learners whose primary language is not English. First, we discuss several critical problems associated with the education of English language learners (ELLs): (a) instructional programs that have not been effective in meeting educational needs, (b) the shortage of adequately qualified teachers, (c) teacher expectations, and (d) teaching practices that predominantly consist of a basic skills/mastery orientation that leads to student compliance and passivity. Second, in response to the concerns of current instructional practices used with ELLs, many educators have advocated that alternative teaching practices be used that emphasize more active student learning and teachers becoming facilitators of learning. Five teaching practices are described in the chapter: (a) cognitively guided instruction, (b) culturally responsive teaching, (c) technology-enriched instruction, (d) cooperative learning, and (e) instructional conversation. These research-based instructional practices all stress a student-centered model of class-

---

This chapter was supported in part by a Department of Education/OERI grant for the National Center for Research on Education, Diversity, and Excellence. The opinions expressed in this article do not necessarily reflect the position, policy, or endorsement of the granting agency.

room instruction, and they have also been found to be beneficial for ELLs. The final sections of the chapter focus on implications for teacher education and research.

Many school reforms in the past decade have not been successful because they neglected to address the recent demographic changes in the United States (Reyes and Valencia, 1993), such as the 53 percent increase of Latinos in the United States between 1980 and 1990 (Chapa and Valencia, 1993). While changes in demographics affect many aspects of society, the impact appears to be most critical for the education of children (Bialystok and Cummins, 1991). The number of K–12 language-minority students has increased by over 50 percent between 1985 and 1991 (García, 1994). Currently about 2.26 million K–12 students in the United States are categorized as "limited English proficient" (U.S. Department of Education, 1992). Several estimates project that the number of school-age children from various language backgrounds will reach about 6 million by the year 2000 (García, 1994). Projections for the year 2000 also indicate that Spanish-speaking students will constitute approximately 77 percent of the total language-minority student population. By the year 2026, language-minority students are projected to make up nearly 25 percent of the K–12 enrollment (García, 1994).

Learners whose primary language is not English have often been described as language-minority students or limited-English proficient students. This description, however, often has derogatory meanings in that it infers that students are deficient in language rather than that these children have mastered another language (LaCelle-Peterson and Rivera, 1994). Consequently, the term "English language learner" has been recently used to describe those students whose first language is not English and who either are beginning to learn English or have demonstrated some proficiency in English (LaCelle-Peterson and Rivera, 1994). The construct of "English language learner" (ELLs) helps educators reframe the problem from one of "blaming" the learners because they have a language "deficiency" or their primary language is not the language of the dominant culture, to a perspective that focuses on the specific educational needs of ELLs because they are learning another language. The use of this construct also helps us reverse the deficit model or view of subordinated students that suggests that it is the individual child or his or her ethnic group that is deficient, and therefore we need to focus on the individual and *not* on the circumstances that affect the child (Trueba and Bartolomé, 1997; Waxman, 1992).

Although Hispanic students constitute the largest group of ELLs, they have the lowest levels of education and the highest dropout rate (Smith, 1995). Hispanic students' educational aspirations and academic performance in science, mathematics, and reading are significantly lower than those of white students (Smith, 1995; U.S. Department of Education, 1997). In addition, approximately 40 percent of Hispanic students are one grade or more below expected achievement levels by the eighth grade, and only about 50 percent graduate "on time" (García, 1994). These facts and reports are especially problematic, given that most Hispanic children reside in urban cities and are immersed in neighborhoods of concentrated poverty where the most serious dropout problems exist (Carson, Huelskamp, and Woodall, 1993). Hispanic students are more than twice as likely to experience poverty as are white students (U.S. Department of Education, 1994). Furthermore, Hispanic children start elementary school with fewer preschool experiences than do white children, and this gap in education widens over time (Smith, 1995).

PROBLEMS ASSOCIATED WITH THE UNDERACHIEVEMENT OF ELLS

Several critical problems have been associated with the underachievement of ELLs. While some educators argue that the most serious concerns are basic funding for ELLs or political beliefs that influence decisions (Melendez, 1993), there are several educational problems that are "alterable" and can lead to educational improvements for ELLs. One of these critical problems is that an increasing proportion of ELLs with limited proficiency in English (nearly 25 percent) are not being served by appropriate instructional programs (U.S. Department of Education, 1992). Furthermore, many of the current instructional programs that ELLs are enrolled in have not been effective in meeting their educational needs (Faltis, 1993). One explanation of why these programs have not been effective is that there have been many implicit assumptions that curricular or instructional innovations that improve the education of English-monolingual students will work equally well for ELLs (LaCelle-Peterson and Rivera, 1994).

A second serious problem associated with the failure of ELLs is the shortage of adequately qualified teachers of ELLs and the preparation of credentialed teachers for ELLs (García, 1994; Gersten and Jiménez, 1998). Teachers of ELLs have to address the "double demands" of ELLs, which include acquiring a second language while learning traditional academic content (Gersten and Jiménez, 1998). Estimates indicate that nearly half of the teachers assigned to teach ELLs have not received any preparation in methods to teach ELLs (García, 1994). Furthermore, the number of teachers prepared to teach ELLs falls short of the tremendous need for teachers of ELLs. In addition, the majority of classroom teachers and school administrators are white, while the proportion of nonwhite and Hispanic students is increasing rapidly (U.S. Department of Education, 1997). Alternative forms of teacher preparation and teacher staff development are being implemented by local school districts to meet the needs of ELLs, but they have generally not been effective in training qualified teachers of ELLs.

A third critical problem has to do with teachers' expectations of ELLs. Many teachers simply view ELLs as low-performing native English-speaking children (Yates and Ortiz, 1991). Some teachers also believe that the academic failure of ELLs is primarily a function of language difficulties (Irvine and York, 1993), and that students must develop speaking proficiency in English before they can be taught to read and write (Díaz-Rico and Weed, 1995). In addition, several studies and reviews of research have found that schools serving ELLs and other minority students often devote less time and emphasis to higher-order thinking skills than do schools serving white students (Coley and Hoffman, 1990; Losey, 1995; Moll, 1986; Padrón and Knight, 1989; Padrón and Waxman, 1993). ELLs and other minority students have often been denied the opportunity to learn higher-level thinking skills because it has been believed that they must demonstrate the ability to learn the basics or lower levels of knowledge before they can be taught higher-level skills (Rivera and Zehler, 1991; Waxman, Padrón and Knight, 1991). Furthermore, there is generally an emphasis on remediation for ELLs and other low-achieving students, which has resulted in teachers' lower expectations for these students and an overemphasis on repetition of content through drill-and-practice (Knapp and Shields, 1990; Lehr and Harris, 1988). The result of these practices may lead to students' adopting behaviors of "learned helplessness" and having a passive orientation to schooling (Coley and Hoffman, 1990). Another prevalent expectation for ELLs is that there needs to be a heavy emphasis on learning English at the expense of learning content (Cummins, 1986; Gersten and Jiménez, 1998).

Finally, a fourth critical problem has to do with the current teaching practices that are prevalent in most classrooms serving ELLs. The most common instructional approach found in schools that serve ELLs is the direct instructional model, where teachers typically teach to the whole class at the same time and control all of the classroom discussion and decision making (Brookhart and Rusnak, 1993; Haberman, 1991; Padrón and Waxman, 1993). This teacher-directed instructional model emphasizes lecture, drill-and-practice, remediation, and student seatwork consisting mainly of worksheets (Stephen, Varble, and Taitt, 1993). Haberman (1991) argues that this overreliance on direct instruction in schools serving minority students constitutes a "pedagogy of poverty." He maintains that this teacher-directed instructional style leads to student compliance, passive resentment, and teacher burn out. Furthermore, he criticizes this orientation because teachers are generally held accountable for "making" students learn, while students usually assume a passive role with low engagement in tasks or activities that are generally not authentic. Cummins and Sayers (1990) similarly argue that this instructional approach creates compliant students who cannot think critically or creatively or solve problems.

Several recent studies have examined classroom instruction for ELLs and found that this "pedagogy of poverty" orientation exists in many classrooms with ELLs (Padrón and Waxman, 1993; Waxman, Huang, and Padrón, 1995). In a large-scale study examining the classroom instruction of ninety teachers from sixteen inner-city middle-level schools serving predominantly ELLs, Waxman, Huang, and Padrón (1995) found that students were typically involved in whole-class instruction and not interacting with either their teacher or other students. About two-thirds of the time, for example, students were not involved in verbal interaction with either their teacher or other students. There were very few small-group activities and very few interactions with other students. Students rarely selected their own instructional activities, and they were generally very passive in the classroom, often just watching or listening to the teacher, even though they were found to be on task about 94 percent of the time. In these classrooms, teachers typically focused on the content of the task or assignment, responded to students' signals, communicated the task's procedures, and checked students' work. Teachers were observed spending very little time interacting with students regarding personal issues, encouraging students to succeed, showing personal regard for students, and showing interest in students' work. They also spent more time explaining things to students rather than questioning, cueing, and prompting students to respond.

In another study examining middle school instruction in mathematics and science in inner-city classrooms serving ELLs, Padrón and Waxman (1993) found that science teachers spent about 93 percent of the time in whole-class instruction, while mathematics teachers spent about 55 percent of the time in whole-group instruction. Students in mathematics classes worked independently about 45 percent of the time, while there was no independent work observed in science classes. In the mathematics classes, there was no small-group work observed, and students worked in small groups in science classes only about 7 percent of the time. Questions about complex issues were not raised by any of the mathematics and science teachers. Furthermore, teachers seldom (4 percent of the time) posed open-ended questions for students in science classes, and they never posed these questions in mathematics classes.

The results of these studies illustrate that classroom instruction in schools serving predominantly ELLs often tends to be whole-class instruction with students working in teacher-assigned activities, generally in a passive manner (i.e., watching or listening). Students are on task most of the time, but about two-thirds of the time there is no verbal interaction with either their teacher or other students. There are very few small-group activities and very few interactions with other students. Teachers were observed keeping students on task most of the time, focusing on the task, communicating the tasks' procedures, praising students' performance, checking students' work, and responding to students' signals (e.g., raising their hands). Teachers also spent more time explaining things to students than questioning, cueing, and prompting students to respond. Teachers were not frequently observed encouraging extended student responses or encouraging students to help themselves or help each other.

In summary, the increasing number of students from culturally and linguistically diverse backgrounds, the high number of minority students dropping out, the lower achievement levels of culturally and linguistically different students, and ineffective instructional programs and classroom instruction constitute critical educational problems for ELLs. Unfortunately, the pedagogically induced learning problems or instructional inadequacies previously described may also account for students' poor academic achievement and low motivation (Fletcher and Cardona-Morales, 1990). Educators need to focus on research-based instructional practices that have been found to be effective for ELLs. Although there have been many programs and school-based interventions that have been found to be beneficial for some types of students at risk of failure, these programs and interventions may not necessarily be effective for ELLs. Teaching practices need to specifically address the concerns of ELLs who come from different cultures and are trying to learn a new language. The next section reviews five teaching practices that have been successfully used with ELLs.

EFFECTIVE TEACHING PRACTICES FOR ELLS

Many educators and policymakers are calling for changing models of teaching and learning that emphasize more active student learning and changing the role of the teacher from a deliverer of knowledge to one of a facilitator of learning (Sheingold, 1990; Wiburg, 1991). The following five teaching practices all stress this changing model of classroom instruction, and they all have been found to be previously successful for ELLs. These research-based instructional practices are (a) cognitively guided instruction, (b) culturally responsive instruction, (c) technology-enriched instruction (d) cooperative learning, and (e) instructional conversation. The following sections briefly describe each of these practices and explain why they are beneficial for ELLs.

Cognitively Guided Instruction

Influenced by theory and research from the field of cognitive psychology, many educators have adopted an information-processing view of teaching and learning (Knight and Waxman, 1991; Shuell, 1993; Waxman, Padrón and Knight, 1991). From this perspective, learning is viewed as an active process, and teaching is a means of facilitating students' active mental processing

(Gagne, 1985). This cognitive approach also suggests that students need to apply cognitive strategies in order to learn (Winne, 1985). Therefore, cognitively guided instruction emphasizes the development of students' cognitive learning strategies and the direct teaching and modeling of cognitive learning strategies as well as techniques and approaches that foster students' metacognition and cognitive monitoring of their own learning (Pressley and Ghatala, 1990; Waxman, Padrón and Knight, 1991). In other words, this instructional practice encourages teachers to emphasize students' psychological processing as well as what is taught and how it is presented (Shuell, 1993). Furthermore, teachers are encouraged to focus on affective, motivational, metacognitive, developmental, and social factors that influence students, since they all occur simultaneously and are critical to students' learning (Presidential Task Force on Psychology in Education, 1993).

From the cognitive perspective, effective instruction (a) activates or assesses students' prior knowledge of content, (b) models or illustrates appropriate learning strategies, and (c) connects both prior knowledge and learning strategies to the new learning objectives (Jones and Friedman, 1988). Another goal of effective instruction is to shift the responsibility of learning from the teacher to the student. This perspective also assumes that individuals have prior knowledge differences and differ in the frequency and types of strategies they bring to the learning context (Jones and Friedman, 1988; Padrón, 1997). Effective teachers are aware of student differences and try to specifically help students who use weak or ineffective strategies or bring in less relevant information to the learning task. For ELLs and other students at risk of failure, strategy instruction may also need to include techniques that address students' affective needs (Coley and Hoffman, 1990). If students, for example, have developed a passive orientation to learning, then the strategy instruction would need to include an affective dimension so that students can perceive themselves as able learners. Strategy instruction for students who view themselves as unsuccessful at reading may need to focus on affective needs of students (Coley and Hoffman, 1990).

Strategy instruction focuses on explicitly teaching students what strategies to use and how they should use them. This instructional approach can be very beneficial for the large number of ELLs who are not doing well in school because once students learn how to effectively use cognitive strategies, some of the individual barriers to academic success faced by this group may be removed. Explicit instruction in strategies and modeling are only the initial steps of successful strategy instruction models (Jones, 1986). The scaffolding approach, which gradually relinquishes control of classroom dialogue and control of strategy use to students, is another important component of successful strategy programs such as Reciprocal Teaching (Brown, Palincsar and Purcell, 1986; Palincsar, 1986; Palincsar and Brown, 1984) and Question-Answer Relationship (QAR) (Raphael, 1984, 1987). Reciprocal teaching takes place in a cooperative instructional environment where the teacher and students engage in a dialogue. Students are instructed in four specific comprehension monitoring strategies: (a) summarizing, (b) self-questioning, (c) clarifying, and (d) predicting. Studies using reciprocal teaching have found that these strategies can successfully be taught to low-achieving students and ELLs and that the use of these strategies increases reading achievement (Palincsar and Brown, 1984; Padrón, 1992; Pressley and Harris, 1990).

There is a growing understanding that effective teaching practices for ELLs should include cognitive strategy instruction (Chamot, Dale, O'Malley and Spanos, 1993; Gersten and Jiménez, 1998; O'Malley and Chamot, 1990; Padrón, 1992, 1993). Several studies conducted with ELLs have focused on their cognitive reading strategies. For example, Padrón, Knight, and Waxman (1986) compare strategies used by bilingual and English-monolingual students. Students read a passage and stopped at predetermined intervals to explain the strategies that they were using in order to comprehend the passage. The results indicated that bilingual and monolingual third- and fifth-grade students were not using the same number of cognitive reading strategies. English- monolingual students indicated using significantly more strategies than did bilingual students—on the average, about twice as many. In another study investigating the relationship between students' perceptions of cognitive reading strategies and gains in reading achievement, Padrón and Waxman (1988) found that certain strategies predict students' gain in reading comprehension.

Cognitive strategy training programs may be an effective means of improving cognitive outcomes of ELLs (Chamot and O'Malley, 1987; O'Malley and Chamot, 1990; Padrón, 1992; Padrón and Knight, 1989). Padrón (1992), for example, found that explicit training of reading strategies significantly improved the reading achievement of ELLs. She randomly assigned eighty-seven third-, fourth-, and fifth-grade Hispanic bilingual students to four instructional groups. Group One was taught using Reciprocal Teaching (see, e.g., Palincsar and Brown, 1984). Group Two was instructed using the Question-Answer Relationships (see e.g., Raphael, 1984; Raphael and Pearson, 1985). Two control groups were used to determine whether it was the strategy training or the additional instruction that increased students' reading achievement. Group Three, therefore, read passages and answered questions, while students in the fourth group remained in their regular classroom and received instruction from their teacher on a subject other than reading. Students who participated in either the Reciprocal Teaching or the Question-Answer Relationship groups scored significantly higher on a standardized reading achievement test than students who participated in the control groups. Chamot and O'Malley (1987) have also developed an effective instructional program for limited-English-proficient students that specifically focuses on strategy instruction. Overall, their research indicates that when strategies are modeled for the students and the students have an opportunity to practice the strategy, learning outcomes improve. Their work also highlights the importance of ELLs being able to use effective learning strategies.

Culturally Responsive Instruction

One of the major educational problems of schools serving diverse student populations is that the curriculum and teaching practices have not reflected the diversity within the population (Waxman and Padrón, 1995). The culture in which many ELLs live often prevents them from acquiring the middle-class cultural patterns on which most school curriculum and instructional materials are based. This phenomenon is often viewed as a mismatch between the culture of the home and the school culture, or a discrepancy between what schools are about and the needs and concerns of students (Au and Kawakami, 1994; Gordon and Yowell, 1994). Many classroom teachers need assistance in acquiring the knowledge and skills necessary to bridge the gap between the culture of the school and the home culture of students.

Culturally responsive instruction is often viewed as a process that addresses these previously mentioned concerns (Erickson, 1987). It emphasizes the serious miscommunication problems that can occur in classrooms when teachers do not understand their students' social and cultural milieu (Lucas and Schecter, 1992). Culturally responsive instruction focuses on the students' needs and culture and tries to create conditions that support the empowerment of students (Darder, 1993). This type of pedagogy is sometimes called (a) culturally sensitive instruction (Boyer, 1993), (b) culturally relevant teaching (Ladson-Billings, 1992, 1995), (c) culturally compatible instruction (Jordan, 1985), (d) culturally sensitive scaffolding (Lee, 1992), (e) culturally responsible pedagogy (Pewewardy, 1994), (f) equity pedagogy (McGee-Banks and Banks, 1995), or (g) multicultural instruction (Saldana and Waxman, 1996, 1997). Culturally responsive instruction emphasizes the everyday concerns of students and tries to incorporate these concerns into the curriculum. Culturally responsive instruction, however, is more than merely including aspects of the students' culture into the curriculum, textbooks, and learning activities. It also focuses on the critical family and community issues that students encounter daily. Culturally responsive instruction helps students prepare themselves for meaningful social roles by emphasizing both social responsibility and academic responsibility. Furthermore, it addresses the promotion of racial, ethnic, and linguistic equality as well as the appreciation of diversity (Boyer, 1993).

Culturally responsive instruction requires a learner-centered instructional approach, where teachers assume the role of a facilitator rather than the source of all knowledge (Branch, Goodwin and Gualtieri, 1993). In this approach, teachers use students' prior knowledge or existing cultural knowledge as a foundation or scaffold to guide students in instructional tasks (Lee, 1992). Some of the benefits of culturally responsive instruction for ELLs are that it (a) improves the acquisition and retention of new knowledge by working from students' existing knowledge base, (b) improves self-confidence and self-esteem by emphasizing existing knowledge, (c) increases the transfer of school-taught knowledge to real-life situations, and (d) exposes students to knowledge about other individuals or cultural groups (Rivera and Zehler, 1991).

There is a large body of research that has found a significant relationship between culturally responsive instruction and students' academic success (Au and Jordan, 1981; Erickson, 1987; Tharp and Gallimore, 1988). There have been only a few studies, however, that have specifically examined culturally responsive instruction for ELLs. One such study found that Latino teachers who engaged in responsive instruction were more likely to recognize and address the academic and social needs of their students (Darder, 1993). This study also found that other successful strategies for ELLs included collaborative group work, cooperative grouping, and more opportunities for student dialogue. These are other effective teaching practices that will be discussed later in this chapter. Furthermore, students had more responsibility for their own learning and students were more involved in the development of curriculum activities and decisions about classroom activities. According to this study, the key difference between Latino and white effective teachers was that Latino teachers were more likely to reinforce and perpetuate students' cultural values. McCollum's (1989) study comparing whole-class lessons taught in third grade by a Spanish-speaking Puerto Rican teacher and an English-speaking white teacher found similar results.

This research provides evidence that instructional practices that address the cultural and linguistic needs of students are effective methods for preparing students to compete in mainstream society. Cummins (1986) argues that students can be "empowered" when teachers provide instruction that adds a second language and culture or "disabled" when teachers neglect the students' language and culture. He adds that this empowerment is necessary for successful learning to occur. The knowledge that students gain from instruction that is culturally relevant to their experiences can empower them to be successful in mainstream society (Osborne, 1996). Unfortunately, there is also evidence that the culture-related instruction is not often included in classrooms (Padrón and Knight, 1989; Saldana and Waxman, 1996, 1997).

Technology-Enriched Instruction

Another instructional practice that can improve the teaching and learning of ELLs is the use of technology in the classroom (Padrón and Waxman, 1996). Unfortunately, several studies have found that technology is not being widely or appropriately used in many classes predominantly composed of ELLs (Arias, 1990; Office of Technology Assessment, 1988; Waxman and Huang, 1995). Fewer than 25 percent of teachers of ELLs use technology in their teaching, and when it is used, it is often for drill-and-practice activities rather than higher-level applications (Cummins and Sayers, 1990; Office of Technology Assessment, 1988; U.S. Department of Education, 1995). In addition, ELLs are less likely than other students to have access to technology in their homes (U.S. Department of Education, 1995).

These inequities in technology use are especially problematic because several systematic reviews of research have found that technology significantly improves students' cognitive outcomes (Niemiec and Walberg, 1992; Ryan, 1991). Furthermore, there are several studies and reviews of research specifically focusing on ELLs that have found that technology is effective for ELLs (Chavez, 1990; Cummins and Sayers, 1990; De Villar, 1990; Merino, Legarreta, Coughran, and Hoskins, 1990; Padrón and Waxman, 1996; Walker de Felix, Johnson, and Shick, 1990). Chavez (1990), for example, examined first- and second-grade students who were instructed to use the "Write to Read" (WTR) Program to develop English writing and reading skills. He found that the use of the WTR Program provided a risk-free environment for ELLs that made the students feel comfortable about expressing their ideas. Students' story writing also showed improvement in sentence structure and the breadth of the content. Merino, Legarreta, Coughran, and Hoskins (1990) found that pairing a limited-English-proficient (LEP) student with a fluent English-proficient (EP) student was effective in producing on-task behavior, equitable turn taking, and cooperative exchanges during computer-based science activities. Dixon's (1995) study also demonstrated the benefits of LEP students working collaboratively with EP students at a computer during mathematics. She found that both LEP and EP students who worked in a computer-based, dynamic instructional environment significantly outperformed students who worked in traditional instructional environments on measures of reflection and rotation concepts and two-dimentional visualization ability.

Other research evidence indicates that multimedia use with ELLs can produce positive effects. Walker de Felix, Johnson, and Schick (1990), for example, developed two interactive videodisc lessons that were tested with fourth-grade English-as-a-second-language (ELS) inner-city students. Their findings provide evidence of the advantages of contextually rich learning environments for ELLs. A final area that holds promise for improving the teaching and learning of ELLs is the use of computer networks and telecommunications. Cummins and Sayers's (1990) work with computer-mediated learning networks for ELLs exemplifies research in this area. They describe a partnership between classes from North and South America where teachers and students work jointly on curricular projects through extensive computer networks. They found that this networking project improved students' academic achievement and also promoted other important outcomes like students' cultural understanding.

Several conceptual articles and research studies have examined the specific ways technology impacts students at risk and ELLs. Instructional technology has been found to be beneficial for students at risk of failure and ELLs in the following ways: (a) it is motivational, (b) it is nonjudgmental, (c) it can individualize learning and tailor the instructional sequence to meet students' needs and rate of learning, (d) it allows for more autonomy, (e) it can give prompt feedback, (f) it provides the students with a sense of personal responsibility and control, (g) it can be less intimidating to students, (h) it gives the students a rich linguistic environment, (i) it diminishes the authoritarian role of the teacher, and (j) it decreases situations where students could be embarrassed in class for not knowing answers (Cantrell, 1993; Mielke and Flores, 1992–1993, Poirot and Canales, 1993–94). Furthermore, some types of technology like multimedia are effective for ELLs and students at risk because they help students connect images, sound, and symbols (Kozma and Croninger, 1992; Poirot and Canales, 1993–94). Multimedia can also connect student learning in the classroom to real-life situations and authentic learning situations (Means and Olson, 1994). In addition, multimedia technology can be especially helpful for ELLs because it can facilitate auditory skill development by integrating visual presentations with sound and animation (Bermudez and Palumbo, 1994; Mielke and Flores, 1992–93).

De Villar and Faltis (1991) specifically discuss the effectiveness of technology for ELLs by describing how computer-integrated instruction facilitates social integration, communication, and cooperation for ELLs. All of these characteristics of technology are especially beneficial for ELLs because they are often disengaged from schools and have generally experienced more failure than success in learning situations. In addition, there is some indication that Latino students are kinesthetic learners and learn better through hands-on activities and in small-group and individualized instruction than through whole-class or direct-instruction approaches (Poirot and Canales, 1993–94). Computers also provide students the opportunity for hands-on learning and working collaboratively in pairs or small groups. Several of the studies previously described (Dixon, 1995; Merino, Legarreta, Coughran, and Hoskins, 1990) illustrate the value of ELLs working collaboratively with English-proficient students. Such pairings have been found to improve students' cognitive outcomes, and they can also benefit the psychosocial development of ELLs.

Another important outcome of technology-enriched classrooms is that they can help reduce or eliminate the teacher-dominated, whole-class, direct instructional approach that exists in most classrooms with ELLs (Cummins and Sayers, 1990; De Villar and Faltis, 1991). Swan and Mitrani (1993), for example, compared the classroom interactions between high school students and teachers involved in (a) computer-based instruction and (b) traditional instruction. They found that student-teacher interactions were more student-centered and individualized during computer-based teaching and learning than with traditional teaching and learning. In another study that examined changes in classroom instruction as a result of technology, Sandholtz, Ringstaff, and Dwyer (1992) found that high access to computers enabled teachers to individualize instruction more. In a national study, Worthen, Van Dusen, and Sailor (1994) found that students who used a computerized integrated learning system (ILS) in both laboratory and classroom settings were more actively engaged in learning tasks than were students in the non-ILS classrooms. Finally, in a study that included many ELLs, Waxman and Huang (1996–97) found that instruction in classroom settings where technology was not often used tended to be whole-class approaches, where students generally listened or watched the teacher. Instruction in classroom settings where technology was moderately used had much less whole-class instruction and much more independent work. These studies all support the notion that technology use in classrooms may change teaching from the traditional teacher-centered model to a more student-centered instructional approach.

Cooperative Learning

McLaughlin and McLeod (1996) describe cooperative learning as an effective instructional approach that stimulates learning and helps students come to complex understandings by discussing and defending their ideas with others. One commonly accepted definition is that "cooperative learning is the instructional use of small groups so that students work together to maximize their own and each other's learning" (Johnson and Johnson, 1991, p. 292). The traditional roles of teacher and student are altered in cooperative learning settings. Instead of lecturing and transmitting material, teachers facilitate the learning process by encouraging cooperation among students (Bejarano, 1987). This teaching practice is student-centered and creates an interdependence among students and teachers (Rivera and Zehler, 1991).

Research studies and syntheses of research have found that cooperative learning structures, like working together in small cooperative groups, promote higher cognitive and affective student outcomes. More specifically, several reviews of the research have found that cooperative learning improves student outcomes such as (a) attitudes toward school and motivation toward learning, (b) social skills, (c) classroom discipline, (d) achievement, retention, and critical thinking, (e) decision making, (f) higher-level thinking skills, and (g) self-esteem (Johnson et al., 1981; Johnson and Johnson, 1984, 1991; Slavin, 1990, 1991).

Cooperative learning has been widely used in classrooms for several decades, but only recently has it gained support as an effective teaching practice for ELLs. As an instructional practice, cooperative grouping impacts ELLs in several different ways: (a) provides opportunities for students to communicate with each other, (b) enhances instructional conversations, (c) decreases anxiety, (d) develops social, academic, and communication skills, (e) enhances self-confidence and self-esteem through individual contributions and achievement of group goals, (f) improves individual and group relations by students' learning to clarify, assist, and challenge each other's ideas, and (g) develops proficiency in English by providing students with rich language experiences that integrate speaking, listening, reading, and writing (Calderón, 1990, 1991; Christian, 1995; García, 1994; Rivera and Zehler, 1991). Cooperative learning is particularly beneficial for ELLs who are learning a second language, because it requires students to engage in meaningful communication about the task at hand, which is the ideal context for language learning. It is especially effective for students who are less fluent in English when they are grouped with students who are more fluent. Such cooperative learning situations are effective, since students are often required to negotiate roles by using linguistic and social strategies (McLaughlin and McLeod, 1996).

Hispanic ELLs tend to prefer cooperative rather than competitive learning situations because they mirror the cooperative attitudes characteristic of work patterns in these students' homes and communities (Charbonneau and John-Steiner, 1988; Rivera and Zehler, 1991). De Avila (1988), for example, used peer cooperation to enable Hispanic ELLs to successfully acquire mathematical concepts. Students had access to materials both in their home and in second languages and were able to use their teacher as a resource as well. The program was successful because ELLs seemed not only to learn more in a cooperative environment working with peers, but also to enjoy working individually with the teacher. Other research has similarly found that cooperative learning is a successful instructional practice for ELLs (Moll, 1988; García, 1994).

García (1988, 1990, 1992, 1994) has been involved in several studies and reviews of research that examined effective instruction for ELLs, and has found that cooperative or collaborative learning is an effective teaching practice. He found that when teachers organized instruction so that students were required to interact with others, these student-student interactions often occurred at higher-cognitive levels. In these classroom settings, students often sought and received help from other students.

Cooperative learning is one instructional practice that relates to several other of the effective practices described in this chapter. For example, cooperative learning can be considered a culturally relevant strategy for Hispanic students because it ties in to the interaction patterns in their home. The instructional discourse that often occurs in these student groups is also highly related to instructional conversation, which will be discussed in the following section.

Instructional Conversation

As we have previously pointed out, classroom instruction for ELLs is typically teacher-centered, dominated by teacher talk and student passivity. Teachers typically dominate classroom discussion and interaction, control all knowledge, and merely pass knowledge on to the students (Gallimore and Goldenberg, 1992). In addition, teachers are generally unresponsive to students' utterances and create very few meaningful interactions that promote language and literacy development (Gallimore and Goldenberg, 1992). While direct-instruction practices may be suited to some knowledge and skill domains that are hierarchically organized in a linear sequence, these practices are not as effective for ill-structured domains or areas that are not hierarchically organized (Gallimore and Goldenberg, 1992). Basic or critical thinking skills are most effectively developed through instructional conversations or dialogue, which is the process of questioning and sharing ideas and knowledge (Tharp, 1997). In other words, instructional conversation is the medium for cognitive development (Tharp and Gallimore, 1988). It is the teaching practice of instructional conversation that addresses the need for a cognitively challenging curriculum and moves us away from the typical recitation patterns currently found in schools.

Instructional conversation is a teaching practice or instructional strategy where teachers and students relate the formal school content to the student's individual, community, and family knowledge (Tharp, 1997). It is through conversation or dialogue that the teacher is able to contextualize instruction to fit the knowledge, skills, values, and culture of the learner. This instructional approach is similar to culturally responsive teaching in that it focuses on the students' cultural knowledge, but it goes beyond that teaching practice because it also explicitly focuses on the processes of forming, expressing, and sharing ideas and knowledge. Furthermore, in instructional conversations, the classroom changes from direct instruction to dialogic teaching, where a teacher constructs lessons based on students' experience and ideas and the classroom becomes a "community of learners."

Some of the important features of instructional conversation include teachers (a) activating and using students' prior knowledge, (b) promoting complex language and expression, (c) minimizing factual questions, (d) responding to and using students' contributions, (e) using connected discourse, and (f) creating a challenging and nonthreatening atmosphere (Gallimore and Goldenberg, 1992). In instructional conversations, teachers also (a) draw students into conversations, (b) create conversational purposes for children to say something, and (c) intentionally create and sustain a conversation that is a means to an instructional end (Gallimore and Goldenberg, 1992).

Instructional conversations are purposeful extended discourses with a teacher and other students that are typically initiated by students when the need arises (Tharp, 1995). As McLaughlin and McLeod (1996) describe it, "instructional conversation is an approach in which a teacher guides students toward discovering a deeper understanding of material through a discussion that incorporates students' ideas and backgrounds. The teacher and students become conversation partners and the whole group participates in constructing a personally meaningful and relevant intellectual creation" (p. 7).

Much of the theoretical and research base for instructional conversation has been summarized by Tharp and Gallimore (1988) based on their work on the Kamehameha Early Education Project (KEEP). Tharp, Gallimore, and their colleagues developed and researched a successful reading program for native Hawaiian students that included instructional conversation as one of its major components. Saunders and Goldenberg (1992) have also substantiated the beneficial effects of an instructional conversation lesson on childrens' understanding of a complex concept. García's (1990) study of effective teachers of ELLs also lends support to the benefits of instructional conversation. He found that effective teachers of ELLs generally elicited student responses at a low cognitive and linguistic level, but then let students take control of the lesson, which resulted in more advanced cognitive and linguistic discussion. In other words, effective teachers of ELLs used instructional conversation as a teaching practice in their classrooms.

Rather than limiting expectations for ELLs by avoiding use of language and discussion during instruction, instructional conversations emphasize the use of oral language through dialogues with teachers and classmates (Durán, Dugan, and Weffer, 1997). Because ELLs often do not have control of the English language, they generally do not participate in classroom discussions. Thus, one of the major benefits of the use of instructional conversation for ELLs is that it is a practice that is designed to provide extended discourse, which is an important principle of second-language learning (Christian, 1995). Instructional conversation also helps ELLs create meaning in the social context of the classroom. As Gardner (1985) describes it, we justify knowledge through a social process by engaging in extended conversations. Joint activity and discourse between teachers and students create a common context of experience within the classroom (Tharp, 1997). Furthermore, since instructional conversations reveal the knowledge, skills, and values of the learner, they allow the teacher to contextualize teaching to fit the needs of each student. This is especially critical for teachers of ELLs, since many of their students come from very diverse backgrounds.

DISCUSSION

Research on effective teaching practices has been conducted for nearly a century, but for the most part, research has not had a substantive impact on today's basic instructional approaches. There has been a shift of focus in some content areas like science and mathematics from the traditional lecture-and-drill approaches to a slightly greater emphasis on teaching for understanding and teaching in investigative ways (McKinney, 1992). These shifts of emphasis, however, will not have any long-term effects unless there are mechanisms to foster their development and use. Teachers must have a strong commitment in order to change their teaching practices. In order to build this commitment, teachers need to believe that these practices will make a difference, and they will also need administrative support and training.

The five instructional practices that are described in this chapter have all been found effective for teaching ELLs, and there are several benefits of incorporating these approaches in schools serving ELLs. In a classroom with many ELLs, instruction becomes extremely complex. Not only does the teacher have to deal with students' language and knowledge-base differences, but teachers also have to interpret content presented in textbooks from a cultural perspective different from that of the student (Padrón, 1991). Instructional conversations and culturally responsive instruction, however, are two practices that can help mechanisms for contextualizing instruction. The implementation of cognitively guided instruction also has several positive components that can improve the education of ELLs. In reciprocal teaching, for example, the text may be read by the students, or the teacher may read the text aloud to students. This technique can be very useful when teaching ELLs, who may experience a great deal of difficulty with the language. Having the teacher read the text provides the students with the opportunity to learn the four comprehension strategies presented in reciprocal teaching, without having to wait until they learn to decode (Padrón, 1991).

Technology-enriched instruction also has the potential for deepening classroom instruction, making it more meaningful, and for assisting the learning of higher-order thinking skills (Niemiec and Walberg, 1992). When technology is used in this way as an instructional tool, it can eliminate the total reliance on direct instructional approaches and empower all students with the thinking skills that will help them help themselves. Technology-enriched environments, however, are a new and very different instructional approach from what teachers have been exposed to in their teacher education programs. Teachers, for the most part, have been trained with direct instructional models, while technology-enriched instruction requires a student-oriented approach that requires the teacher to assume a facilitator or coaching role. Technology-enriched instruction also requires some knowledge about technology that needs to be provided on an ongoing basis by the school or district.

The teaching practices reported here are not meant to be presented as dichotomous, coherent instructional programs, but rather as different practices or strategies that can be implemented simultaneously into the classroom. The principles and conditions of culturally responsive instruction (e.g. respect for diversity) for example can be taught and applied through cooperative learning (Le Blanc and Skaruppa, 1997). From a cognitively guided teaching perspective, some methods such as reciprocal teaching are explicitly designed for students to construct knowledge through the social process of cooperative learning. Other aspects of cooperative learning techniques such as discussion, debate, negotiation, and compromise reflect aspects of instructional conversation. The search for the "one best method" or approach to classroom instruction for ELLs may be futile, but the practices reported in this chapter indicate that there are several effective teaching practices for ELLs.

Implications for Teacher Education

One of the major challenges for teacher educators is to disseminate the research that has been conducted in this field to preservice and classroom teachers (Olmedo, 1992). Teacher educators need to identify and conceptualize effective teaching practices that promote meaningful interactions in the classroom and then help teachers develop the knowledge and skills needed to implement such instruction (Gallimore and Goldenberg, 1992). Teacher education programs at both the in-service and preservice levels should ensure that teachers are provided with appropriate knowledge and training of effective instructional practices for teaching ELLs. Prospective teachers, in particular, need to have field experiences and student teaching opportunities in culturally diverse settings. Teacher education programs should also develop teachers who can recognize and change the pedagogy of poverty (Brookhart and Rusnak, 1993). School administrators and instructional supervisors should similarly recognize the dangers of existing instructional practices and encourage teachers to change their current practices. The implementation of these instructional approaches must be carefully orchestrated and will require a strong commitment from teachers, since these approaches are new and differ from what teachers have typically been exposed to in their teacher preparation programs.

To prepare teachers for these new instructional approaches, teacher education programs should (a) provide the knowledge base about the cognitive and affective processes that influence learning, (b) include information about general and domain-specific metacognitive strategies and how they can be effectively taught to students of differing abilities and backgrounds, (c) encourage preservice teachers to "think aloud" during explanations so that they can model metacognitive thinking for their students, and (d) focus on learner-centered instructional approaches (Presidential Task Force on Psychology in Education, 1993). This will call for a change in policy that will need to empower teachers with the authority to implement such changes as well as to support teachers so that they will feel sufficiently supported and valued (Presidential Task Force on Psychology in Education, 1993). In order to carry out such changes, teachers need to be given more opportunity to restructure their classroom environment. In addition, training should be provided, wherein teachers are active participants and collaborators in the training process (Gallimore and Goldenberg, 1992).

Several other factors must also be addressed in implementing these instructional approaches that are related to teacher preparation. Teachers may need to receive more information on how to address the cultural and linguistic differences represented in their classrooms. Boyer (1993), for example, argues that culturally responsive teaching requires ethnic literacy development of all those who teach. Staff-development procedures become crucial to the implementation of these instructional interventions, since many teachers have not been exposed to strategy training procedures, instructional technology, instructional conversation, or ways to incorporate cultural pluralism into their instruction. Furthermore, since many teachers do not believe that these practices are beneficial, particularly for ELLs, teacher training may need to specifically address issues related to teachers' attitudes and perceptions of ELLs. Teachers of ELLs are presented with complex classroom situations. They must diagnose students' needs in terms of their knowledge and language and of learning strategies they know, those they do not know, or those they do know but do not use. In addition, teachers in these classrooms must also deal with different cultural backgrounds and in many instances with different levels of language proficiency. The variety of languages found in many classrooms today and the difficulty in assessing the students' level of proficiency make diagnosis difficult. Therefore, teacher education programs must help teachers readily diagnose students' background knowledge and learn how to address student differences in the classroom. University faculty may also need to change their repertoire of teaching patterns in order to meet the challenge of preparing teachers to use these instructional approaches (Le Blanc and Skaruppa, 1997). Finally, teacher education faculty should model these teaching practices and provide opportunities for preservice and in-service teachers to engage in such practices (Le Blanc and Skaruppa, 1997).

Implications for Research

Although research on effective teaching for ELLs has made significant progress over the past decade, there are still additional areas that need further investigation. In order to capture all the processes and nuances that occur in classrooms composed predominantly of ELLs, triangulation procedures are needed to collect data from multiple perspectives (Evertson and Green, 1986). Collecting multiple measures or indicators of classroom processes may provide us with a more comprehensive picture of the quality of classroom instruction provided for ELLs as well as what practices are most effective for them and why they are effective. Further classroom research focusing on instruction for ELLs should also examine the social context surrounding instruction because it provides important information on how instructional aspects such as classroom interaction differ according to settings, topics, situations, activities, and purposes (Losey, 1995).

Further correlational, longitudinal, and especially experimental research is needed to examine the effects of these instructional practices on students' cognitive, affective, and behavioral outcomes. In particular, we need to examine the extent that these practices enhance ELLs' higher-level thinking, motivation, and educational aspirations. Since not all of these approaches have been incorporated into an integrated program for improving teaching and student learning, evaluative research studies will need to examine the impact of such interventions. Other research questions that still need to be investigated in this area include examining (a) the ideal or optimum levels at which these practices should be used, (b) how teachers' beliefs, attitudes, and expectations influence their verbal interactions and classroom instruction and how they can be improved, and (c) what other district- or school-level factors (e.g., district policies, school organization, or school climate) influence the teaching practices used with ELLs. More studies are also needed to examine *how* schools and teachers can improve their classroom instruction. It should be pointed out that the instructional practices described in this chapter do not explicitly focus on issues such as when and how to introduce English-language instruction, which is another important issue that should be addressed in future research. These and similar issues still need to be examined so that we can continue to understand and improve the education of ELLs.

SUMMARY

While most of the teaching practices summarized in this chapter are based on theoretical and conceptual frameworks, there are still concerns related to whether too little attention has been placed on the development of general instructional theory for ELLs. Classroom settings for ELLs, however, are quite complex, and a general instructional theory for ELLs may not sufficiently help teachers understand how to improve their teaching practices. Educational reformers have typically searched for "simplistic answers" to our wide array of educational problems (Good, 1988). Reformers have generally focused on solving educational problems without taking into account the growing diversity of students in our schools. We need to ensure that instructional improvements focus on the needs of students. It should be pointed out that the most important issues related to effective classroom instruction is not the form (i.e., simple characteristics of instruction such as large- or small-group teaching) it takes, but the quality of the instruction (Good, 1988). The teaching practices described in this chapter all need to be taught well. Furthermore, there is an affective component to all of these practices that needs to be considered as well. Given the problems associated with low expectations for ELLs, we need to ensure that teachers have high expectations for ELLs and provide them academic tasks that are complex and challenging (Rivera and Zehler, 1991). Teachers also need to create warm, positive classroom environments and be supportive of all students and of alternative cultural perspectives (Branch, Goodwin, and Gualtieri, 1993). One of the most important factors for establishing an effective school and classroom learning environment is having teachers who are positive, supportive, and care about students (Phelan, Davidson and Cao, 1992; Waxman, 1992), which is especially critical for ELLs.

In conclusion, the five instructional practices described here are promising new directions in the education of ELLs. While these instructional practices are not necessarily recent developments in education, they can be considered new because they have not been widely used in teaching ELLs. Although the focus in this chapter is on instruction for ELLs, these practices should not be limited to them. The research base suggests that they are effective for students at risk of failure as well as most other students. Once teachers begin to critically examine their existing teaching practices, they may then acknowledge the value of more student-centered practices like the ones described here. Once that occurs, teachers may begin to tailor and adapt them for their own classroom needs.

REFERENCES

Arias, M. B. (1990). Computer access for Hispanic secondary students. *Computers in the Schools*, 7(1/2), 243–256.

Au, K., and Jordan, C. (1981). Teaching reading to Hawaiian children: Finding a culturally appropriate solution. In H. Trueba, G. Guthrie, and K. Au (eds.), *Culture and the bilingual classroom: Studies in classroom ethnography* (pp. 139–152). Rowley, Mass.: Newbury House.

Au, K. H., and Kawakami, A. J. (1994). Cultural congruence in instruction. In E. R. Hollins, J. E. King, and W. C. Hayman (eds.), *Teaching diverse populations: Formulating a knowledge base* (pp. 5–23). Albany: State University of New York Press.

Bejarano, Y. (1987). A cooperative small-group methodology in the language classroom. *TESOL Quarterly*, 21, 483–504.

Bermúdez, A. B., and Palumbo, D. (1994). Bridging the gap between literacy and technology: Hypermedia as a learning tool for limited English proficient students. *The Journal of Educational Issues of Language Minority Students, 14,* 165–184.

Bialystok, E., and Cummins, J. (1991). Language, cognition, and education of bilingual children. In E. Bialystok (ed.), *Language processing in bilingual children* (pp. 222–232). New York: Cambridge University Press.

Boyer, J. B. (1993). Culturally-sensitive instruction: An essential component of education for diversity. *Catalyst for Change, 22*(3), 5–8.

Branch, R. C.; Goodwin, Y.; and Gualtieri, J. (1993). Making classroom instruction culturally pluralistic. *The Educational Forum, 58,* 57–70.

Brookhart, S. M., and Rusnak, T. G. (1993). A pedagogy of enrichment, not poverty: Successful lessons of exemplary urban teachers. *Journal of Teacher Education, 44*(1), 17–26.

Brown, A. L.; Palincsar, A. S.; and Purcell, L. (1986). Poor readers: Teach, don't label. In U. Neisser (ed.), *The school achievement of minority children: New perspectives* (pp. 105–143). Hillsdale, N.J.: Erlbaum.

Calderón, M. (1990). *Cooperative learning for limited English proficient students.* Baltimore: Center for Research on Effective Schooling.

Calderón, M. (1991). Benefits of cooperative learning for Hispanic students. *Texas Research Journal, 2,* 39–57.

Cantrell, J. (1993). Technology's promise for at-risk students. *Thrust for Educational Leadership, 23*(2), 22–25.

Carson, C. C.; Huelskamp, R. M.; and Woodall, T. D. (1993). Perspectives on education in America: An annotated briefing. *Journal of Educational Research, 86,* 259–309.

Chamot, A. U.; Dale, M.; O'Malley, J. M.; and Spanos, G. A. (1993). Learning and problem solving strategies of ESL students. *Bilingual Research Journal, 16*(3 and 4), 1–34.

Chamot, A. U., and O'Malley, J. M. (1987). The cognitive academic language learn-ing approach: A bridge to the mainstream. *TESOL Quarterly, 21,* 227–249.

Chapa, J., and Valencia, R. R. (1993). Latino population growth, demographic characteristics, and educational stagnation: An examination of recent trends. *Hispanic Journal of Behavioral Sciences, 15,* 165–187.

Charbonneau, M. P., and John-Steiner, V. (1988). Patterns of experience and the language of mathematics. In R. R. Cocking and J. P. Mestre (eds.), *Linguistic and cultural influences on learning mathematics* (pp. 91–100). Hillsdale, N.J.: Lawrence Erlbaum.

Chavez, R. C. (1990). The development of story writing within an IBM Writing to Read Program Lab among language minority students: Preliminary findings of a naturalistic study. *Computers in the Schools, 7*(1/2), 121–144.

Christian, D. (1995). Two-way bilingual education, In C. L. Montone (ed.), *Teaching linguistically and culturally diverse learners: Effective programs and practices* (pp. 8–11). Santa Cruz, Calif.: National Center for Research on Cultural Diversity and Second Language Learning..

Coley, J. D., and Hoffman, D. M. (1990). Overcoming learned helplessness in at-risk readers. *Journal of Reading, 33,* 497–502.

Cummins, J. (1986). Empowering minority students: A framework for interventions. *Harvard Educational Review, 56,* 18–36.

Cummins, J., and Sayers, D. (1990). Education 2001: Learning networks and educational reform. *Computers in the Schools,* 7(1/2), 1–29.

Darder, A. (1993). How does the culture of the teacher shape the classroom experience of Latino students? The unexamined question in critical pedagogy. In S. W. Rothstein (ed.), *Handbook of schooling in urban America* (pp. 195–221). Westport, Conn.: Greenwood.

De Avila, E. A. (1988). Bilingualism, cognitive function, and language minority group membership. In C. B. McCormick, G. E. Miller, and M. Pressley (eds.), *Cognitive Strategy research: From basic research to educational applications* (pp. 104–121). New York: Springer-Verlag.

De Villar, R. A. (1990). Second language use within the non-traditional classroom: Computers, cooperative learning, and bilingualism. In R. Jacobson and C. Faltis (eds.), *Language distribution issues in bilingual schooling* (pp. 133–159). Clevedon, England: Multilingual Matters.

De Villar, R. A., and Faltis, C. J. (1991). *Computers and cultural diversity: Restructuring for school success.* Albany: State University of New York Press.

Díaz-Rico, L. T., and Weed, K. Z. (1995). *The crosscultural, language, and academic development handbook.* Needham Heights, Mass.: Allyn & Bacon.

Dixon, J. K. (1995). Limited English proficiency and spatial visualization in middle school students' construction of the concepts of reflection and rotation. *Bilingual Research Journal,* 19, 221–247.

Durán, B. J.; Dugan, T.; and Weffer, R. E. (1997). Increasing teacher effectiveness with language minority students. *The High School Journal,* 84, 238–246.

Erickson, F. (1987). Transformation and school success: The politics and culture of educational achievement. *Anthropology and Education Quarterly,* 18, 335–356.

Evertson, C., and Green, J. (1986). Observation as inquiry and method. In M. C. Wittrock (ed.), *Handbook of research on teaching* (3rd ed., pp. 162–207). New York: Macmillan.

Faltis, C. J. (1993). Programmatic and curricular options for secondary schools serving limited English proficient students. *The High School Journal,* 76, 171–181.

Fletcher, T. V., and Cardona-Morales, C. (1990). Implementing effective instructional interventions for minority students. In A. Barona and E. E. García (eds.), *Children at risk: Poverty, minority status, and other issues in educational equity* (pp. 151–170). Washington, D.C.: National Association of School Psychologists.

Gagne, E. (1985). *The cognitive psychology of school learning.* Boston: Little Brown.

Gallimore, R., and Goldenberg, C. N. (1992). Tracking the developmental path of teachers and learners: A Vygotskian perspective. In F. K. Oser, A. Dick, and J-L. Patry (eds.), *Effective and responsible teaching: The new synthesis* (pp. 203–221). San Francisco: Jossey-Bass.

García, E. E. (1988). Attributes of effective schools for language minority students. *Education and Urban Society,* 20, 387–398.

García, E. E. (1990). Instructional discourse in "effective" Hispanic classrooms. In R. Jacobson and C. Faltis (eds.), *Language distribution issues in bilingual schooling* (pp. 104–117). Clevedon, England: Multilingual Matters.

García, E. E. (1992). Effective instruction for language minority students: The teacher. *Journal of Education,* 173(2), 130–141.

García, E. (1994). *Understanding and meeting the challenge of student cultural diversity*. Boston: Houghton Mifflin.

Gardner, H. (1985). *The mind's new science: A history of the cognitive revolution*. New York: Basic Books.

Gersten, R., and Jiménez, R. (1998). Modulating instruction for language minority students. In E. J. Kameenui and D. W. Carnine (eds.), *Effective teaching strategies that accommodate diverse learners*. Columbus, Ohio: Merrill.

Good, T. L. (1988). Observational research . . . grounding theory in classrooms. *Educational Psychologist, 25*, 375–379.

Gordon, E. W., and Yowell, C. (1994). Cultural dissonance as a risk factor in the development of students. In R. J. Rossi (ed.), *Schools and students at risk* (pp. 51–69). New York: Teachers College Press.

Haberman, M. (1991). Pedagogy of poverty versus good teaching. *Phi Delta Kappan, 73*, 290–294.

Irvine, J. J., and York, D. E. (1993). Teacher perspectives: Why do African-American, Hispanic, and Vietnamese students fail? In S. W. Rothstein (ed.), *Handbook of schooling in urban America* (pp. 162–173). Westport, Conn.: Greenwood.

Johnson, D. W., and Johnson, R. (1984). *Circles of learning*. Alexandria, Va.: Association for Supervision and Curriculum Development.

Johnson, D. W. and Johnson, R. T. (1991). Classroom instruction and cooperative grouping. In H. C. Waxman and H. J. Walberg (eds.), *Effective teaching: Current research* (pp. 277–293). Berkeley, Calif.: McCutchan.

Johnson, D. W.; Maruyama, G.; Johnson, R.; Nelson, D.; and Skon, L. (1981). Effects of cooperative, competitive, and individualistic goal structures on achievement: A meta-analysis. *Psychological Bulletin, 89*, 47–62.

Jones, B. F. (1986). Quality and equality through cognitive instruction. *Educational Leadership, 43*(7), 4–11.

Jones, B. F., and Friedman, L. B. (1988). Active instruction for students at risk: Remarks on merging process-outcome and cognitive perspectives. *Educational Psychologist, 23*, 299–308.

Jordan, C. (1985). Translating culture: From ethnographic information to educational program. *Anthropology and Education Quarterly, 16*, 105–123.

Kaufman, P., and Frase, M. J. (1990). *Dropout rates in the United States: 1989*. Washington, D.C.: U.S. Department of Education, National Center for Educational Statistics.

Knapp, M. S., and Shields, P. M. (1990). Reconceiving academic instruction for the children of poverty. *Phi Delta Kappan, 71*, 753–758.

Knight, S. L., and Waxman, H. C. (1991). Students' cognition and classroom instruction. In H. C. Waxman and H. J. Walberg (eds.), *Effective teaching: Current research* (pp. 239–255). Berkeley, Calif.: McCutchan.

Kozma, R. B., and Croninger, R. G. (1992). Technology and the fate of at-risk students. *Education and Urban Society, 24*, 440–453.

Ladson-Billings, G. (1992). Culturally relevant teaching: The key to making multicultural education work. In C. A. Grant (ed.), *Research and multicultural education: From the margins to the mainstreams* (pp. 106–121). London: Falmer.

Ladson-Billings, G. (1995). But that's just good teaching! The case for culturally relevant pedagogy. *Theory into Practice, 34*, 158–165.

LeBlanc, P. R., and Skaruppa, C. (1997). Support for democratic schooling:

Classroom level change via cooperative learning: *Action in Teacher Education, 19*(1), 28–38.
Le Celle-Peterson, M., and Rivera, C. (1994). Is it real for all kids? A framework for equitable assessment policies for English language learners. *Harvard Educational Review, 64,* 55–75.
Lee, C. D. (1992). Literacy, cultural diversity, and instruction. *Education and Urban Society, 24,* 279–291.
Lehr, J. B., and Harris, H. W. (1988). *At risk, low-achieving students in the classroom.* Washington, D.C.: National Education Association.
Losey, K. M. (1995). Mexican-American students and classroom interaction: An overview and critique. *Review of Educational Research, 65,* 283–318.
Lucas, T., and Schecter, S. R. (1992). Literacy education and diversity: Toward equity in the teaching of reading and writing. *The Urban Review, 24,* 85–103.
McCollum, P. (1989). Turn-allocation in lessons with North American and Puerto Rican students: A comparative study. *Anthropology and Education Quarterly, 20,* 133–158.
McGee-Banks, C. A., and Banks, J. A. (1995). Equity pedagogy: An essential component of multicultural education. *Theory into Practice, 34,* 152–158.
McKinney, K. (1992) *Improving math and science teaching.* Washington, D.C.: Office of Educational Research and Improvement, U. S. Department of Education.
McLaughlin, B., and McLeod, B. (1996). *Educating all our students: Improving education for children from culturally and linguistically diverse backgrounds* (Vol. 1). Santa Cruz, Calif.: National Center for Research on Cultural Diversity and Second Language Learning.
Means, B., and Olson, K. (1994). The link between technology and authentic learning. *Educational Leadership, 51*(7), 15–18.
Melendez, M. (1993). Bilingual education in California: A status report. *Thrust for Educational Leadership, 22*(6), 35–38.
Merino, B. J.; Legarreta, D.; Coughran, C. C.; and Hoskins, J. (1990). Interaction at the computer by language minority boys and girls paired with fluent English proficient peers. *Computers in the Schools, 7*(1/2), 109–119.
Mielke, A., and Flores, C. (1992–1993). Bilingual technology equalizes opportunities in elementary classrooms. In L. M. Malave (ed.), *Annual conference journal: NABE '92–'93* (pp. 81–92). Washington, D.C.: National Association for Bilingual Education.
Moll, L. C. (1986). Writing as communication: Creating strategic learning environments for students. *Theory into Practice, 25*(2), 102–107.
Moll, L. (1988). Educating Latino students. *Language Arts, 64,* 315–324.
Niemiec, R. P., and Walberg, H. J. (1992). The effects of computers on learning. *International Journal of Educational Research, 17,* 99–108.
Office of Technology Assessment (1988). *Power on: New tools for teaching and learning.* Washington, D.C.: U.S. Government Printing Office.
Olmedo, I. M. (1992). Teacher expectations and the bilingual child. *Action in Teacher Education, 14*(2), 1–8.
O'Malley, J. M., and Chamot, A. U. (1990). *Learning strategies in second language acquisition.* Cambridge, England: Cambridge University Press.
Osborne, A. B. (1996). Practice into theory into practice: Culturally relevant pedagogy for students we have marginalized and normalized. *Anthropology and Education Quarterly, 27,* 285–314.

Padrón, Y. N. (1991). Commentary on dialogues promoting reading comprehension. In B. Means, C. Chelemer, and M. S. Knapp (eds.), *Teaching advanced skills to at-risk students: Views from research and practice* (pp. 131–140). San Francisco: Jossey-Bass.

Padrón, Y. N. (1992). Strategy training in reading for bilingual students: *Southwest Journal of Educational Research into Practice, 4,* 59–62.

Padrón, Y. N. (1993). The effect of strategy instruction on bilingual students' cognitive strategy use in reading. *Bilingual Research Quarterly Journal, 16*(3 & 4), 35–51.

Padrón, Y. N. (1997). Latino students and reading: Understanding these English language learners' needs. In K. Beers and B. Samuels (eds.), *Into focus: Understanding and creating middle school readers* (pp. 105–124). Norwood, Mass.: Christopher-Gordon.

Padrón, Y. N., and Knight, S. L. (1989). Linguistic and cultural influences on classroom instruction. In H. P. Baptiste, J. Anderson, J. Walker de Felix, and H. C. Waxman (eds.), *Leadership, equity, and school effectiveness* (pp. 173–185). Newbury Park, Calif.: Sage.

Padrón, Y. N.; Knight, S. L.; and Waxman, H. C. (1986). Analyzing bilingual and monolingual students' perceptions of their reading strategies. *The Reading Teacher, 39,* 430–433.

Padrón, Y. N., and Waxman, H. C. (1988). The effect of students' perceptions of their cognitive strategies on reading achievement. *TESOL Quarterly, 22,* 146–150.

Padrón, Y. N., and Waxman, H. C. (1993). Teaching and learning risks associated with limited cognitive mastery in science and mathematics for limited-English proficient students. In Office of Bilingual Education and Minority Language Affairs (eds.), *Proceedings of the Third National Research Symposium on Limited English Proficient Students: Focus on middle and high school issues* (Vol. 2, pp. 511–547). Washington, D.C.: National Clearinghouse for Bilingual Education.

Padrón Y. N., and Waxman, H. C. (1996). Improving the teaching and learning of English language learners through instructional technology. *International Journal of Instructional Media, 23*(4), 341–354.

Palincsar, A. S. (1986). The role of dialogue in providing scaffolded instruction. *Educational Psychologist, 21*(1/2), 73–98.

Palincsar, A., and Brown, A. (1984). Reciprocal teaching of comprehension-fostering and comprehension-monitoring activities. *Cognition and Instruction, 1,* 117–175.

Pewewardy, C. D. (1994). Culturally responsible pedagogy in action: An American Indian magnet school. In E. R. Hollins, J. E. King, and W. C. Hayman (eds.), *Teaching diverse populations: Formulating a knowledge base* (pp. 77–92). Albany: State University of New York Press.

Phelan, P.; Davidson, A. L., and Cao, H. T. (1992). Speaking up: Students' perceptions on school. *Phi Delta Kappan, 73,* 695–704.

Poirot, J. L., and Canales, J. (1993–94). Technology and the at-risk: An overview. *The Computing Teacher, 21*(4), 25–26, 55.

Presidential Task Force on Psychology in Education (1993). *Learner-centered psychological principles: Guidelines for school redesign and reform.* Washington, D.C.: American Psychological Association.

Pressley, M., and Ghatala, E. S. (1990). Self-regulated learning: Monitoring learning from text. *Educational Psychologist, 25*, 19–33.

Pressley, M., and Harris, K. R. (1990). What we really know about strategy instruction. *Educational Leadership, 48*(1), 31–34.

Raphael, T. (1984). Teaching learners about sources of information for answering questions. *Journal of Reading, 27*, 303–311.

Raphael, T. (1987). Research on reading: But what can I teach on Monday? In V. Richardson-Koehler (ed.), *Educators' handbook: A research perspective* (pp. 26–49). New York: Longman.

Raphael, T., and Pearson, P. D. (1985). Increasing students' awareness of sources of information for answering questions. *American Educational Research Journal, 22*, 217–235.

Reyes, P., and Valencia, R. R. (1993). Educational policy and the growing Latino student population: Problems and prospects. *Hispanic Journal of Behavioral Sciences, 15*, 258–283.

Rivera, C., and Zehler, A. M. (1991). Assuring the academic success of language minority students: Collaboration in teaching and learning. *Journal of Education, 173*(2), 52–77.

Ryan, A. W. (1991). Meta-analysis of achievement effects of microcomputer applications in elementary schools. *Educational Administration Quarterly, 27*, 161–184.

Saldana, D. C., and Waxman, H. C. (1996). The integration of multicultural education in urban middle level schools. *Issues in Middle Level Education, 5*(2), 9–29.

Saldana, D. C., and Waxman, H. C. (1997). An observational study of multicultural teaching in urban elementary schools. *Equity and Excellence in Education, 30*(1), 40–46.

Sandholtz, J. H.; Ringstaff, C.; and Dwyer, D. C. (1992). Teaching in high-tech environments: Classroom management revisited. *Journal of Educational Computing Research, 8*, 479–505.

Saunders, W., and Goldenberg, C. (1992, April). *Effects of instructional conversations on transition students' concepts of friendship: An experimental study.* Paper presented at the annual meeting of the American Educational Research Association, San Francisco.

Sheingold, K. (1990). Restructuring for learning with technology: The potential for synergy. In K. Sheingold and M. S. Tucker (eds.), *Restructuring for learning with technology* (pp. 9–27). New York: Center for Technology in Education, Bank Street College of Education.

Shuell, T. J. (1993). Toward an integrated theory of teaching and learning. *Educational Psychologist, 28*, 291–311.

Slavin, R. E. (1990). Research on cooperative learning: Consensus and controversy. *Educational Leadership, 47*(4), 52–55.

Slavin, R. E. (1991). Synthesis of the research on cooperative learning: *Phi Delta Kappan, 48*(5), 71–82.

Smith, T. M. (1995). *The educational progress of Hispanic students.* Washington, D.C.: U.S. Department of Education, National Center for Educational Statistics.

Stephen, V. P.; Varble, M. E.; and Taitt, H. (1993). Instructional strategies for minority youth. *The Clearing House, 67*, 116–120.

Swan, K., and Mitrani, M. (1993). The changing nature of teaching and learning in computer-based classrooms. *Journal of Research on Computing in Education, 26,* 40–54.

Tharp, R. G. (1995). Instructional conversations in Zuni classrooms. In C. L. Montone (ed.), *Teaching linguistically and culturally diverse learners: Effective programs and practices* (pp. 12–13). Santa Cruz, Calif.: National Center for Research on Cultural Diversity and Second Language Learning.

Tharp, R. G. (1997). *From at-risk to excellence: Research, theory, and principles for practice.* Santa Cruz, Calif.: Center for Research on Education, Diversity and Excellence.

Tharp, R. G., and Gallimore, R. (1988). *Rousing minds to life: Teaching, learning, and schooling in social context.* Cambridge, England: Cambridge University Press.

Trueba, E. T., and Bartolomé, L. I. (1997). *The education of latino students: Is school reform enough?* (Digest No. EDO-UD-97-4). New York: ERIC Clearinghouse on Urban Education, Teachers College, Columbia University.

U.S. Department of Education. (1992). *The condition of bilingual education in the nation: A report to the Congress and the President.* Washington, D.C.: Author.

U.S. Department of Education (1994). *The condition of education 1994.* Washington, D.C.: U.S. Department of Education, National Center for Education Statistics.

U.S. Department of Education. (1995). *The condition of education 1995.* Washington, D.C.: U.S. Department of Education, National Center for Education Statistics.

U.S. Department of Education (1997). *The condition of education 1997.* Washington, D.C.: U.S. Department of Education, National Center for Education Statistics.

Walker de Felix, J.; Johnson, R. T.; and Shick, J. E. (1990). Socio- and psycholinguistic considerations in interactive video instruction for limited English proficient students. *Computers in the Schools, 7*(1/2), 173–190.

Waxman, H. C. (1992). Reversing the cycle of educational failure for students in at-risk school environments. In H. C. Waxman, J. Walker de Felix, J. Anderson, and H. P. Baptiste (eds.), *Students at risk in at-risk schools: Improving environments for learning* (pp. 1–9). Newbury Park, Calif.: Sage.

Waxman, H. C., and Huang, S. L. (1995). An observational study of technology integration in urban elementary and middle schools. *International Journal of Instructional Media, 22*(4), 329–339.

Waxman, H. C., and Huang, S. L. (1996–97). Classroom instruction differences by level of technology use in middle school mathematics. *Journal of Educational Computing Research, 14*(2), 147–159.

Waxman, H. C.; Huang, S. L.; and Padrón, Y. N. (1995). Investigating the pedagogy of poverty in inner-city middle level schools. *Research in Middle Level Education, 18*(2), 1–22.

Waxman, H. C., and Padrón, Y. P. (1995). Improving the quality of classroom instruction for students at risk of failure in urban schools. *Peabody Journal of Education, 70*(2), 44–65.

Waxman, H. C.; Padrón, Y. N.; and Knight, S. L. (1991). Risks associated with students' limited cognitive mastery. In M. C. Wang, M. C. Reynolds, and H. J. Walberg (eds.), *Handbook of special education: Emerging programs* (Vol. 4, pp. 235–254). Oxford, England: Pergamon.

Wiburg, K. M. (1991). Teaching teachers about technology. *Computers in the Schools, 8*(1/2/3), 115–129.

Winne, P. (1985). Steps toward promoting cognitive achievements. *The Elementary School Journal, 85*, 673–693.

Worthen, B. R.; Van Dusen, L. M., and Sailor, P. J. (1994). A comparative study of the impact of integrated learning systems on students' time-on-task. *International Journal of Educational Research, 21*, 25–37.

Yates, J. R., and Ortiz, A. A. (1991). Professional development needs of teachers who serve exceptional language minorities in today's schools. *Teacher Education and Special Education, 14*(91), 11–18.

8

Improving Classroom Teaching and Learning: What American Educators Can Learn from International Research

Lorin W. Anderson

Although comparative education has been a recognized discipline for almost two centuries (Epstein, 1994), the studies conducted under the auspices of the International Association for the Evaluation of Educational Achievement (IEA) over the past thirty years have had a profound and rather unique effect on educational thought and practice throughout the world. This effect has been both direct—through the results of the studies themselves (Degenhart, 1990; Pelgrum and Plomp 1991; Rosier and Keeves, 1991; Keeves, 1992; Postlethwaite and Wiley, 1992; Purves, Lehmann, and Degenhart, 1992; Burstein, 1993; and Elley, 1993)—and indirect—because many researchers began their own studies by accepting the differences among countries in students' achievement, as identified by various IEA studies (Farrell, 1989; Stevenson, 1990; Stigler and Stevenson, 1991; Sato, 1993).

Both sets of studies share a common theme—a desire to move beyond simply describing these differences to explaining them and, ultimately, benefiting from these tentative explanations (Keeves and Adams, 1994). From the earliest study (Husen, 1967) to the present, the IEA studies have attempted to identify factors associated with achievement differences between countries. Similarly, studies comparing American and Japanese schools (Stevenson, 1990; Stigler and Stevenson, 1991; Sato, 1993) or the educational systems of developing countries and industrialized countries (Farrell, 1989) have explored possible reasons for the achievement differences between countries or groups of countries.

In the past thirty years, international researchers have identified several factors consistently related to higher levels of achievement, many of which are integrally related to the teaching-learning process as it occurs within classrooms throughout the world. Examples of such factors include opportunity to learn, structure, and feedback.

In some countries, the research supporting these factors has been embraced and used (Bathory, 1989; Marklund, 1989). In the United States, however, these same findings have generally been greeted with skepticism and defensiveness (Westbury, 1992).

The purpose of this chapter is twofold: (1) to describe a conceptual framework that can be used to integrate the results of international studies of classroom teaching and learning; and (2) within that framework, to summarize what educators in the United States can learn from studies conducted by researchers from other countries.

A CONCEPTUAL FRAMEWORK

The centerpiece of the conceptual framework is the lesson. Like the proverbial elephant, a lesson is more easily recognized than it is defined. Virtually everyone, however, can identify with the piano lesson, the reading lesson, or the physics lesson. Stigler and Stevenson (1991) use the analogy of a story to describe a lesson:

> A good story is highly organized; it has a beginning, middle, and end; and it follows a protagonist who meets challenges and resolves prob-

lems that arise along the way. Above all, a good story engages the reader's interest in a series of interconnected events, which are best understood in the context of the events that precede and follow it. [P. 14]

Just as the sequence of events provides contextual clues for understanding what is happening within a story, each lesson takes its meaning partly from the curricular unit in which it is embedded. Units are generally defined by the topics being taught or a related set of skills to be learned. Thus, we may have a lesson on Robert Frost within a unit on American poets (a topical organization) or a lesson on division within a unit on "working with fractions" (a skill-oriented organization).

From a social-psychological perspective, lessons generally take place within classrooms (although they can occur in hallways, or playgrounds, or in other nonclassroom locations). Regardless of their location, teachers are expected to *organize* these settings in ways that support the lessons and must *manage* them in ways that the lesson itself is paramount. In simplest terms, then, classroom organization is a matter of the teacher's arranging the physical and social environment in ways that maximize the probability that students will "learn their lessons." In contrast, classroom management requires the teacher doing what is necessary to minimize the time that disrupts or distracts from the lesson.

There is a clear relationship between classroom organization and classroom management. Stated simply, the better the organization, the less classroom management that is needed. In classrooms in which students are engaged in activities that possess what Kounin and Sherman (1979) term "holding power" (that is, the activities themselves hold students' attention without direct teacher intervention), the need for classroom management is likely to be minimum. Conversely, classrooms that are poorly planned and organized (e.g., needed materials are not available or available in limited numbers, "overly social" students are seated in the same group) pose a real challenge for the best of classroom managers. In any case, the ways in which classrooms are organized and managed impact directly on the success or failure of each lesson.

Figure 8-1 visually represents the relationships of classroom, units, and lessons. In this example, there are seventeen lessons divided into two units (unit 1 with five lessons and unit 2 with twelve lessons), the teaching of which takes place in the context of a classroom that is organized and managed by a teacher.

Figure 8-1
The Relationship of Classrooms, Units, and Lessons

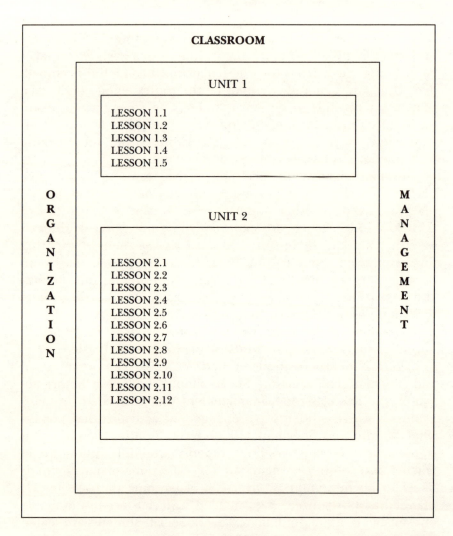

In addition to its place within the curricular unit, each lesson has an internal structure. Numerous components of this structure have been identified (Gump, 1987; Wragg, 1994). Figure 8-2 shows many of the components most frequently mentioned, including (1) the purpose of the lesson, (2) the time allocated to the lesson and pace with which students move through the lesson, (3) the activities engaged in by the students, (4) the roles and responsibilities of teachers and students, and (5) the ways in which lesson progress is assessed and evaluated.

Figure 8-2
The Structure of a Lesson

LESSON U.1*

Purpose/objective (e.g., factual recall, conceptual understanding, problem solving, noncognitive)
Activities (e.g., classroom discourse, recitation, demonstration, group work, seatwork, student reports)
Teacher and Student Roles and Responsibilities (e.g., teacher = direct, indirect, absent; student = competitive, cooperative, individualistic; student = engaged, passive; student = assignments)
Time and Pacing (e.g., time allocated for lesson, rate at which students move through the lesson, steering group)
Assessment and Evaluation (e.g., "what counts," standards)

* *Note:* u.1 refers to the unit number (u) and the lesson number (1). Thus, 5.3 would refer to the third lesson within the fifth unit.

Lesson Purpose

Each lesson has a purpose. This purpose may be referred to as an *objective* (Hunter, 1984), as an *academic focus* (Wragg, 1994), or by some other term. Regardless of what words are used to denote purpose, the purpose is generally stated in terms of the content to be covered during the lesson (e.g., a lesson on the Battle of Bunker Hill) or what students are to learn from the lesson (e.g., a lesson in which students are to learn how to distinguish acids from bases).

Allocated Time and Pacing

Time is the feature most frequently associated with the concept of lesson. Piano lessons last for either thirty minutes or an hour. In high schools, a fifty-minute class period is typically devoted to a single history lesson. Occasionally, lessons may transcend class periods, as when a discussion of the significance of the Louisiana Purchase continues from Tuesday to Wednesday.

Pacing has two definitions. The first is the rate at which the material in the lesson or unit is covered. Using this definition, the pace of the lesson is the amount of material (e.g., pages, problems) covered per unit of time (Anderson and Torrey, 1994). Teachers who expect students to cover a chapter every two weeks are moving at a more rapid rate than those who expect students to cover a chapter every three weeks.

The second definition of pacing emphasizes the person or thing responsible for determining the rate at which the lesson progresses (Stodolsky, 1988). Within this definition, there are three possible "pacers": the teacher, the student(s), or some mechanical or technological means (e.g., videotapes, computers). In most classrooms throughout the world, teachers control the pace of the lessons (Anderson, Ryan, and Shapiro, 1989).

Lesson Activities

Lesson activities refer to the events of the lesson. From his research, Berliner (1983) developed a fairly extensive list of lesson activities. The list includes reading circles, seatwork, two-way presentations (e.g., discussions), one-way presentations (e.g., lectures), mediated presentations (e.g., movies, videotapes, computers), silent reading, construction, games, play, and housekeeping. To this list, Stodolsky (1988), who refers to lesson activities as instructional formats, has added recitations, group work, student reports, task preparation, tutorial, and tests. These sixteen categories include the vast majority of activities that occur in classrooms throughout the world (Anderson, Ryan, and Shapiro, 1989).

Roles and Responsibilities of Teachers and Students

While all five of the components of lessons are interrelated, this interrelationship is most evident in the component "roles and responsibilities of teachers and students." Stated simply, the appropriate roles and responsibilities of teachers and students depend primarily on the lesson activities. When lecturing, teachers generally assume an active role; students, on the other hand, tend to be rather passive. During lectures, teachers are expected to talk, while students are expected to listen (and perhaps take notes—a slightly more active role).

For other activities, however, the roles and responsibilities of teachers and students are not quite so clear. During group work, students are expected to perform in a more active role, while teachers are expected to be more passive. However, some students may be quite passive, while some teachers may be fairly intrusive.

In addition to differentiating the roles and responsibilities of teachers from those of students, the expected relationships among the students themselves may change as lesson activities change. "Seatwork" generally means that students are expected to work by themselves. In fact, conversations between or among students may be seen by teachers as disruptive or evidence of cheating. "Group work," on the other hand, implies that students are to work together. Thus, conversations are not only encouraged, but expected (Johnson and Johnson, 1989). However, simply seating students together does not mean they should or do work together (Galton, Simon, and Croll, 1980).

Assessment and Evaluation

Teachers must determine how well each lesson is going and how well their students are learning, and they may do so in several ways: They may observe students' attention and involvement (Jackson, 1967), they may ask questions (Gall, 1989), or they may give assignments (e.g., worksheets, quizzes) (Pellicer and Anderson, 1995). After assessing the lesson and students' progress, teachers make a variety of decisions: Should I go on to the next lesson or review the previous one? Which students seem to need a little more help and how can I provide it without disrupting the whole class? To which students should I assign higher marks and to which should I assign lower ones?

Assessment and evaluation are also means of providing feedback to students concerning their learning progress (or lack thereof). The feedback given can range from the simple acknowledgment of correctness or incorrectness (knowledge of results), to praise and encouragement (reinforcement), to statements that link a student's performance to his or her effort or ability (attributional feedback).

THE KNOWLEDGE BASE GLEANED FROM INTERNATIONAL CLASSROOM RESEARCH

The conceptual framework described in the previous section serves two purposes. First, it provides a useful organization for discussing the results of international studies of classroom teaching and learning. Second, it enables connections to be made across the studies. In this section, the focus is on what international researchers have contributed to our understanding of each of the five major components of the conceptual framework. In the final two parts of this section, research on two related issues, teacher planning and the classroom environment, will be summarized briefly.

Lesson Purpose

Traditionally in this country, lesson purpose is generally aligned with the content to be covered (e.g., perimeter in geometry, *Leaves of Grass* in English literature, the Battle of Hastings in world history, viruses in science) or equated with some modification of the taxonomy of educational objectives (Bloom et al., 1956). (See, for example, Stodolsky, 1988.)

While content-oriented statements emphasize what is to be taught, objectives specify what students are expected to learn. Thus, for example, students may be expected to memorize the formula for computing perimeter, understand the meaning of perimeter, know when the computation of perimeter is appropriate, or analyze the relation of perimeter and area for various geometric shapes. These are four quite different objectives within the same topic.

International researchers have provided alternative ways of thinking about lesson purpose. Borrowing from the cognitive psychologist David Norman (1978), Bennett and Desforges (1988), for example, have identified four types of lesson objectives. They are incremental lessons (in which students are expected to recall, recognize, and discriminate among new ideas, procedures, or skills), restructuring lessons (where students are expected to invent or discover an idea, process, or pattern inherent in the new material or knowledge already stored in students' memories), enrichment lessons (in which students are expected to apply familiar skills to new problems), and practice lessons (where students are to "fine tune" skills on familiar problems or exercises). Whereas incremental and restructuring lessons are somewhat related to the frequently mentioned distinction between lower-order and higher-order objectives in Bloom's taxonomy (Anderson, 1994), enrichment and practice lessons move our consideration beyond the individual lesson to the context within which the lesson is taught; namely, the instructional unit.

This concern for the contextual meaning of a lesson became a central focus in the IEA Classroom Environment Study (Anderson, Ryan, and Shapiro, 1989). In this study, four lesson purposes were identified: *introducing* new content, expanding on new content to the point of *mastery*, *reviewing* previously taught content to help students remember it (e.g., connecting a new lesson to a previously taught one, preparing for an upcoming test), and reviewing previously taught content for the purpose of *correcting* identified errors and misunderstandings.

Much has been learned about lesson purpose from international research. First, while lesson purposes are many and varied, the vast majority of lessons worldwide tend to emphasize memorization, rather superficial understanding, and the routine use of well-taught skills (McKnight et al., 1987; Anderson, Ryan, and Shapiro, 1989; Purves, 1989). Furthermore, those countries with consistently higher achievement scores also tend to have lessons that emphasize explanation over rote learning (Mayer, Sims, and Tajika, 1995) or, at the very least, use problems to contextualize the necessary memorization (Stigler and Stevenson, 1991).

Second, the extent to which the lesson topics correspond with the topics included on the tests used to make international comparisons varies from one country to the next and from one classroom to the next within countries (McLean, 1988; Anderson, Ryan, and Shapiro, 1989; Westbury, 1992). Interestingly, it is the within-country variation that quite likely accounts for the between-country differences. For example, whereas almost *all* students in Japan may receive a reasonable amount of instruction on a particular topic on test, a fairly large proportion of students in the United States may receive little, if any, instruction on that test topic. For example, on the average, Japanese eighth graders outperform United States eighth graders on the statistics subtest of the mathematics achievement test (McLean, 1988). Statistics is taught in virtually every Japanese classroom, but may or may not be taught in the typical American classroom.

Third, the number of review lessons is quite large in most countries. In the IEA Classroom Environment Study, approximately two of every five lessons were primarily for the purpose of review (Anderson, Ryan, and Shapiro, 1989). Furthermore, there tends to be an emphasis on introductory lessons in most countries (McLean, 1988). In McLean's words, "This tendency to touch a topic and move on before the majority of students have mastered it is common in North America, but not in Japan and in other countries where high achievement is observed" (p. 36).

At first blush, the data on the number of review lessons and the number of introductory lessons appear to be contradictory. It may be, however, that extensive review is needed because the material was not learned well in the first place. In any case, the number of mastery lessons tends to be very small in most countries.

Allocated Time and Pacing

Allocated time refers to the number of days, hours, and minutes devoted to particular subject matters or specific lessons within a subject area. Countries differ widely in the number of years they require students to study particular subject matters (Anderson and Postlethwaite, 1989). Furthermore, within subject matters, as mentioned previously, a great deal of time at certain grade levels may be allocated to specific topics (e.g., fractions) while little, if any, time is allocated to others (e.g., algebra) (Muthen et al., 1995). Not surprisingly, students achieve more in those subject matters they study for more years (Carroll, 1975; Bathory, 1989) and on those topics that are emphasized in their study (McLean, 1988).

As mentioned earlier, pacing has multiple definitions. International research contributes to our understanding of pacing, however it is defined. Quite obviously, review lessons slow the pace of instruction. In the IEA Classroom Environment Study (Anderson, Ryan, and Shapiro, 1989), more than 60 percent of the lessons observed in Nigeria were seen by teachers as serving the purpose of review. In the Republic of Korea, in contrast, fewer than 10 percent of the observed lessons were intended by teachers as review lessons. Thus, it should not be surprising that the Republic of Korea is among the top of the achievement distribution in many international comparisons, while Nigeria is near the bottom.

In most traditional elementary and secondary classrooms, pacing is controlled by the teacher. Mortimore and colleagues (1988) summarized this point quite clearly following their study of classrooms in the United Kingdom: "The vast majority of teachers preferred ... to retain almost complete control over the amount of time spent on the work, and the way in which the work was under-taken, except in areas that the teacher considered peripheral" (p. 83).

Since teachers generally control the pace of instruction, it seems reasonable to question how they make pacing decisions. One of the main contributors to our understanding of these decisions is Dahllof, a Swedish researcher who formulated the concept of "steering group" within his frame factor theory (Dahllof, 1971). A steering group is a small group of students whom the teacher uses as a reference point in deciding when to move from one teaching point to the next. According to Dahllof, a teacher makes pacing decisions based on his or her interpretation of the dynamic interplay among three factors—the time allocated to particular topics or units, the total amount to be learned in the units or course, and the time students in the steering group apparently needed to learn the material (Torper, 1994).

Lesson Activities

International classroom research makes it clear that activities are a key component in all lessons. In fact, in the IEA Classroom Environment Study (Anderson, Ryan, and Shapiro, 1989), classroom activities were coded into one of nine specified categories derived primarily from Berliner's work (1983), with a tenth category ("other") to be used if the observed activity did not fit into one of the previous nine categories. The frequency with which observers used the "other" category ranged from zero percent in Canada to 8.7 percent in Israel, with a median across countries of 0.7 percent. Thus, a limited number of clearly specified activities is used by teachers throughout the world.

Furthermore, lessons almost always consist of multiple activities. For example, lectures may precede discussions, which precede seatwork. Similarly, task preparation may lead to group work, which is followed by recitation and, finally, housekeeping. In the IEA Classroom Environment Study, the average number of activities within lessons conducted by teachers in four countries (Canada, Hungary, the Republic of Korea, and Thailand) ranged from slightly less than three to slightly more than five. Regardless of the specific type of activity occurring in the classroom, four aspects of the activity tend to be very important to student learning: structure, clarity, involvement, and meaning. One of the major findings of international studies is that the type of activity matters less than how the activity is presented to students (structure, clarity), how students engage in the activity (involvement), and how the activity and their participation in it is interpreted by students (meaning).

Structure. Lessons should be properly structured and that structure should be communicated to students (Mortimore et al., 1988; Tomic and Van der Sijde, 1989). In the context of this research, the term "structure" has two meanings. The first corresponds with the description of lesson offered by Stigler and Stevenson (1991) (and summarized earlier in this chapter). The second meaning of the term "structure" implies that the structure of the lesson should help students understand the structure of the subject matter being taught (Mortimore et al., 1988; Renkl and Helmke, 1992).

Structure does not mean that teachers must be in control of the lesson. Structuring a cooperative learning lesson, for example, may involve the teacher posing problems, forming groups of students, assigning tasks to groups of students, and assigning roles and responsibilities to students within groups (Johnson and Johnson, 1989). Once this initial cooperative learning structure is in place, the teacher's role becomes less direct and more unobtrusive. Because of this change in teacher role, the success of a cooperative learning lesson is clearly in jeopardy without appropriate problems, tasks, groups, roles, and responsibilities being assigned to and accepted by students.

Clarity. Lessons must be communicated in ways that are clear to students. Clarity should be apparent in the texts that accompany the lesson (Mayer et al., 1995) as well as the means teachers use to present the lesson to students (Cruickshank and Metcalf, 1994). The use of verbal markers, examples, illustrations, cognitive modeling, and reasonable redundancy all contribute to increased clarity (Anderson, 1989; Cruickshank and Metcalf, 1994; Mayer et al., 1995).

Involvement. For lesson activities to be successful, students must be involved or engaged in them (Fisher, 1994). In much classroom research, active participation is defined as the amount or percentage of time students are on task (Anderson, Ryan, and Shapiro, 1989; Weinert and Helmke, 1995). Structure and clarity tend to enhance student involvement in learning (Anderson, Ryan, and Shapiro, 1989), as does substantive interaction between teachers and students during the lesson (e.g., academic monitoring, academic feedback) (Fisher, 1994).

Meaning. The final aspect of lesson activities is meaning. Meaning implies understanding what is to be learned within the context of what is already known (Weinert and Helmke, 1995). Nuthall and Alton-Lee (1993) have made this point quite succinctly:

> When we related the students' recall of the content of their class experience to our data on their actual experience, it became apparent that what the students had stored in memory was an interpretative representation of that experience.... [That is, students' recall] consisted of a coherent and elaborated reconstruction of the original classroom experience. [P. 811]

Nuthall and Alton-Lee went on to describe examples of the process by which reconstruction—this search after meaning (Schnotz and Ballstaedt, 1994)—occurred in their studies of nine- to twelve-year-old children in New Zealand.

Meaning is clearly related to the second definition of structure mentioned previously. In fact, reconstruction implies there must be some original construction or structure communicated to students. However, meaning is also related to the first definition of structure—namely, the structure of the lesson itself. Stigler and Stevenson (1991) use the term "coherence" in this regard. Irrelevant comments, frequent shifts from topic to topic, inefficient transitions from activity to activity, and outside interruptions (e.g., unexpected visitors, public address announcements) all contribute to the lack of coherence. Lessons that exemplify coherence are likely to be more effective lessons.

Roles and Responsibilities of Teachers and Students

As mentioned earlier, appropriate roles and responsibilities of teachers and students depend a great deal on the lesson activities. They also depend on the teacher's theory of learning and the function classroom activities serve within that theory. Bennett and Desforges (1988) provide an excellent example of these relationships:

> Learning [is] a covert, intellectual process involving the development and restructuring of existing conceptual schemes.... Teaching affects achievement through pupil thought processes, that is, teaching influences pupil thinking, and pupil thinking mediates learning.... The tasks on which students work structure to a large extent what information students select from the environment and how they process it.... To understand the effects of teaching on learning, it is necessary to ascertain the extent to which the intellectual demand of assigned work is [appropriately] matched to children's [prior] attainments. [P. 222]

Within this framework, teachers have a major responsibility: to assign tasks to students that match the students' level of prior knowledge and learning. After performing this responsibility, the teachers' role shifts to serving as a guide to learning rather than a giver of knowledge, and as a facilitator of learning rather than a causal agent. In this country, this role has been captured quite well by Sizer (1984), who contends that the prevailing metaphor governing the teaching-learning process should be "student-as-worker, teacher-as-coach."

There is some evidence that this role is not assumed by large numbers of teachers in very many countries (Anderson, Ryan, and Shapiro, 1989). There is additional evidence, however, that this role is more comfortably assumed by teachers in Japan (Sato, 1993; Stigler and Stevenson, 1991) than by those in the United States.

Because lessons occur within classrooms, another responsibility of teachers is to create classroom environments that support and enhance the lesson. A great deal of international research supports four key elements of such an environment: cohesiveness, satisfaction, goal direction, and organization (Fraser, 1989). The first element, cohesiveness, deals with the social dimension of the classroom environment, whereas the second, satisfaction, deals with the affective dimension. Interestingly, however, the remaining two elements overlap substantially with the lesson structure shown in Figure 8-2. Goal direction corresponds primarily with lesson purpose; organization, with time, pacing, and activities.

Teachers' responsibilities extend beyond their classrooms. They must prepare for their lessons, grade papers, and complete various administrative tasks (e.g., complete book order forms, mark report cards). While these responsibilities are clearly supportive of excellence in teaching, American teachers, unlike their Japanese counterparts, are expected to find time for them or do them on their own time. As a consequence, American teachers often find themselves having to steal lesson time to attend to this "multitude of chores" (Stigler and Stevenson, 1991).

Assessment and Evaluation

During lessons, teachers throughout the world tend to use questions to check lesson progress and the level of student understanding (Anderson, Ryan, and Shapiro, 1989). In the IEA Classroom Environment Study, the majority of questions asked by teachers in the majority of countries called for memory of previously taught material and required short answers from students. Across countries, there were similarities and differences in what teachers did after students gave incorrect responses or did not respond. Only rarely did teachers in any country give the answer themselves or tell students the answers were wrong. In some countries (e.g., Israel and Nigeria), the most frequent reaction was to redirect the question to another student. In other countries (e.g., Canada, Hungary), the typical reaction was to ask follow-up or probing questions of the student to whom the question originally was asked.

One of the more interesting findings of the study was that across countries, teachers who perceived their students to be of lower ability spent more time assessing and evaluating them by asking questions and probing. One interpretation of this finding is that teachers are less certain that they are "getting across" to their low-ability students.

Near the end of a lesson, teachers may assign homework for the purpose of providing opportunities for review and practice and, once again, checking for understanding. The issue of homework suggests two major differences between American and Asian teachers and parents. The homework given to Japanese students by their teachers emphasizes the process used to find the answer or solve the problem, rather than the answer or solution. The converse tends to be true of homework given to American students (Sato, 1993). Similarly, mathematics textbook exercises in Japan emphasize explanation of material, rather than memorization of it. Again, the reverse is generally true in mathematics textbooks used in this country (Mayer, Sims, and Tajika, 1995).

With respect to parents and homework, Chinese and Japanese mothers spend more time providing homework assistance than do American mothers (Chen and Stevenson, 1989). Interestingly, however, "spending time on homework because my parents want me to" was a response more frequently given by American children than by their Chinese or Japanese counterparts.

Regardless of the method used to assess student lesson learning, monitoring and record keeping are critically important (Mortimore et al., 1988). Furthermore, teachers who not only monitor but make adjustments in their teaching tend to produce higher-achieving students (Anderson, Ryan, and Shapiro, 1989).

Summary

Several generalizations can be derived from the results of international research on classroom teaching and learning. Six of the more important ones follow.

1. *The purpose of each lesson is perhaps best understood by its place in the curriculum unit within which it is embedded.* Introductory, mastery, review, practice, correction, and enrichment lessons all take their meaning from the unit context.
2. *Lessons in which the emphasis is on explanation rather than rote memorization and on knowledge and skills that are sufficiently important to be included on end-of-year examinations tend to result in higher levels of achievement.*
3. *Increasing the pace of instruction (within reasonable limits) will quite likely result in increased student achievement.* In this regard, minimizing the number of review lessons and, perhaps, incorporating the needed review within introductory, mastery, and enrichment lessons will increase the instructional pace.
4. *Constructs such as structure, clarity, involvement, meaning, monitoring, feedback, coherence, cohesiveness, satisfaction, goal directedness, and organization should be incorporated into a theoretical framework that is then used to guide teaching practices and teacher decision making.*
5. *While substantive teacher-student interaction is critical to lesson success, excessive teacher control of the classroom and the lesson is not (and, in fact, may be detrimental).* Accepting the principles of and research on cognitive psychology means that teachers need be less directive in their classrooms and

instead emphasize task selection and presentation, by questioning, cuing, responding, prompting, and encouraging.
6. *When teachers assume this less directive role, they then must spend sufficient amounts of time away from their students.* This time away from students is used to plan, ready the classroom (e.g., ensure the availability of needed materials; arrange chairs, tables, and desks), read professional journals, and share ideas and practices with colleagues (which may involve visiting other teachers' classrooms).

CONCLUSION

What can American educators learn from international classroom research? There are several answers to this question. I would suggest first that international classroom research provides a mirror by which we can more clearly see ourselves. I vividly recall my wonderment when I read Joe Farrell's (1989) summary of a study in the Philippines on textbook availability. The results of this study suggested that providing one book for every two primary students instead of one book for every ten primary students resulted in substantial achievement gains in science, mathematics, and Filipino. "Textbook availability" would never be included as a variable in classroom research in this country. Like many things, we Americans take textbooks for granted.

This mirror also shows us possibilities—things we are not doing now, but could do if we wanted to. As mentioned in the previous section, we could speed up the pace of instruction (which would quite likely increase student achievement), if we reduced the number of review lessons included in the curriculum. We could increase the depth of student understanding of a subject matter if we emphasized explanations rather than memory, provided worked-out examples of problems, and assumed a more "guidelike, coachlike" role as teachers. All these ideas are possible. The question is whether they are likely to be used.

In this regard, this mirror clarifies what it would take to move from the realm of possibility to reality. American teachers may express a desire for more time for planning and grading papers (an important element of feedback). We know that the Chinese elementary school teachers teach three hours per day, thereby having additional time for planning and paper grading. But we also know that the size of classes in Chinese elementary schools is substantially larger than that in American elementary schools (Stigler and Stevenson, 1991). Are American teachers willing to trade larger classes for the necessary amounts of nonteaching time?

This mirror can be used to develop a sound conceptual framework that transcends our often parochial view of life in schools and that can be used to guide both practice and research. By using this mirror, common research questions can be identified and collaborative research efforts and methodologies can be used to address the most critical and fundamental of these questions.

Finally, this mirror can be used to reflect our educational problems toward those who provide the political and economic support for American education. In this regard, we would be wise to remember the words of Erland Ringborg, then Director General of the National Board of Education in Stockholm, Sweden:

> Critics of the IEA sometimes bewail the tendency of politicians to latch onto superficial comparisons between countries as a means of scoring political points. Personally, I feel that we should refrain from this kind of moralizing and acknowledge the realities of politics. If the [studies] have the scientific substance we assume, then let us instead turn the whole thing to the best possible account. Let us supply our politicians with national averages and ranking orders and also with those analyses of the underlying systematic factors that may serve to explain the results. [Quoted in Marklund, 1989, p. 44]

REFERENCES

Anderson, L. W. (ed.) 1989. *The effective teacher: Study guide and readings.* New York: Random House.

Anderson, L. W. (1994). Research on teaching and teacher education. In L. W. Anderson and L. A. Sosniak (eds.) *Bloom's taxonomy: A forty-year retrospective.* Chicago: University of Chicago Press.

Anderson, L. W., and Postlethwaite, T. N. (1989). What IEA studies say about teachers and teaching. In A. Purves (ed.). *International comparisons and educational reform* (pp. 73–86). Washington, D.C.: Association for Supervision and Curriculum Development.

Anderson, L. W.; Ryan, D. W.; and Shapiro, B. J. (1989). *The IEA classroom environment study.* Oxford, Eng.: Pergamon Press.

Anderson, L. W., and Torrey, P. (1994). Instructional pacing. In T. Husen and T. N. Postlethwaite (eds). *International encyclopedia of education* (2nd ed., pp. 2867–2870). Oxford, Eng.: Pergamon Press.

Bathory, Z. (1989). How two educational systems learned from comparative studies: The Hungarian experience. In A. Purves (ed.). *International comparisons and educational reform* (pp. 45–50). Washington, DC: Association for Supervision and Curriculum Development.

Bennett, S. N., and Desforges, C. (1988). Matching classroom tasks to students' attainments. *Elementary School Journal, 88,* 221–234.

Berliner, D. C. (1983). Developing conceptions of classroom environments: Some light on the T in classroom studies of ATI. *Educational Psychologist, 18*(1), 1–13.

Bloom, B. S.; Engelhart, M.; Furst, E., Hill, W.; and Krathwohl, D. R. (1956). *The taxonomy of educational objectives: Handbook 1, the cognitive domain.* New York: Longman.

Burstein, L. (ed.) (1993). *The IEA study of mathematics* (Vol. 3). Oxford, Eng.: Pergamon Press.

Carroll, J. B. (1975). *The teaching of French as a foreign language in eight countries.* New York: John Wiley and Sons.

Chen, C., and Stevenson, H. (1989). Homework: A cross-cultural examination. *Child Development, 60,* 551–561.

Cruickshank, D., and Metcalf, K. (1994). Explanation in teaching and learning. In T. Husen and T. N. Postlethwaite (eds). *The international encyclopedia of education* (2nd ed., pp. 6143–6149). Oxford, Eng.: Pergamon Press.

Dahllof, U. (1971). *Ability grouping, content validity, and curriculum process analysis.* New York: Teachers College Press.

Degenhart, R. E. (1990). *Thirty years of international research: An annotated bibliography of IEA publications (1960–1990).* The Hague, Netherlands: IEA.

Elley, W. B. (1993). *Reading literacy in 30 countries.* Oxford, Eng.: Pergamon Press.

Epstein, E. H. (1994). Comparative and international education: Overview and historical development. In T. Husen and T. N. Postlethwaite (eds). *International encyclopedia of education* (2nd ed., pp. 918–923). Oxford, Eng.: Pergamon Press.

Farrell, J. (1989). International lessons for school effectiveness: The view from the developing world. In M. Holmes, K. A. Leithwood, and D. F. Musella (eds.). *Educational policy for effective schools* (pp. 53–70). New York: Teachers College Press.

Fisher, C. W. (1994). Academic learning time. In T. Husen and T. N. Postlethwaite (eds). *International encyclopedia of education* (2nd ed., pp. 20–23). Oxford, Eng.: Pergamon Press.

Fraser, B. (1989). Twenty years of classroom climate work: progress and prospect. *Journal of Curriculum Studies, 21,* 307–327.

Gall, M. (1989). Synthesis of research on teachers' questioning. In L. W. Anderson (ed.) *The effective teacher: Study guide and readings.* New York: Random House (pp. 301–306).

Galton, M.; Simon, B.; and Croll, P. (1980). *Inside the primary classroom.* London: Routledge and Kegan Paul.

Gump, P. (1987). Activities: Structure and function. In M. J. Dunkin (ed.) *International encyclopedia of teaching and education.* Oxford, Eng.: Pergamon Press.

Hunter, M. (1984). *Mastery teaching.* El Segundo, Calif.: TIP Publications.

Husen, T. (ed.) (1967). *International study of achievement in mathematics: A comparison of twelve countries* (Vols. 1 and 2). Stockholm: Almqvist and Wiksell.

Jackson, P. W. (1967). *Life in classrooms.* New York: Teachers College Record.

Johnson, D., and Johnson, R. (1989). Cooperative learning. In L. W. Anderson (ed.) *The effective teacher: Study guide and readings* (pp. 175–184). New York: Random House.

Keeves, J. (1992). *The IEA study of science: Changes in science education and achievement, 1970 to 1984.* Oxford, Eng.: Pergamon Press.

Keeves, J., and Adams, D. (1994). Comparative methodology in education. In T. Husen and T. N. Postlethwaite (eds). *International encyclopedia of education* (2nd ed., pp. 948–958). Oxford, Eng.: Pergamon Press.

Kounin, J. S., and Sherman, L. W. (1979). School environments as behavior settings. *Theory into Practice, 18,* 145–149.

McKnight, C. C.; Crosswhite, F. J.; Dossey, J. A.; Kefer, E.; Swafford, J. O.; Travers, K. J.; and Cooney, T. J. (1987). *The underachieving curriculum: Assessing U. S. school mathematics from an international perspective.* Champaign, Ill.: Stipes.

McLean, L. (1988). Lessons for administrators from large-scale assessments of teaching and learning. In M. Holmes, K. A. Leithwood, and D. F. Musella (eds.). *Educational policy for effective schools* (pp. 31–52). New York: Teachers College Press.

Marklund, I. (1989). How two educational systems learned from comparative studies: The Swedish experience. In A. Purves (ed.). *International comparisons and educational reform* (pp. 45–50). Washington, DC: Association for Supervision and Curriculum Development.

Mayer, R.; Sims, V.; and Tajika, H. (1995). A comparison of how textbooks teach mathematical problem solving in Japan and the United States. *American Educational Research Journal, 32,* 443–460.

Mortimore, P.; Sammons, P.; Stoll, L.; Lewis, D.; and Ecob, R. (1988). *School matters.* Berkeley: University of California Press.

Muthen, B.; Huang, L-C.; Jo, B.; Khoo, S-T.; Goff, G. N.; Novak, J. R.; and Shih, J. C. (1995). Opportunity-to-learn effects on achievement: Analytical aspects. *Educational Evaluation and Policy Analysis, 17,* 355–370.

Norman, D. (1978). Notes towards a complex theory of learning. In A. M. Lesgold (ed.). *Cognitive psychology and instruction* (pp. 39–48). New York: Plenum.

Nuthall, G., and Alton-Lee, A. (1993). Predicting learning from student experiences of teaching: A theory of student knowledge construction in classrooms. *American Educational Research Journal, 30,* 799–840.

Pelgrum, W. J., and Plomp, T. (1991). *The use of computers in education worldwide: Results from the IEA "Computers in education" survey in nineteen educational systems.* Oxford, Eng.: Pergamon Press.

Pellicer, L. O., and Anderson, L. W. (1995). *Handbook for teacher leaders.* Thousand Oaks, Calif.: Corwin Press.

Postlethwaite, T. N., and Wiley, D. (1992). *The IEA study of science II: Science achievement in twenty-three countries.* Oxford, Eng.: Pergamon Press.

Purves, A. (1989). The IEA studies and reform in reading, writing, and literacy instruction. In A. Purves (ed.) *International comparisons and educational reform* (pp. 87–98). Washington, DC: Association for Supervision and Curriculum Development.

Purves, A. C.; Lehmann, R.; and Degenhart, R. E. (eds.) (1992). *The IEA study of written composition II: Education and performance in fourteen countries.* Oxford, Eng.: Pergamon Press.

Renkl, A., and Helmke, A. (1992). Discriminant effects of performance-oriented and structure-oriented mathematics tasks on achievement growth. *Contemporary Educational Psychology, 17,* 47–55.

Rosier, M., and Keeves, J. (1991). *The IEA study of science I: Science education and curricula in twenty-three countries.* Oxford, Eng.: Pergamon Press.

Sato, N. (1993). Teaching and learning in Japanese elementary schools: A context for understanding. *Peabody Journal of Education, 68*(4), 111–153.

Schnotz, W., and Ballstaedt, S-P. (1994). Teaching and testing for comprehension. In T. Husen and T. N. Postlethwaite (eds). *International encyclopedia of education* (2nd ed., pp. 964–969). Oxford, Eng.: Pergamon Press.

Sizer, T. (1984), *Horace's Compromise.* Boston: Houghton-Mifflin.

Stevenson, H. (1990). Mathematics achievement of children in China and the United States. *Child Development, 61,* 1053–1066.

Stevenson, H. (1993). Why Asian students still outdistance Americans. *Educational Leadership, 50*(5), 63–65.

Stigler, J., and Stevenson, H. (1991). How Asian teachers polish each lesson to perfection. *American Educator, 15*(1), 12–20, 43–47.

Stodolsky, S. (1988). *The subject matters.* Chicago: University of Chicago Press.

Tomic, W., and Van der Sijde, P. C. (1989). *Changing teaching for better learning.* Amsterdam: Swets & Zeitlinger.

Torper, U. (1994). Frame factors. In T. Husen and T. N. Postlethwaite (eds). *International encyclopedia of education* (2nd ed., pp. 2375–2377). Oxford, Eng.: Pergamon Press.

Weinert, F. E., and Helmke, A. (1995). Interclassroom differences in instructional quality and interindividual differences in cognitive development. *Educational Psychologist, 30,* 15–20.

Westbury, I. (1992). Comparing American and Japanese achievement: Is the United States really a lower achiever? *Educational Researcher, 21*(5), 18–24.

Wragg, E. (1994). In T. Husen and T. N. Postlethwaite (eds). *International encyclopedia of education* (2nd ed., pp. 3385–3389). Oxford, Eng.: Pergamon Press.

Part III
Constructivist Perspectives on Teaching

9

Narrative, Teaching, and Teacher Thinking

Linda S. Behar-Horenstein

For many decades, quantitative research methods have dominated inquiry into teachers' behavior. More recently, narrative inquiry has been employed to analyze teaching and teacher thinking. The practice has generated controversy and excitement among educators. Advocates of narrative inquiry believe that story research offers a thick and rich description of teachers' experiences in context-specific situations. Such descriptions are thought to play a powerful meditative role for teachers who engage in active reflection. These descriptions have been credited with guiding practice through the illumination of tacit wisdom and with assisting teachers through the generation of practice-based theory. Narrative researchers proclaim that story represents an enormous database from which to develop new understandings about the relationships among phenomena in educational contexts. However, empiricists have raised several questions about the utility, authenticity, and claims of veracity suggested by storytelling researchers. (For example, empiricists typically confront narrative researchers with the contention that *every* teacher has a story.) These concerns

---

This chapter was adapted from Behar-Horenstein, L. S., and Morgan, R. R. (1995). Narrative, teaching, and teacher thinking: Perspectives and possibilities. *Peabody Journal of Education* 70(2), 139–161 and a presentation made by the author at the Annual Meeting of the American Educational Research (San Francisco, Calif., April, 1995) entitled, "Toward an understanding of teaching and teacher thinking: Contributions from story research."

beg the question of whether the research community will ultimately sanctify storytelling work as a viable methodological approach. While educators strive to determine which research method is best for analyzing teachers' behavior, debates between narrative and empirical researchers have reached new levels of argumentation.

In this chapter, I explore the utility of narrative as a legitimate educational research tool and discuss the (a) definitions and conceptions of narrative/story; (b) conceptual and theoretical frameworks that guide narrative and technical/empirical forms of research, (c) advantages, criticisms, and limitations of story; and (d) epistemological issues concerning the assumptions underlying the interpretation and the conceptual roots of story research. Finally, future directions for narrative inquiry are examined in an effort to offer story a vital role in research about teachers. This discussion concludes with the presentation of a conceptual framework designed to move us beyond philosophizing about the viability of story research as a methodological approach.

CONCEPTIONS OF STORY AND NARRATIVE FORMS OF INQUIRY

Story is a narrative with a very specific syntactical shape (Scholes, 1981, 1982) and subject matter that allows for, and encourages, the projection of human values on the story. Story emphasizes the connections between what humans think, know, and do as well as the reciprocal relationships between the way that human thinking shapes behavior and knowing shapes thinking. As an entity with its own parameters (beginning, middle, and end), story has a dynamic that is created and interpreted through a person's own experiences or by a participant observer who offers a vicarious interpretation of an individual's personal story. A synthesis of the lived experiences results in a narrative that occurs through a process of active construction and reconstruction. Temporality and causality are involved in this reconstruction process. These factors, related to the time, place, specific situation, and cultural context, provide a framework for interpreting the events and outcomes within a story.

The similarities between story and other forms of representation are illustrious. For example, when comparing story and musical works, it becomes evident that the structure of a story parallels that of a musical composition. Consider the elements embedded in a composer's production. Musical works have an introduction and a development, a recapitulation, a variation on a theme, and a denouement. As the theme is developed, the listener may become acutely engaged in attending to the melody, often referred to as the thematic content, or may focus on the harmony, the dynamics, the tonality, the metric movement, the intervalic patterns, and the tempo.

Comparable to the ways in which an individual processes hearing or reading a story, the listener constructs his or her own personal experience and meaning while listening to a musical composition. There is no assurance that the listener's experience is synonymous with the composer's intentions. The listener's experience is unique—contextualized and embedded in his or her previous experiences, tacit knowledge, and connectedness to the exposition.

Much like listeners use musical components to construct meaning when they hear a musical composition, narrative researchers employ codes and conventions to construct stories, relay their interpretations (as exemplified in music by melody, dynamics, and harmony), convey the sequence of incidents (demonstrated by meter, intervalic patterns, and tempo in music), and describe a synthesis of events that occurs by way of a story (illustrated in music by development, recapitulation, variation on a theme, and denouement). By its very nature, a story involves an agent who acts to achieve goals that can be interpreted in understandable ways. Story establishes the "ordinary" and the demonstration of the truth as it is experienced.

Story or narrative inquiry belongs to the classroom ecology paradigm that includes sociolinguistic meditative research on teaching, as well as qualitative, interpretive, and psychoanalytic forms of inquiry (Martin and Sugarman, 1993). Story or narrative inquiry is an ethnographic form of qualitative research that involves telling or recounting. The uses of narrative forms of inquiry are exemplified by microanalyses of teacher-student classroom interactions within specific curriculum areas (Clandinin and Connelly, 1988, and Connelly and Clandinin, 1990, 1988, 1986), documentations of teachers' reflections (Cochran-Smith and Lytle, 1993, 1990; Elbaz, 1991; Kagan, 1988; Leinhardt, 1990; Schon 1987; Shulman, 1987; and Yinger, 1987), and microanalyses of social and community factors that influence schooling, teaching, and learning (Peshkin, 1978).

Story research emphasizes learning how to teach and seeks to elucidate teachers' ways of knowing. The use of narrative inquiry is predicated on the belief that teachers' thought processes, not solely their behavior, are essential to the knowledge base of research on teachers' thinking. It is important to bear in mind that the knowledge that results from narratives is qualitatively different from formal theoretical knowledge. Formal theoretical knowledge represents the synthesis of interactions taking place within a particular context and the classroom situations in which knowledge is transformed into action. In contrast, story knowledge attempts to relate predefined observables to a theoretical context. In story, the teacher is the unit of analysis.

By highlighting the teacher, credence is given to an assumption that teachers bring a specialized set of social relationships and experiences to the classroom that are important components in the development of knowledge. Although the practical knowledge that coalesces as practitioners interact in the classroom results in knowledge in action, that quality of knowledge is integrally interwoven with the teachers' expertise. One must exercise caution when interpreting the meaning of practical knowledge. The validity of classroom experience may be misleading, since teachers are generally very isolated while experiencing and perceiving events. The perceptions that teachers form may be limited by the depth and breadth of their own experience or bias. In contrast, others have argued that teachers' active reflection on their own classroom experience acts as a powerful instructor that facilitates teachers' development of beliefs and perceptions of themselves as learners and helps them acquire practical knowledge (Connelly and Clandinin, 1986). Narrative research acknowledges the importance of the teacher's role by underscoring the value of teacher autonomy and reflection.

The overall purpose of story research is to fill a gap in the knowledge base of teaching by crafting a mode for teachers' voices and providing a means to understand the interpretive frames that teachers use to improve their classroom practices (Cochran-Smith and Lytle, 1990). Narratives emphasize teachers' own interpretations of context-specific classrooms, by elucidating the context in which decisions are made. Narrative research provides an avenue to bring about a conscious awareness of teachers' professional reasoning. The common thread in narrative studies is the overarching emphasis on the validity of teachers' judgments drawn from their own experiences.

Sparks-Langer and Bernstein-Colton (1991) claim that several benefits are derived from research that uses teacher narrative. First, by creating a detailed description of a teacher's everyday life, these studies are believed to heighten an awareness regarding what motivates teachers' actions. Second, teachers' narratives provide material for instructional case study. Third, gained as a result of self-reflection, narratives can encourage the development of teachers' insight. Sparks-Langer and Bernstein-Colton (1991) contend that narrative research represents a bridge to a new way of thinking about teachers' thinking. In contradistinction, it is thought that many contemporary researchers who are philosophically opposed to the use of empirical forms of methodological inquiry have chosen to employ the sociolinguistic techniques (literary analysis and psychoanalysis) of the humanities in the context of educational research.

Meaning that evolves from using the narrative inquiry paradigm emerges from the use of interpretive and analytical frameworks. Narrative inquiry attempts to convey an understanding of the events in specific educational contexts under investigation by generating rich and thick descriptions and without relying on causal, associative data treatments and analyses. One of the fundamental assumptions underlying the application of narrative methodology lies in the belief that the interaction of teachers' personal biographies with particular situations helps them understand their own use and application of practical knowledge. Narrative inquiry also seeks to explicate teachers' ways and origins of knowing by analyzing their reflective thought processes and related behaviors.

Few would disagree that environmental factors, such as the contextual, organizational, or bureaucratic structures indigenous to specific school environments, also influence teachers' thinking, behaviors, and reflection in action. However, it is somewhat remarkable that little attention has been given to understanding the ways in which these environmental structures actually influence teachers' behavior or mediate their display of practical knowledge. Generally, it is understood that individual responses can perhaps be predicted in laboratory settings or role-play situations. In real-world or actual contexts, however, planned responses may be sacrificed for behaviors that are perceived as normative within the context of the culture in which they are expressed. Teachers may experience pressure to conform to the contextual influences of the power structures within which they have to co-exist.

CONCEPTUAL FRAMEWORKS

Advantages of Story

Advocates for the use of story research assert that it has unique benefits. They claim that these benefits can not be realized solely by the use of empirical methodologies. Proponents for story research claim that

1. Stories give meaning and convey a sense of experience;
2. Stories acts as a frame to counter the technical and empirical modes of inquiry that have dominated research on teachers' thinking;
3. Stories portray women's specialized way of knowing (Belenky, Clinchy, Goldberger, and Tarule, 1986; Helle, 1991) and provide them with a representative voice in the research literature; and
4. Storied knowledge can be organized into explanatory frameworks in which the cultural and contextual variables that serve as interpretive lenses for comprehending one's experiences can be analyzed.

Advocates for storytelling research also suggest that experienced teachers use narrative structures (story) as a frame for organizing, interpreting, and integrating their use and application of curriculum knowledge (Gudmundsdottir, 1991). They claim that the documentation of stories offers educators and researchers unique access to teachers' specialized ways of knowing (Carter and Doyle, 1987). The documentation of stories, it is believed, can illuminate the relationship between teachers' intended actions and actual experiences. Because teachers experience their work as a complexity of social events driven (in part) by knowledge they have derived from other teachers' stories, proponents of story believe that knowledge results in teachers' acquisition of event-structured knowledge (Carter, 1993; Carter and Doyle, 1987; Carter and Gonzales, 1990) that promotes expertise in teaching.

Criticisms of Story

Critics of story claim that storytelling suffers from an absence of an "authenticity judge" (Klein and Greene, 1993) and an inability to "... distinguish a scholarly interpretation of a classroom event from that of a delirious observer" (Salomon, 1991, p. 10). Some researchers suggest that the use of story research results from a researcher's inability to use experimental design methods and statistical techniques for data analysis. Essentially, story is portrayed as an indefensible form of inquiry and a victim of the fluidity that characterizes the context in which data are collected. Even Connelly and Clandinin (1990), who rely heavily on narrative inquiry in their own research, seem to suggest that perhaps narrative inquiry provides a research agenda that gives "curriculum professors something to do" (Schwab, 1983). Others have criticized story for placing extreme emphasis on teachers' personal meaning and exaggerating the significance of the writer. They say that such an unbalanced presentation tends to confer unwarranted authenticity on teachers' experience (Carter, 1993) and rewards narcissism. Basic problems of knowledge claims associated with elevating teachers' stories to a "privileged status" have yet to be systematically addressed.

In an overall sense, storytelling is a variation on reflection. Through reflection, individuals analyze, question, or privately re-evaluate their own behavior and perceptions. While engaged in reflection,[1] individuals may consider the wisdom and perceptions of others. Reflection is essential to the processes involved in analysis, but clearly this technique is not new; reflection has been around for more than fifty years. The ability to reflect is a quality of good practitioners who are intuitive individuals. Thus, some researchers assert that the use of the term "reflection" is faddish.

Limitations of Story and Narrative

Several limitations regarding the disadvantages of story have been cited:

1. The relationship between story and reality as defined by the experiences of an outside observer does not necessarily portray a one-to-one correspondence;
2. Selecting a story for teaching purposes conveys a particular conception of teaching to students. Since these descriptions are open to multiple meanings, the complexities portrayed

---

[1] *Reflection* refers to the process of engaging in thoughtful, deliberative thinking about an event, subject matter, an idea, or a purpose.

sometimes lead to confusion in teaching (Carter, 1993). The possibilities for different interpretations are also a function of the perspectives and experiences that students engaged in the study of story bring to the task.
3. Story does not represent a consensually agreed upon or scholarly curriculum. Therefore the use of story as curriculum for training teachers raises questions regarding what knowledge is worth most. One must wonder, if told stories represent those of solely the dominant culture, how does this curriculum promote pedagogical practice for people of color, women, underrepresented populations, and the underprivileged classes? How do the contextualized ethnography research findings embedded in case studies help us better understand what teachers should consider doing in classrooms?
4. The interpretations that emerge from narrative inquiry are not open to verification, since they emanate from beliefs that are the collaborative construction of the teacher (interviewee) and researcher (interviewer).
5. The generalizability and utility of interpretations are also open to argumentation. A person's interpretations of narratives are influenced by belief systems that are a product of his or her own cultural framework. Are neutrality or unbiased perceptions possible? Can we claim that the evidence derived from interpretations truly corresponds to an objective reality or renders any universally valid principles or laws (Greene, 1994)?
6. Paradigmatic assumptions about the value of various research methodologies also play a role in interpretations that emerge from narrative research. Story has been criticized for amplifying moralistic, narcissistic, and omnipotent representations. Calling our attention to these concerns, Hargreaves (1994) suggests that the voice given to teachers through narrative research has come to represent teachers as an entity. He claims that this notion is a highly morally laden and prescriptive voice, not an empirical or actual representation of all teachers. Hargreaves points out that latter career teachers do not necessarily exemplify "care" for their students. Research on teachers' thought and voice is replete with teachers who are humanistic and caring, but not with those who are cynical or who lack knowledge or an understanding of pedagogy. Although the re-

search literature amplifies the positive, moral characteristics of teachers, these qualities are not necessarily common to the representation of all teachers.

According to Hargreaves (1994), this moral singularity of teachers' voice needs to be deconstructed. Research on teaching shows that didactic moralistic instruction seems to dominate classrooms even today. Many teachers tend to see classrooms from their position of power, authority, privileged status, and role instead of from the viewpoint of their students. One can build a strong case for the notion that understanding teachers' voice should be a priority, but we must be careful not to romanticize these "voices" or accord them unwarranted authenticity. One of the most poignant criticisms leveled against stories is that they amplify a sense of narcissism, by exemplifying delusions of omnipotence and highlighting the sense of a boundless self (Hargreaves, 1994). If narrative inquiry is likely to be accepted by the research community at large, these concerns obligate disputation or serious consideration about whether or not to modify the techniques involved in the process of gathering storytelling data.

EPISTEMOLOGICAL ISSUES

Assumptions Underlying Interpretation

Connelly and Clandinin (1990) claim that the primary value of narrative inquiry resides in its quality as subject matter and its capacity to render life experiences. However, certain difficulties exist, since falsehood may be substituted for meaning and narrative truth by using criteria that engenders significance, value, and intention. Meanings told do not necessarily represent the interviewer's interpretation of the teacher (interviewee). Furthermore, secondary or tertiary levels of interpretations may be falsely created. Methodological errors in interpretation of narrative can occur from attempts to generalize the events of story. One may misrepresent the truth and alter actualities by fabricating a recounting of the events. Narrative smoothing (Spence, 1986) may result from an obscurity of facts, leaving open questions of what is not being told. Gadamer (1960) concurs and reminds us that "The interpreter experiences two claims: one from the object of the interpretation ... and one from the interpreters' own lived circumstances" (pp. 124–125). "Prejudgments and prejudices can not be set aside, since they have so much to do with shaping those *interpretations*" (italics added) (Greene, 1994, p. 438).

Sanctifying and formulating an epistemology to support storytelling work is insufficient for creating a new paradigm for research on teacher thinking without addressing the assumptions that underlie this method or without considering those posited by empirical researchers. Researchers are still grappling with the issue that story has been criticized on epistemological grounds because the criteria of acceptance are rooted in contextualism. Moreover, the interpretations gathered from story data do not necessarily yield practical information, because the meanings embedded in story are not always accessible to the reader. Nespor and Barlyske (1991) contend that when researchers use narratives as a tool for constructing knowledge, they are describing, discovering, or identifying objects that really exist. However, those researchers use teachers' constructions of the object, which has been fashioned according to the needs of the researchers. In this sense, narratives are used to express relations of power and the political agendas of researchers, not as a tool to discover truth and expand the pluralistic knowledge base of research on teacher thinking.

Nespor and Barlyske point out the fallacy associated with the premise that narratives index fundamental structures of thought or experience, as Bruner (1986), Connelly and Clandinin (1990), Gergen and Gergen (1986), Polkinghorne (1988), and others suggest. The representational fallacy is that entities that emerge within story actually preexist and contribute to the creation of that discourse. Researchers reify narrative discourse, make inferences from nonobservable mental processes, and then use discourse as evidence for the existence of the inferred processes. Thus a sophisticated and esoteric, but circular and indefensible, system of reasoning has been created to forge the acceptance of a nontraditional method of research. In spite of these epistemological issues, the number of publications and presentations grounded in narrative research has recently burgeoned. Is narrative research actually more prevalent than the empirical and technical (traditional) forms of inquiry than has been previously acknowledged? How much of our current research, case studies, and the like are grounded in empirical interpretations that represent forms of story?

Connelly and Clandinin (1990, pp. 7–9) have defined criteria for narrative as grounded in a white, educated, and Anglo-American society. This perspective contradicts their assumption that narrative reflects basic human cognitive structures that mirror normative methodological inquiry. The historical specificity that defines criteria for narrative is class biased, gender biased, and culturally biased if the criteria of acceptance are based solely on the value system of the dominant culture and middle-class standards. Using these criteria as the standard ignores the diversity, richness, and thickness of experience that narrative can exemplify.

Narrative is a culturally specific communication that imposes certain societal structural characteristics. For example, there may be difficulty in determining whose narrative is being told, that of the teacher (interviewee) or the researcher (interviewer). According to Willinsky (1989), representation is always a matter of power that should be treated with skepticism. Recounting one's history and related social events does not always portray the lived experience of the teacher's discourse. An account may be told through the lived experiences or interpretation of the researcher; however, the latter may reflect the researcher's desire for recognition (Crapanzano, 1980, pp. 9–10).

Conceptual Roots of Story

Epistemologically, story is conceptually rooted in mentalistic psychology, as opposed to behavioral psychology. Kendler (1993) stated that the differences between these branches of psychology are methodological, not theoretical. He asserted that selecting behavior as the dependent variable does not negate the use of hypotheses about mentalistic processes as long as theoretical mentalistic assumptions have testable behavioral implications. In contrast, the behaviorists would argue that by promoting techniques of self-observation, "the unbiased scrutiny of experience" (MacLeod, 1968) is unachievable because conscious experience is private and available only to the self-observer, although most people are incapable of self-awareness. Behaviorists also claim that it is only when an event can be observed by more than one person that socially agreed upon criteria can be adopted that might lead to agreement about what has been observed.

The overarching dilemma is that researchers engaged in narrative inquiry can not provide veracity or socially agreed upon criteria by which to judge the content and value of story. Pondering the notion of either/or perspectives, Keller (1985) contends that this dichotomy is akin to the male/female opposition. She links the abstract and objectivist to masculine modes of thinking and self-interpretation, but challenges male claims to universalism and neutrality. Greene (1994) concurs with Keller and states, "For mainstream and technical thinkers (often including some doctrinal Marxists), so-called *subjective* views are suspect in part because they are associated with embeddedness or situatedness and, by extension, with the female" (p. 433).

Psychology can not resolve the debate over whether qualitative or quantitative methodology is better. However, psychology can shed light on the consequences of adopting competing principles. The dilemma facing the empiricists is that they can not provide value-free information devoid of expressions that reveal the researcher's political or value commitments. Some will insist that behavioral methodology seeks to attain political power control, not truth (explanation). On the other hand, the subjective conceptions associated with qualitative research can be criticized for failure to distinguish between those value judgments (emphasis on controlled observations, use of comparisons groups, statistical significance) intrinsically associated with empiricism, and those that can be detached from empirical evidence.

One of the major issues that empiricists have yet to grapple with lies in the limitations associated with the knowledge claims that empirical researchers offer. As Greene (1994) asserts,

> Too many researchers still find it difficult to confront the effects of technicism on their thinking or to face the problem of objectivity. The desire for precision and disinterestedness continues on, sometimes as a corrective against what is viewed as uncontained relativism and reliance on mere *opinion*. [P. 432]

Another limitation associated with empiricism is its inability to discern if the quality of research illuminates the social consequences associated with competing methodologies. Technocratic research varies in its ability to empirically predict consequences associated with assumptions underlying qualitative and quantitative methods of research. Second, knowledge claims that emanate from the notional quality of behavioral concepts may or may not be socially defensible.

The difficulty associated with narrative inquiry as a phenomenological and mentalistic conception of psychology resides in its inability to offer persuasive knowledge claims that society can trust. Kendler's (1993) claim that empirical researchers need to abandon their assumptions that quantifiable research can identify definitive principles that describe predictable human behavior should be instructive to those who believe that a strict use of empirical methodology can guide teaching and teacher education programs. Kendler also suggests that empiricists must give up the notion that a gap between what is and what ought to be can be bridged only by empirical evidence.

Kendler receives support from Martin and Sugarman (1993), who contend that research on teaching that relies primarily on an empirical enterprise is ill-fated because of an overemphasis on methodology. Furthermore they assert that empirical researchers have failed to adequately address the epistemological problems that confront assumptions underlying their work. Much of the empirical research on teaching (a) lacks an underlying theory that identifies specific variables; (b) provides an insufficient description of the characteristics of focal variables that are particularly worthy of empirical scrutiny; or (c) fails to explain why empirically based evidence is pragmatically unmanageable (Martin and Sugarman, 1993). One might ask how research based on narrative inquiry can be advocated when it seems to be based purely on rationally biased assumptions.

Current debates about research on teachers have focused primarily on using methodological and epistemological paradigms instead of on providing a theoretically defensible argument for the empirical preoccupation. However, as Martin and Sugarman have pointed out, during the proliferation of empirical studies, no new scientific understandings or heuristics have been made available for practitioners.

FUTURE DIRECTIONS

Although the use of story is an emergent power in educational research, teachers' stories do not provide us with a political or paradigmatic base from which to create new understandings. Contextual parameters need to be established in order to illuminate the potential contributions of research that relies on story.[2] One avenue to capitalizing on the unrealized benefits of story

---

[2] I. Goodson: personal communication, April 8, 1994.

research may involve macrolizing the location of story. *Macrolizing* means to take a macro or global perspective and move beyond the analysis of individual stories as they exist in micro or singular educational contexts. Macrolizing refers to the process of creating a quantifiable database and analyzing all of the stories that emerge in a particular location by assessing common themes, patterns, or traits that emerge across locations. Since the ultimate aim of story or narrative research is to mediate pedagogically, politically, and educationally what we want to share, the categorization and organization of information gleaned from story research seems to be a logical progression from accumulating individual stories.

A review of the research literature on narrative inquiry reveals that the predominant purpose of story resides in its ongoing efforts to create an awareness about what teachers do and how they teach. Each teacher's story seeks to impart something of a practical nature regarding how that particular teacher copes with instructional and curricular matters in the context of his or her environment. However, the emergent insights derived from one's own story or a study of stories have implications only in the context in which the story was located. What does continued research on classroom ecology using narrative as the methodological vehicle portend for training teachers? Perhaps the time is ripe to create teacher education programs that use individualistic, sociolinguistic, and psychoanalytically anchored approaches to teacher preparation (Combs, 1965). Perhaps storytelling research offers unrealized instructional potential to teacher educators.

Clearly we need to reassess the potential utility of story and bring narrative methodology to a more sophisticated level of productiveness. Suppose, for example, that we obtained narratives from the teachers in several schools and created a database of multiple stories and organized the descriptive findings that emerged from narrative studies into analytical or classificatory systems. Perhaps patterns or classificatory systems of action would coalesce and reveal how teachers use story or how professional reasoning guides their practice. An analysis of these classificatory systems of action might also highlight the reciprocal relationships between teachers' thinking process and their behaviors. Subsequently, tangible connections between practice and theory might be synthesized. By organizing the data into logical categories, quantifying multiple stories, as well as the contextual and demographic variables related to the occurrences of and characterizations of self-awareness, the applicability of story research might be substantiated.

Methodological approaches in other fields might be instructive to educators conducting research on teachers. Consider the potential utility of methods used in health care. Within medicine, particularly psychiatry, patients' case histories have been documented and chronicled. They became codified sources for illustrating classificatory systems of mental disorders. Subsequently, this information became a database for the diagnostic statistical manuals in which characterizations of symptomatology have been organized. Volumes of case studies have been written into books to guide the effective treatment of patients. These textbooks continue to be used as primary sources for training psychiatrists, psychoanalysts, and psychologists. Using the sociolinguistic approaches employed by narrative inquiry, the findings from story research might serve to highlight effective teaching practices for students in "characteristic" or "chronicled" situations or within context-specific environments.

CONCLUSIONS

Stories are important because they constitute a legitimate arena of formal knowledge about teaching. Storied research makes knowledge about teachers' expertise accessible and provides perspectives on teaching and learning that can not be known by other forms of inquiry. However, while all forms of research rely on assumptions, it is crucial to question assumptions that underlie different conceptions of research inquiry. Most of us would probably support the notion that absolute truths will never be known about the truths of assumptions.

Concerns about the limitations of narrative research techniques have focused on the descriptive nature of narrative and have highlighted the lack of objective standards to guide improvement or gauge effectiveness. To be truly effective, narrative research should be evaluated in consideration of standards that would be used to ensure appropriate classroom practice. Changes in teachers' practice will also be necessary. Teachers will need to progress beyond the development of their own idiosyncratic theory and practice to use these standards in their classrooms (Buchmann, 1986). Furthermore, incomplete considerations about story should involve examining the possibilities for the use of story research that have not been suggested previously. Using narrative as the sole form of methodological inquiry will require agreed upon and rigorous methodological procedures, clear conceptualizations, the formulation of key assumptions, and common referents that have precise meanings and consistent usage.

Given the importance of stories, the next step should focus on rendering story knowledge accessible. Three approaches to conducting related studies are discussed. The first would involve looking at recurring patterns across different contexts and variables. To aid in this process, a conceptual framework consisting of four process-oriented principles is offered. These principles include (a) situating teachers' stories in relationship to other stories; (b) contextualizing stories in relationship to other considerations; (c) raising questions about story in relationship to social and political considerations; and (d) regrounding stories (Hargreaves, 1994).

The implementation of the first principle is predicated on increasing the use of story and building large databases of multiple stories. For example, suppose that teachers' stories were compiled for all teachers within several public and private (elementary, middle, junior high, special education, and secondary) schools. Teachers would maintain daily journals. Using content-analysis procedures, the entries in each journal would be examined. As a result, recurrent themes could be identified, categorized, and quantified within and across all journals.

Related to the second principle, themes would be categorized in relationship to demographic teacher variables (gender, age, level of education, area of subject matter expertise, socioeconomic status, race, and ethnicity), and school variables (the geographical location and type of school). If similarities across variables and contexts within thematic categories became apparent, then techniques might be employed to test for significance. Correlation techniques might be used to test for significant relationships among various subgroups and across variables and themes. Path analysis might also be used. Path-analysis techniques permit testing the validity of causal inferences for pairs of variables while controlling for the effects of other variables.

Using programs such as SAS, path models can be specified and the influence of exogenous variables (which correspond to independent constructs) on endogenous variables (which correspond to dependent variables), as influenced by other variables present in an educational context (location), can be estimated. Limitations on the meaningfulness of parameters are predicated on the researcher's ability to demonstrate the extent to which models can be shown to fit the data. If the pattern of variances and covariances derived from the model do not differ significantly from the pattern of variances and covariances related to the observed variables, then a given model is said to fit the data (Leithwood, Jantzi, and Fernandez, 1993). This evidence might serve to identify strengths and weaknesses of storytelling as a research tool. Corresponding to the third principle, these activities would cause researchers to raise questions about story themes that emerged in relationship to social and political considerations. A total analysis of the findings would then lead to regrounding stories as suggested by the fourth principle.

A second approach to expanding the use of story might involve examining the outcomes of certain emergent themes among teachers, such as teacher isolation, working with a student with disabilities, and professional disequilibrium (Cochran-Smith and Lytle, 1993, p. 231) during a teacher's transition from a novice to an advanced beginner. If teachers' actions were dissimilar for each situation reported, we might ponder if their behavior was coincidental, or influenced by one or more variables. Having actual data to look at, rather than relying on preferences or hunches, is the most appropriate means for exploring the meaning of teachers' behavior.

A third approach would consist of having several researchers analyze teachers' stories. There can be little doubt that the interviewer interjects his or her interpretive reality while recounting a teacher's story. Consider if one teacher's story was distributed among a group of researchers rather than just to one or two. What is the likelihood that the analysis or identification of thematic content would be the same? How do we separate the framework of one's own culture, experiences, or tacit knowledge from their interpretation of teachers' stories? If we gathered seven to ten teacher stories, and asked five to seven researchers to analyze the content, what degree of agreement or interrater reliability might be achieved?

There have been vociferous debates about the limitations of story and empiricism. While many of these arguments are difficult to evaluate, proaction rather than reaction is needed. Surely, there are other productive approaches to take in addressing this matter, instead of remaining paralyzed in unresolvable debates.

A marriage of empiricism and mentalistic psychology is not unreasonable given that the underlying assumptions from both camps can not be verified. Research in the field may be strengthened by a combination of these methods. The power of story to make new things possible and important in educational research becomes a reality when the researchers' aims are focused on expanding our understanding rather than on providing the one right methodology. If we begin to quantify the contexts in which teachers' themes occur, then the potential value of story as an educational research tool may be known. The substantial and quantified framework offered by these approaches may affirm the belief that by engaging educators regardless of gender, class, and culture and by giving them a voice, then story or narrative research can be used as a vehicle to direct and change lives (Noddings, 1991).

We are coming full circle in our exploration of what constitutes truth, knowledge, and viable educational research approaches. However, ultimately, we must disengage from the notion of renegotiating which research method is worth most for understanding teachers' behavior. Instead we must examine the essential means by which research methodology can inform practice. If we do not challenge the value or utility of story as a viable methodology, we will remain mired in the undisciplined and circular discourse that characterizes the debates between narrative and empirical researchers. To challenge these assumptions might give rise to an emergent linkage that I believe exists in *macrolizing* the location of multiple stories. Operationalizing this concept will require the creation of a classificatory system supported by an empirically derived system. The development of this classificatory system will serve to illustrate the relationship among teachers' reflection, thought, beliefs, and actions. Finally, attempts to codify thematic material will serve to exemplify the notional value of story and illustrate the importance of this methodology in the training of future educators.

REFERENCES

Belenky, M.; Clinchy, B.; Goldberger, N.; and Tarule, J. (1986). *Women's ways of knowing*. New York: Basic Books.

Bruner, J. (1986). *Actual minds, possible worlds*. Cambridge, Mass.: Harvard University Press.

Buchmann, M. (1986). Role over person: Morality and authenticity in teaching. *Teachers' College Record, 87,* 529–544.

Carter, K. (1993). The place of story in the study of teaching and teacher education. *Educational Researcher, 22*(1), 5–12, 18.

Carter, K., and Doyle, W. (1987). Teachers' knowledge structures and comprehension processes. In J. Calderhead (ed.), *Exploring teachers' thinking* (pp. 79–98). Hillsdale, N.J.: Erlbaum.

Carter, K., and Gonzalez, L. (1990, April). Beginning teachers' knowledge of classroom events. Paper presented at the Annual Meeting of the American Educational Research Association, Boston.

Clandinin, D. J., and Connelly, F. M. (1988). Studying teachers' knowledge of classrooms: Collaborative research, ethics, and the negotiation of narrative. *The Journal of Educational Thought., 22*(2A), 269–282.

Cochran-Smith, M., and Lytle, S. (1990). Research on teaching and teacher research: The issues that divide. *Educational Researcher, 19*(2), 2–11.

Cochran-Smith, M., and Lytle, S. (1993). *Inside/outside: Teacher research and knowledge.* New York: Teachers College Press.

Connelly, F. M. and Clandinin, D. J. (1986). On narrative method, biography, and narrative unities in the study of teaching. *Journal of Research in Science on Teaching, 24*(4), 293–320.

Connelly, F. M., and Clandinin, D. J. (1988). *Teachers as curriculum planners: Narratives of experience.* New York: Teachers College Press.

Connelly, F. M., and Clandinin, D. J. (1990). Stories of experience and narrative inquiry. *Educational Researcher, 19*(5), 2–14.

Combs, A. W. (1965). *The professional education of teachers: A perceptual view of teacher preparation.* Boston: Allyn & Bacon.

Crapanzano, V. (1980). *Tuhami.* Chicago: University of Chicago Press.

Elbaz, F. (1991). Research on teachers' knowledge: The evolution of a discourse. *Journal of Curriculum Studies, 23,* 1–19.

Gadamer, H. G. (1960). *Truth and method.* New York: Seabury Press.

Gergen, M., and Gergen, K. (1986). The social construction of narrative accounts. In K. Gergen and M. Gergen (eds.) *Historical social psychology* (pp. 173–189.) Hillsdale, N.J.: Lawrence Erlbaum.

Goodson, (1994). Personal communication. April 4, 1994.

Greene, M. (1994). Epistemology and educational research: The influence of recent approaches to knowledge. *Review of Research in Education, 20,* 423–426.

Gudmundsdottir, S. (1991). Story-maker, story-teller: Narrative structures in curriculum. *Journal of Curriculum Studies, 23,* 207–218.

Hargreaves, A. (April, 1994). Dissonant voices: Teachers and the multiple realities of restructuring. Paper presented at the Annual Meeting of the American Educational Research Association. New Orleans.

Helle, A. P. (1991). Reading women's autobiographies: A map of reconstructed knowing. In C. Witherell and N. Noddings (eds.), *Stories lives tell: Narrative and dialogue in education* (pp. 233–249). Chicago: University of Chicago Press.

Kagan, D. M. (1988). Teaching as critical problem solving: A critical examination of the analogy and its implications. *Review of Educational Research, 58*(4), 482–505.

Keller, E. F. (1985). *Reflections on gender and science.* New Haven, Conn.: Yale University Press.

Kendler, H. H. (1993). Psychology and the ethics of social psychology. *American Psychologist, 48*(10), 1046–1053.

Kleine, P. F., and Greene, B. A. (1993). Story telling: A rich history and a sordid past—a response to Berliner (1992). *Educational Psychologist, 28*(2), 185–190.

Leinhardt, G. (1990). Capturing craft knowledge in teaching. *Educational Researcher, 19*(2), 18–25.

Leithwood, K; Jantzi, D.; and Fernandez, A. (April, 1993). Secondary school teachers' commitment to change: The contributions of transformational leadership. Paper presented at the Annual Meeting of the American Educational Research Association. Atlanta, Ga.

MacLeod, R. B. (1986). Phenomenology. In D. L. Stills (ed.) *International encyclopedia of the social sciences, 12*, 68–72. New York: Macmillan and Free Press.

Martin, J., and Sugarman, J. (1993). Beyond methodolatry: Two conceptions of relations between theory and research in research on teaching. *Educational Researcher, 22*(8), 17–24.

Nespor, J., and Barlyske, J. (1991). Narrative discourse and teacher knowledge. *American Educational Research Journal, 28*(4), 805–823.

Noddings, N. (1991). Stories in dialogue: Caring and interpersonal reasoning. In C. Witherell and N. Noddings (eds.), *Stories lives tell: Narrative and dialogue in education* (pp. 155–170). New York: Teachers' College Press.

Peshkin, A. (1978). *Growing up in America: Schooling and the survival of community.* Chicago: University of Chicago Press.

Polkinghorne, D. (1988). *Narrative knowing and the human sciences.* Albany, N.Y.: State University of New York Press.

Salomon, G. (1991). Transcending the qualitative-quantitative debate: The analytic and systematic approaches to educational research. *Educational Researcher, 20*, 10–18.

Scholes, R. (1981). Language, narrative, and anti-narrative. In W. J. T. Mitchell (ed.), *On narrative* (pp. 200–208). Chicago: University of Chicago Press.

Scholes, R. (1982). *Semiotics and interpretation.* New Haven, Conn.: Yale University Press.

Schon, D. A. (1987). *Educating the reflective practitioner.* San Francisco: Jossey-Bass.

Schwab, J. J. (1983). The practical 4: Something for curriculum professors to do. *Curriculum Inquiry, 13*(3), 239–265.

Shulman, L. S. (1987). Knowledge and teaching: Foundations of the new reform. *Harvard Educational Review, 57*(1), 1–22.

Sparks-Langer, G. M., and Bernstein-Colton, A. (1991). Synthesis of research on teachers' reflective thinking. *Educational Leadership, 48*(6), 37–44.

Spence, D. P. (1986). *Narrative truth and historical method.* New York: Norton and Company.

Willinsky, J. (1989). Getting personal and practical with personal practical knowledge. *Curriculum Inquiry, 19*(3), 247–264.

Yinger, R. (1987). Learning the language of practice. *Curriculum Inquiry, 17*(3), 293–318.

10

Perspectives on Classroom Management in Learning-Centered Classrooms

Carolyn M. Evertson and Catherine H. Randolph

Definitions of classroom management abound. When we hear the term, often we think only of discipline systems—ways of managing student behavior based on teacher control of behavior. The impetus behind such a conception of management is a particular view of learning: one that demands that we get students in their seats, quiet and listening. If our definition of learning changes, however, such images, which have always been limited, become dangerously limiting as well. Silent children seated in straight rows portray the history of American education, not its future.

Currently, teachers are being encouraged or required to provide a significantly different set of experiences for students. "Schools, previously asked to ensure the development of basic skills, are now required to teach all students a new, broad range of cognitive skills. . . . (Council of Chief State School Officers [CCSSO], 1990, p. 2). Classrooms in which such transformations of learning are taking place will look different, just as their goals will be different. Higher-order learning "is complex; yields multiple solutions; requires interpretation and the use of multiple criteria;

involves uncertainty and finding structure in apparent disorder; demands self-regulation of thinking processes; and requires considerable mental effort" (CCSSO, 1990, p. 3). This is a kind of learning for which a model of management based on behavior control is woefully inadequate.

Assignments with cognitive and procedural complexity place new demands on teachers and students and are, therefore, likely to be more complex to manage (Bossert, 1979). Classroom management and the curriculum are thus interrelated (Doyle and Carter, 1984; Randolph and Evertson, 1995), an especially important point to consider in light of recent recommended changes in curriculum and practice.

Rather than review exhaustively past research on classroom management, this chapter will present and argue for the need for a complex conception of classroom management that parallels a more complex view of learning. The chapter will focus on the gap between conceptions of curriculum and conceptions of pedagogy. What we intend to do is (1) establish a definition and conceptualization of management; (2) provide examples intended to illustrate the relationship between management and instruction; and (3) propose questions to guide further inquiry into the management of complex learning tasks.

DEFINING CLASSROOM MANAGEMENT

It is helpful in any examination of classroom management to take time to establish definitions carefully, because conceptions of classroom management may be tied to research done at various points in the evolution of the concept during the twentieth century. During this time, the term "classroom management" has gone from describing discipline practices and behavioral interventions to serving as a more all-encompassing descriptor of teachers' actions. The first part of this chapter will briefly trace this evolution, identifying its implications and the potential misconceptions that often accompany discussions of management.

What Is Meant by Classroom Management?

The popular press equates the term "classroom management" with discipline, or the correction of misbehavior. We argue instead

Classroom Management

for a view of management that includes all that teachers must do to encourage learning in their classrooms, including proactively setting up an environment that encourages learning and discourages wasting time, and orchestrating instruction in ways that promote and maintain student engagement. We propose a holistic definition of classroom management, one that emphasizes teachers' ongoing choices and actions rather than narrow responses to misbehavior. "[M]isbehavior and teacher interventions can be understood only in terms of their relation to processes of orchestrating order in classrooms.... [T]hey are part of the fabric of the ecological system that defines and sustains order" (Doyle, 1986, p. 418). It is this whole "fabric" that we want to consider in this discussion of management. Our goal will be to address the intersection of management and content, and how together they impact learning. In doing so, we will be discussing management from a sociocognitive perspective.

HISTORY AND CURRENT DIRECTION OF CLASSROOM MANAGEMENT RESEARCH

In order to define classroom management, it may be helpful to begin with a brief sketch of the history of research in this area. By tracing the line of inquiry from past to present, we will try to illuminate some of the major questions and theoretical stances that have driven the field and thus differentiate our current approach from much of that work. What we will present here is by no means a complete review of the field; for this we refer readers to Doyle's (1986) thorough work. Instead, we intend to focus on the research on classroom management that informs our present work.

One way of viewing the intersection of learning and pedagogy is to consider both in terms of where they fall along two continua: from behavioral/external to cognitive/internal, and from individual to group or social (see Figure 10-1).

Definitions of learning and content that fall in the behavioral/individual quadrant would logically be paired with definitions of pedagogy/management falling in the same quadrant. Similarly, as newer models of learning emphasize its social and cognitive nature, thinking about management must also shift. In the following section we will trace the development of this shift.

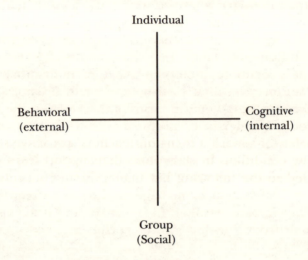

Figure 10-1
A Map for Locating Definitions of Learning and Pedagogy

Behavioral/Individual Approaches to Classroom Management

The field of classroom management has been, and in some cases remains, heavily behavioral in orientation, with chief focus on the individual. Early investigations into classroom management were prompted by an interest in fixing misbehavior, which is centrally an individual issue (Doyle, 1986). The behavioral psychological model saw the root of behavioral problems as conditioning and therefore sought to alter existing behavior in individuals through modification, incentive, and reward systems. Thus, a good deal of research in the 1960s and 1970s focused on behavior analysis and the appropriate application of rewards and deterrents. The central focus was on the individual and the individual's misbehavior. This approach to management paralleled the behaviorist, mostly individual view of learning predominant at the time.

Approaches to Managing Classroom Groups

Central to the shift from individual to group in the focus of research on classroom management was the work of Jacob Kounin, beginning in the late 1960s. Kounin's interest was in teacher desists and the effect of the desist on the students around the student who was reprimanded. He learned that there was little correspondence between desists and effective management. Once misbehavior broke out, there was no superior strategy for ending it. Instead, the distinction between effective and ineffective managers was in their ability to prevent and identify misbehavior *before* it had a chance to become disruptive (Kounin, 1970).

Kounin's work led to extensive research on proactive strategies for group management. This research on effective teaching over the past twenty years showed that the ability of teachers to organize and manage their classrooms directly impacts students' opportunities to learn, and the work also extended the concept of "classroom management" past a focus on reactive control of deviant behavior toward a focus on teachers' proactive strategies for creating conditions in classrooms that support learning. This research led to the following key management concepts.[1]

Room arrangement is essential to establishing a classroom environment in which all students have the opportunity to succeed. How the available physical space is used can have important implications for how students participate in class activities and how they may interact with the teacher and with each other. Studies in elementary and secondary classrooms have shown that effective teachers plan for the arrangement of furnishings to accommodate different types of activities, to minimize problems with disruptive movement in the classroom, and to facilitate monitoring of student work and behavior.

Studies focusing on how teachers started the school year indicated that effective managers *planned rules and procedures* in advance and had clearly in mind the ways that they would function in the classroom. Specific routines promote smooth and quick transitions between activities and thus add to instructional time. Such routines also reduce disruption that can lead to behavior problems. They help maintain lesson flow, continuity, and students' engagement in academic work.

Effective teachers developed procedures not only to *hold students accountable*, but also to help them become accountable for both academic work and behavior. These teachers made sure that they checked students' work regularly, provided feedback and correctives, and rechecked to make certain students were learning concepts correctly.

---

[1] These findings have been described and explored elsewhere (e.g., Evertson and Emmer, 1982; Evertson, Emmer, Sanford, and Clements, 1983; Evertson, 1985; Evertson, 1989), and readers are referred to those sources for further information.

One way effective managers anticipated potential problems was to *discuss with students rules and procedures, the rationales for these regulations, and the accompanying rewards and penalties.* These teachers provided evidence that rules and procedures are more likely to be followed if students have a clear idea of the expected behaviors and the consequences for their cooperation or noncooperation. Ultimately, a teacher's goal is to help students develop self-control and manage their own behavior. A clear understanding of the consequences of a given behavior can be a step toward this end.

Effective managers regularly *monitored* their classes or groups and watched for signs of student confusion. Teachers are unlikely to be able to deal with student inattention or stop misbehavior before it spreads if they do not see it in the first place. Likewise, teachers can appear inconsistent in reinforcing their classroom rules and procedures if they are not aware of infractions. If some students are consistently out of the teacher's line of sight, it may signal to these students that they are not as accountable for their work or behavior as others in the class. All of these things can lead to management problems that can become more severe as time goes on. Still, the importance of monitoring does not lie only in the detection of potential behavior problems. Monitoring also provides teachers with important information about student performance, the appropriateness of assignments, and the like. Effective managers monitored actively, moving around the room to touch base with all students, rather than focusing on only those who could be seen from the front.

Effective managers were aware of student needs as they *organized instruction.* Activities in these classrooms were paced so that students had enough to do; assignments reflected an awareness of student attention spans and interests; and down time between assignments or activities was minimized.

Teachers in classrooms that ran smoothly had *instructional clarity*: they described their objectives clearly, gave precise instructions for assignments, and responded to students' questions with understandable explanations.

The principles listed above were derived from classrooms in which teachers took key responsibility for directing all activity. While this work on management clearly moved from an emphasis on the individual to an emphasis on the group, management and learning in these classrooms was still on the behavioral end of the continuum presented in Figure 10-1. A potential weakness for applying these findings from the late 1970s to today's classrooms is that the classrooms in which these studies were conducted, and from which these principles were derived, looked very different from the classrooms we are encouraging teachers to orchestrate today. For the most part, teachers in these classrooms led whole-group lessons consisting of lecture, recitation, and seatwork from the front of the room, or met with ability-based small groups while other students worked silently and singly at their desks. Such classrooms are a far cry from the dynamic, active, interactive settings described and promoted in current professional literature. How, then, do these principles apply to today's very different settings? Answering this question requires a closer look at the nature of classrooms as social and cultural entities.

CONTRIBUTIONS OF SOCIOCULTURAL STUDIES TO CLASSROOM MANAGEMENT

A number of studies have examined classrooms as social and communicative settings, and their findings are central to understanding classroom management from a sociocognitive perspective. As attempts are made to rethink, restructure, and rework curriculum, and as classrooms continue to become more and more diverse with respect to students' ethnic origins, primary languages, and abilities and disabilities, issues of classroom management that have been dormant have once again become central.

Research on classroom processes during the last twenty years has highlighted important structural features of well-organized classrooms. These features include identification of students' social and academic participation patterns. However, knowing that these features exist falls short of helping us understand how they evolve in any given classroom. Unfortunately, progress toward understanding the interplay among participants and factors that influence what occurs in classrooms has been slow. The challenges that hinder our understanding stem in part from what has been a false dichotomy in the ways we view relationships between classroom management and instructional processes (Evertson and Weade, 1991).

That is, effective management has typically been regarded as a matter of first-order importance, or a necessary precondition, after which effective instruction follows (cf. Evertson, Emmer, Sanford, and Clements, 1983; Emmer, Sanford, Clements, and Martin, 1983). Such a view is contradicted by the reality of classroom life. Observers note, for instance, that when they watch the ongoing stream of talk and interaction in the real time and space of a classroom, distinctions between management and instruction become blurred (Zumwalt, 1986, cited in Evertson and Weade, 1991).

Sociocultural theorists argue that a child's experience during a lesson involves three concurrent strands: (1) responding to curriculum content; (2) managing the classroom culture; and (3) participating in sociocultural processes (Alton-Lee, Nuthall, and Patrick, 1993). Students are thus highly active in interpreting when and how they may participate (Green and Weade, 1985).

Defining Classroom Management from a Sociocognitive Perspective

Incorporating information from sociocultural studies of classrooms allows us to interpret classroom management principles for learning-centered classrooms. Models of learning in classrooms fall into the social cognitive quadrant of Figure 10-1. As we have argued elsewhere (Randolph and Evertson, 1994; 1995), changes in classrooms from teacher-centered to student-centered instruction imply major changes in the roles of both teachers and students, the expectations participants have of each other, and the definitions of teaching and learning that ultimately evolve in the setting. For example, in one process writing classroom (explored by Randolph, 1993), teacher and student roles are redefined to include teacher tasks in the job of studenting and student tasks in the job of teaching. The teacher delegates authority over some areas of classroom control, including the nature of the text, the form of an individual's participation, and leadership of large-group discussions. She exposes the improvisational nature of writing and teaching as processes, and defines herself as a learner. As a result, teacher and students share power over knowledge as they negotiate both content and management.

Students, particularly those who are unfamiliar with this kind of classroom, must be prepared for these changes and taught their new roles. Consider the example of whole-class discussion presented in Table 10-1.

Table 10-1
Continuum of Task Demands Varying by Level of Teacher-Directedness

Unitask		Multitask
Recitation	Teacher-Led Discussion	Student-Led Discussion
Teacher tasks	*Teacher tasks*	*Teacher tasks*
Ask questions	Ask most questions	Ask framing questions
Nominate individual responders	Nominate responders	Nominate initial responder
Evaluate accuracy of responses	Reflect responses back to group	Respond to student questions
	Manage student responses to each other	Observe, provide management support as necessary
Student tasks	*Student tasks*	*Student tasks*
Listen to teacher	Listen to teacher	Listen to teacher, peers
Volunteer to respond	Volunteer to respond	Volunteer to respond
Give correct answer	Respond to ideas of teacher and other students	Call on peers
		Respond to teacher and other students
Purpose of activity	*Purpose of activity*	*Purpose of activity*
Evaluate success of transfer of knowledge from teacher and/test	Evaluate success of transfer of knowledge from teacher and/text	Explore student understandings
	Encourage knowledge growth	Encourage knowledge growth
		Create new knowledge
Assessment	*Assessment*	*Assessment*
Based on number of correct answers	Based on number of correct answers and new ideas	Based on number of correct answers, new ideas, building of new communal knowledge

Students in column 1 (recitation) have predictable tasks to perform as part of the group's discussion. They are expected to be familiar with the content being drilled in the recitation, and content in this format has a particular definition: facts or right or wrong statements, with their origins in either a teacher or textbook presentation. In a recitation setting, teacher and students are likely to agree closely on what the content is and on whether students' answers are right or wrong. In the case of disagreement, there is often an outside source (e.g., a textbook, worksheet, or teacher's guide) to which participants can refer for clarification. There are also particular demands for participation: students are usually asked to raise their hands and respond individually to the teacher when called on by her or him. While there may be some variation in the formality and rigidity of these rules, in all cases the teacher remains the arbiter of both acceptable content and appropriate participation.

Contrast these demands with those made on students in column 3 (discussion). These students are also expected to be familiar with the content under discussion, but "content" is likely to take on a different meaning. In this format, content may be much more widely conceptualized, possibly including students' past experiences, opinions, independent research findings, and new ideas sparked by the ongoing conversation, as well as the more traditional textbook and teacher information, which form the foundation of a recitation. In contrast to a recitation, participants in a discussion may have disagreements about the appropriateness or relevance of a particular comment to a discussion. Students' content demands may thus include not only sharing information, but also defending that information as a valid and valuable contribution to the topic under discussion.

Students' participation demands in a discussion are also very different from those demands in a recitation. There may still be rules requiring participants to raise their hands, or there may not. Often, students in a true discussion are expected to talk to each other rather than to the teacher, and to nominate the next speaker rather than waiting for the teacher to do so (e.g., Randolph, 1993). Arbiters of participation and content are likely to be students rather than the teacher.

Clearly, as this single example shows, activities that can be described as "teacher-centered" make greatly different demands on teachers and students than do activities that can be described as "student-centered." Where, then, is the overlap in managing these distinctly different settings? Whether a teacher is leading a recitation or a discussion, it is clear that students must have certain questions clarified for them:

What is my role here?
What counts as knowledge and knowing?
How do I get to participate?
What behaviors or comments will be considered appropriate or inappropriate?

In other words, in both settings, students must be taught the content and participation demands that will be in place. No matter how student-centered a classroom is intended to be, it is the teacher's responsibility to think through these demands, to assist students in thinking them through, and to make sure that they are made visible to all participants, so that all have equitable opportunities to participate successfully.

A straightforward example of teaching roles to students, and of the overlap between content and management, comes from one process writing classroom (Randolph, 1993), where a frequently recurring activity involved students reading aloud to the rest of the class. During each six-week unit, students read favorite examples of particular genres (for example, during the first unit each child brought a favorite children's book to share), they read aloud their own work in progress, and they read their final drafts as a form of publication. Review of the teacher's instructions to students on each of the first few occasions that these activities occurred demonstrates her careful attention to defining student roles.

On the first day of class, the teacher began to establish content expectations by explaining that the class, called "English" on student programs, would in fact involve speaking, listening, reading, and writing. As students participated in activities on the first few days of school, the teacher continually referred back to these content goals and to the implications of those goals for student participation. At the start of each class during the first unit where students stood to read aloud, the teacher reviewed the roles of speaker and listener: speakers were to get the audience's attention and to read loudly and clearly; listeners were to pay attention and respond. She consistently reminded students that in taking on these roles, they were practicing speaking, listening, and reading.

Another example can be seen in examining the classrooms envisioned in Schools for Thought, a project of the Learning Technology Center at Peabody College, Vanderbilt University (Bruer, 1993). One common activity structure in these upper-elementary-school classrooms is the use of small-group inquiry centers, through which students rotate daily to weekly. Each center has an activity related to a central content theme; in a particular unit, for example, students may work together to create a map at one center, to do independent research at another, to create a computer-based demonstration at another, and so on. In order to implement such a complex model effectively, teachers must plan proactively for the kinds of skills and knowledge students will need. Their planning must include not only "academic" (content-related) knowledge and skills, but also procedural knowledge and skills, of the kinds discussed above. Students in these settings will have to know

How and when to move from group to group
What is an appropriate noise/voice level for group interaction
How, when, and from whom to get help with academic content
How, when, and from whom to get help with procedural content
How, when, and where to obtain needed materials

Clearly, those teachers who attempt to jump into content instruction without teaching students the requisite skills for participation are likely to have greater difficulty in facilitating student investigations than are those who approach the teaching of procedural skills directly. Teachers who take time at the beginning to teach units with lower content demands and higher emphasis on procedures are more likely to have classrooms that function effectively and truly facilitate student learning in the long run.[2]

Johnston has outlined how teachers in Schools for Thought classrooms must alter their ways of thinking about one central classroom management concept, monitoring. He points out that an exclusively procedural approach to monitoring will be inadequate; instead, these teachers must carefully monitor for both behavioral and academic goals, acknowledging their interwoven nature. As teachers circulate to observe small groups in process, a procedural approach would merely assess whether participants' interactions were within acceptable parameters for on-task behavior. A purely academic approach might mean that teachers listen for only key words and concepts in deciding whether the discussions were proceeding appropriately. Johnston, however, advises teachers to take a step back from either of these approaches, to consider both social and academic goals for the activity. Socially, teachers want students to be interacting; however, these interactions must be seen in light of the cognitive goals for the interaction, which involve making connections with students' previous experiences and constructing new knowledge. As teachers monitor, then, they must examine progress toward both types of goals. Their responses to students must reflect the multiple purposes for the activity, pushing students in their explorations of content as well as in maintaining appropriate behavior.

---

[2] J. Johnston: personal communication, September 25, 1995.

FLAWED ASSUMPTIONS ABOUT CLASSROOM MANAGEMENT

The preceding discussion points up some flaws inherent in three common beliefs about the nature of classroom management. The first is that management is largely, if not completely, an activity carried out by the teacher. This idea would be adequate if students were passive recipients of learning in classrooms. In fact, however, sociocultural studies have documented the ways in which all classroom activities are influenced by both the teacher and the students. When viewed from a social interaction perspective, classroom lessons are products. They are outcomes of dynamically evolving actions of and interactions between teacher and students. A social expectation is not merely stated and adhered to, just as it might be listed in a student handbook or among a set of "rules" posted on a classroom wall. In a similar vein, the academic content of a lesson is not a given; it cannot be inferred from a curriculum guide or a scripted lesson plan. Instead, expectations are signalled and various interpretations of these signals are supported or rejected through the participants' talk and actions. Information is revealed to participants in a time-ordered, topic-by-topic, and bit-by-bit fashion. As these bits evolve, they link together to form a coherent "text" of the evolving lesson. Meanings, however, are not simply extracted by students; they are actively constructed. In order to gain access, participants must monitor what is being said (or written or read), how it is being considered, what is being accepted or rejected in relation to the topic-at-hand, and how others are responding to the information provided. Management, instead of being a teacher activity, is jointly negotiated by teacher and students as they interact across the school year.

A second flawed belief about classroom management is that it is a content-free set of behaviors. In this view, management is something that takes place in order to prepare students for content, which comes later. This isolation of management from content is faulty. As Marshall (1990) argues,

> A social constructivist conception [of learning] implies that we need to focus on the social context within which academic tasks are presented and within which academic cognitions are constructed. For example, the social context of the classroom conveys messages about what counts as learning, such as whether the product or the process is important.

> Teachers and students construct this context through their interactions with each other and within and around lessons (Green, Weade, and Graham, 1988). The meaning of lessons and the goals of school are constructed as well through opportunities provided and the interactions between the individuals in these contexts. For example, when teachers present writing lessons as worksheets to complete, the interactions surrounding the task convey a different message about learning and writing than when teachers introduce writing lessons as avenues for the expression and construction of new ideas. [P. 97]

Thus, as the teacher makes management decisions, she or he is also communicating messages about the nature of the content being managed. Rather than being content-free, management subtly serves to define content.

A third problematic belief is that classroom management is a set of discrete behaviors. "Most teaching researchers, whether experimental psychologists interested in instructional design . . . or effectiveness researchers, have tended to view classroom processes in a restricted sense as actions (explaining, prompting, reinforcing) that directly foster learning rather than as the sum total of what teachers do in classroom settings" (Doyle, 1986, p. 392). This belief is tenable only given a particular conception of what a classroom is. If classrooms are settings characterized by a series of isolated events that when added together equal learning, then management can be viewed as one aspect of these isolated events. Learning in this case is thought of as beads on a string, and classrooms are places where teachers take beads from their collections and hand them to students (Evertson and Murphy, 1992). When the model of learning described earlier in the statement from the CCSSO is adopted, this beads-on-a-string image must be replaced, and this change has implications for our conception of management.

PRINCIPLES OF EFFECTIVE CLASSROOM MANAGEMENT

Returning now to the principles of classroom management presented earlier in this chapter, we will present the bedrock of the principles that is applicable, we believe, to settings of any type. First, it is clear that effective management is proactive. Research clearly indicates that a comprehensive management system begins from the first day of school, as opposed to a focus on consequences once undesired behavior has occurred. Effective teachers, regardless of their philosophy of teaching, must think through what students will need to know in order to participate successfully, and teach those skills. The more complex instruction is, the more important teachers' assessment of these needs becomes.

Second, effective teachers take an active role in monitoring students' academic and social progress. Depending on the purposes for a particular activity, their definitions of "on-task" will be different, and their response to a type of behavior will vary, but all teachers will keep close tabs on how their students are participating. Clearly the need for effective management exists in both more and less traditional settings. In both cases, smooth, well-running classrooms where time, space, and materials are used efficiently maximize the opportunities students have to engage material in a meaningful way. The difference can be identified by defining terms such as "efficient" and "well-running" in classrooms where "engaging material in a meaningful way" is also defined differently.

Management demands in a classroom where learning is defined sociocognitively are significantly different from those in a classroom where it is defined behaviorally. As long as curriculum is conceived of as something that is delivered from teacher to students, management must be conceived of as a tool for student control, a way of getting students quiet, in their seats, and ready to receive information. If, however, we believe curriculum is actively constructed by all of the participants in a setting, then the purpose of management becomes to facilitate active inquiry and collaboration among students. In a learning setting, the well-managed classroom will not necessarily be the quiet classroom, and on-task behavior is likely to look quite different than it does in a work setting. "Good" managers in both settings will be reflective. However, their reflections are likely to focus on different issues, about which they will come to different conclusions.

Third, and perhaps most important, is recognition that management and instruction interact in the classroom. A central misconception about classroom management is that it is a content-free set of behaviors. In this view, management is something that takes place in order to prepare students for content, which comes later. This isolation of management from content is flawed. In fact, we argue that as a teacher makes management decisions, she or he is also communicating messages about the nature of the content being managed. As teachers and students negotiate rules for interacting with content and with each other, and as they define the roles that each participant is allowed to play in the classroom community, they establish a set of meanings that impacts what academic content can be learned. Management actions communicate information to students about the knowledge and participation that are valued in a particular setting. Our first task, then, must be to determine the kinds of messages about knowledge and participation that we want to communicate. The messages sent by management actions must be consistent with the kinds of learning we want to encourage.

As we discuss management in classrooms where learning is defined sociocognitively, it is important to recognize that learning, however it is defined, takes place in all classrooms. The important question becomes, what is learned? It is important to consider both the academic and social lessons being taught and learned in any given classroom at any given time, and to recognize that these messages inevitably influence each other, and cannot be considered separately. Teachers must ask themselves the questions presented in Figure 10-2.

CONCLUSIONS

Too frequently, the image that the term "classroom management" calls to mind is one of a teacher disciplining a student's errant behavior. While correction of deviant behavior is an important issue in the classroom, it is only one aspect of classroom management. As we redefine classroom management, there are some key points that we would like to make in conclusion.

Good classroom management practices are inseparable from good instructional practices. Good management and organization must focus more on the content and substance of what is being managed and less on the "look of engagement" (Bloome, Puro, and Theodorou, 1989). Good management is necessary for learning, but it does not stand alone. Recent research has found that in classrooms with high levels of student engagement but meager academic content, students learn little (Weade and Evertson, 1988); it should be obvious but remains worth saying that effective classroom management must not be seen as an end in itself, but as a contributing factor in student learning.

Classroom Management

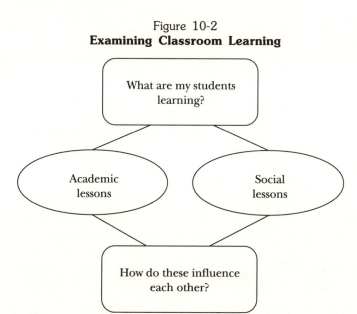

Figure 10-2
Examining Classroom Learning

As teachers move from traditional teacher-centered approaches to more student-centered approaches, principles of good management (such as clearly stating expectations, enacting a system of routines and procedures, etc.) do not change, although the individual and group goals may change.

Developing a classroom management system is not just a matter of enacting a few rules and procedures. The initiation of any activity or set of activities will necessarily involve some planning, implementing, and maintaining. For example, the introduction of a new unit may require that students participate in the classroom in different ways; changes in expectations for participation can mean changes in the classroom arrangement that could require different rules, procedures, and expectations for academic performance and may alter the ways students can demonstrate their knowledge. Each of these shifts in classroom tasks and activities can mean new cycles of planning, implementing, and maintaining. The teacher's task remains one of orchestrating these events in ways that serve curriculum goals and students' needs.

Directions for Future Research

Future research must address these questions: How can classroom management and organization support students' substantive learning? What is the nature and quality of the learning that is supported? We suggest an agenda that will be profitable for expanded research in the future.

Clearly, more images of newer classroom settings are needed. Descriptive studies of successful practice in inquiry-oriented classrooms, whole-language classrooms, and so on will provide such images. At present, there is little agreement on what constitutes effective practice in these settings; the first work should therefore be exploratory and interpretive rather than experimental or hypothesis-testing.

One example is the program of work by Adrienne Alton-Lee, Graham Nuthall, and colleagues (e.g., Alton-Lee, Nuthall, and Patrick, 1993; Nuthall and Alton-Lee, 1990). These researchers examine teaching and learning from multiple perspectives in order to fully examine the settings in which they work. Their thoroughly contextualized case studies are models for the work that must be expanded in the future. As they argue, "To focus on the instructional dimension without attending to the lived culture of the classroom context makes invisible some of the most significant questions about both the learning and the well-being of children in classrooms" (Alton-Lee, Nuthall, and Patrick, 1993, pp. 82–83).

Another approach involves in-depth, ethnographic case studies of such classrooms (e.g., Randolph, 1993). For this work to be meaningful, it must examine management in the context of instruction in a given classroom over an extended period of time, with attention to the roles and relationships that develop through the interactions of teachers and students. In order to preserve the history and connectedness of events over time, such studies should begin at the beginning—possibly during the first days of school—and continue throughout most of the year. In this work it is impossible to isolate curriculum from teachers' management decisions.

Researchers must also examine the relationships between classrooms and the school communities of which they are a part. Often, teachers' management and instructional decisions are constrained by norms and expectations of schools; these interactions must be recognized and explored if teaching reforms are to take hold in any meaningful ways (Evertson and Murphy, 1992).

Centrally, future research must recognize that past perspectives on classroom management have been limited to concerns about control of student behavior. These views constrain our ability to develop classrooms as learning settings in which both teacher and students are active learners. As research in classroom management explores new kinds of classroom settings, we as educators must make the central distinction between control of behavior and control of behavior for a purpose: the support of learning for all participants.

REFERENCES

Alton-Lee, A.; Nuthall, G.; and Patrick, J. (1993). Reframing classroom research: A lesson from the private world of children. *Harvard Educational Review, 63*(1), 50–84.

Bloome, D.; Puro, P.; and Theodorou, E. (1989). Procedural display and classroom lessons. *Curriculum Inquiry, 19*(3), 265–291.

Bossert, S. (1979). *Tasks and social relationships in classrooms: A study of instructional organization and its consequences.* Cambridge: Cambridge University Press.

Bruer, J. T. (1993). *Schools for thought: A science of learning in the classroom.* Cambridge, Mass.: The MIT Press.

Council of Chief State School Officers (CCSSO). (1990). *Restructuring learning for all students: A policy statement by the Council of Chief State School Officers on improved teaching of thinking.* Washington, D.C.: CCSSO.

Doyle, W. (1986). Classroom management. In M. Wittrock (ed.). *Handbook for research on teaching* (3rd ed., pp. 392–431). New York: Macmillan.

Doyle, W., and Carter, K. (1984). Academic tasks in classrooms. *Curriculum Inquiry, 14*(2), 129–149.

Emmer, E. T.; Sanford, J. P.; Clements, B. S.; and Martin, J. (1983, March). *Improving junior high classroom management.* Paper presented at the annual meeting of the American Educational Research Association, Montreal. (ERIC Document Reproduction Service # ED 234 021.)

Evertson, C. M. (1985). Training teachers in classroom management: An experiment in secondary classrooms. *Journal of Educational Research, 79*, 51–58.

Evertson, C. M. (1989). Improving elementary classroom management: A school-based training program for beginning the year. *Journal of Educational Research, 83*(2), 82–90.

Evertson, C. M., and Emmer, E. T. (1982). Effective management at the beginning of the school year in junior high classes. *Journal of Educational Psychology, 74*, 485–498.

Evertson, C. M., and Murphy, J. F. (1992). Beginning with the classroom: Implications for redesigning schools. In H. H. Marshall (ed.), *Redefining student learning: Roots of educational change* (pp. 293–320). Norwood, N.J.: Ablex.

Evertson, C. M.; Emmer, E. T.; Sanford, J. P.; and Clements, B. S. (1983). Improving classroom management: An experiment in elementary classrooms. *Elementary School Journal, 84*, 173–188.

Evertson, C. M., and Weade, R. (1991). The social construction of classroom lessons. In H. Waxman and H. Walberg (eds.) *Effective teaching: Current research* (pp. 135–159). Berkeley, Calif.: McCutchan.

Green, J. L., and Weade, R. (1985). Reading between the words: Social cues to lesson participation. *Theory into Practice, 24*(1), 14–21.

Green, J. L.; Weade, R.; and Graham, K. (1988). Lesson construction and student participation: A sociolinguistic analysis. In J. L. Green and J. O. Harker (eds.). *Multiple perspective analysis of classroom discourse* (pp. 11–47), Norwood, N.J.: Ablex.

Kounin, J. S. (1970). *Discipline and group management in classrooms.* New York: Holt, Rinehart and Winston.

Marshall, H. H. (1990). Beyond the workplace metaphor: Toward conceptualizing the classroom as a learning setting. *Theory into Practice, 29*(2), 94–101.

Nuthall, G. A., and Alton-Lee, A. (1990). Research on teaching and learning: Thirty years of change. *The Elementary School Journal, 90,* 547–570.

Randolph, C. H. (1993). *An ethnographic study of classroom interaction and literacy learning in a fifth/sixth grade writing class.* Unpublished doctoral dissertation, Vanderbilt University, Nashville, Tenn.

Randolph, C. H., and Evertson, C. M. (1994). Images of management for learner-centered classrooms. *Action in Teacher Education, 16*(1), 55–64.

Randolph, C. H., and Evertson, C. M. (1995). Managing for learning: Rules, roles, and meanings in a writing class. *Journal of Classroom Interaction, 30*(2), 17–25.

Weade, R., and Evertson, C. M. (1988). The construction of lessons in effective and less effective classrooms. *Teaching and Teacher Education, 4*(3), 189–213.

11
Social-Constructivist Perspectives on the Teaching of Science

Kenneth Tobin

The enduring problems in science education have recently been cast in terms of new theoretical frames. In the past decade, constructivism has increasingly been mentioned in the definitions of problems and their solutions (Tobin, 1993). In many contexts (e.g., requests for proposals issued by funding agencies), constructivism, which is a way of thinking about knowledge and coming to know, was prescribed as a mandatory way of thinking about teaching and learning science. There was a tendency to equate constructivism with particular activities rather than a way of thinking about knowing and coming to know. Teachers were exhorted to employ constructivist ways of teaching by arranging students in small groups and providing them with greater autonomy. Trends such as these not only diminish the power of constructivism as a way of thinking but also take the focus off critical dimensions of teaching and learning. Instead of examining any activity and asking how it might be improved by thinking about learning from a constructivist perspective, there has been a tendency, for example, to advocate small-group activities over whole-class activities and student-focused activities over teacher-focused activities. The purpose of this chapter is to explore some of the applications of social constructivism to the practice of teaching and learning science. Four main sections explore learning through co-participation, learning with understanding, organizing students for learning, and assessing what students have learned.

LEARNING SCIENCE THROUGH CO-PARTICIPATION

Science is a form of discourse that has evolved as a relatively recent activity of humankind. The goal of science is to make sense of a universe of phenomena in terms of viable knowledge. To be accepted as scientific, knowledge must meet several tests. First, it must be coherent with other viable knowledge claims. Second, it must be accepted by members of the scientific academy through a process of peer review. Third, it must withstand conceptual and empirical challenges in repeated attempts to refute its viability. Skeptical acceptance of scientific knowledge claims is a part of acting scientifically. Thus, even at the earliest of stages, an idea is carefully scrutinized in relation to what else is known, and efforts are made to refute claims associated with the knowledge. In the event that knowledge withstands those tests, the activity of gaining acceptance becomes increasingly social as attempts are made to convince others of the acceptability of what is claimed. When viewed in this way, it is apparent that science can be regarded as a form of argument during which ideas are formulated and then argued out in a social forum in which efforts are made to persuade peers to a particular point of view. The process necessarily involves the production of evidence and discussions about the extent to which the evidence fits the knowledge claim.

If science is viewed as a form of discourse, then learning science can be considered as learning a new way to make sense of experience. Discourse as it is used here refers to a "social activity of making meanings with language and other symbolic systems in some particular kind of situation or setting" (Lemke, 1995, p. 8). Lemke also noted that

> Instead of talking about meaning making as something that is done by minds, I prefer to talk about it as a *social practice* in a community. It is a kind of *doing* that is done in ways that are characteristic of a community, and its occurrence is part of what binds the community together and helps to constitute it as a community. In this sense we can speak of a community, not as a collection of interacting individuals, but as a system of doings, rather than a system of doers. [P. 9]

Social-Constructivist Perspectives on the Teaching of Science

In a school science community, one might expect to see students engage in ways such that, over a period of time, the discourse of a class would become more sciencelike. If the essence of science is to examine the coherence of evidence and knowledge claims, then one might expect a form of discourse in science classrooms that involves students routinely in arguments over the efficacy of the warrants for knowledge claims. As has been advocated by Kuhn (1993), science could be regarded as a form of argument in which emerging conceptual understandings are related to evidence and the extent of the fit with canonical science.

If students are to learn science as a form of discourse, it seems imperative that they are able to adapt their language resources as they practice science in a setting in which others who know science assist them to learn by engaging activities in which co-participation occurs (Schon, 1985). As it is used here, co-participation implies the presence of a shared language that can be accessed by all participants to communicate with one another such that meaningful learning occurs. The shared language must be negotiated and would enable all participants in a community to engage the activities of the community. Students receive opportunities to practice and observe others practice such that at any time a person might be both a teacher and a learner with respect to others in the community. Co-participation implies a concern for facilitating one another's learning, and peer teaching is a critical constituent of such an environment. During interactions among participants, respect would be shown for the knowledge of others, and efforts would be made to find out why particular claims were regarded as viable. There would be concern for knowing in a way that is scientific, and the knowledge that is learned within the community would be consistent with canonical science. Within this evolving knowledge community, concern would be shown for what is known by learners at any given time and how they can represent what they know.

Power, which is constituted in the discourse, would be equitably distributed among the teacher and students such that knowledge claims that made no sense would be clarified and discussion would occur until such time that a learner was satisfied that she or he now understood. In a setting in which co-participation was occurring, students would have the autonomy to ask when they did not understand, and the focus would always be on what students know and how they can represent what they know. Students would not feel that they could not understand and that their only recourse was to accept what was being said as an article of truth based on faith that other authoritative sources understand the warrants for the viability of a claim. Thus, co-participation would involve discussions in which participants test one another's understandings and are sensitive to their roles as both teachers and learners.

UNDERSTANDING SCIENCE

From the perspective of constructivism, learning is a social process of making sense of experience in terms of what is already known. In that process, learners create perturbations that arise from attempts to give meaning to particular experience through the imaginative use of existing knowledge. The resolution of these perturbations leads to an equilibrium state whereby new knowledge has been constructed to cohere with a particular experience and prior knowledge. An often misunderstood aspect of constructivism is that the theory incorporates a value position that any construction is as viable as another. Such a position ignores the social component of knowledge, that is, that knowledge must be viable not only personally but also in the social contexts in which actions occur. Viability is thereby determined with respect to the actions of an individual and the extent to which those actions facilitate the attainment of goals in particular social contexts. Accordingly, teachers should be on the lookout for naive theories or incorrect knowledge held by students. The teacher, representing society, has an obligation to educate students, to assist them to learn what is currently regarded by society as viable knowledge. Accordingly, if a teacher perceives the constructions of any individual to be inviable, it is the teacher's duty to structure learning environments to facilitate the process of learning what society regards as appropriate at that particular time.

To understand can be thought of in at least three senses. First, and in the most trivial meaning of the term, one can know in a limited way, in which case links with other science knowledge are not extensive. Examples of limited understanding would include knowing the names of things, facts, and definitions. Linkages between what is known might not be solely within a domain of science. For example, a link might be from something scientific to something nonscientific, as occurs when students remember the colors of the spectrum associated with sunlight by remembering that the first initial and order of the constituent colors correspond to a boy's name, Roy G. Biv. As well as memorizing the name, a learner must remember a one-to-one correspondence between the name and the first letter of a color. If these links are recalled, an individual is able to reconstruct the order of colors when white light is dispersed.

Some individuals will stop at this point in their quest for understanding and others will go beyond it. Having reconstructed the colors to describe a spectrum, this knowledge can be related to dispersion, diffraction, and refraction to form a semantic web that can then be expanded to include properties of electromagnetic radiation such as wavelength, frequency, and velocity. New knowledge can be connected into the semantic web as a learner postulates a connection and then examines the extent to which the new knowledge coheres with existing knowledge. With some conceptual reorganization, learners can develop relational understandings by constructing webs of relationships for given scientific subject matter. Relational and limited understanding are ends of a continuum that differ in the number and quality of the linkages formed within a domain of knowledge.

At some stage in the process of learning, an individual might have a goal of linking scientific knowledge to his or her actions in the world outside of the classroom. Thus, knowledge of science is used to create patterns of understanding from everyday life experiences. We refer to this process as developing transformational understanding, in that scientific knowledge is transformed in such a way as to cohere with the beliefs of an individual's lifeworld, and is used as a basis for actions that extend beyond what might be regarded as science related. Many of the goals included in such reports as the National Science Education Standards (National Research Council, 1996) are consistent with transformational understanding. For example, the goals listed in the draft of the National Science Education Standards are to educate students such that they can

- Use scientific principles and processes appropriately in making personal decisions
- Experience the richness and excitement of knowing about and understanding the natural world

- Increase their economic productivity
- Engage intelligently in public discourse and debate about matters of scientific and technological concern (National Research Council, 1996, p. 13)

ORGANIZING STUDENTS FOR LEARNING

Thinking about science from a social-constructivist perspective helps science educators to decide what might constitute a science curriculum. Since all knowledge must be individually constructed, it makes no sense to begin by thinking solely about the disciplines of science in the absence of learners. Furthermore, since all learning is social, it makes no sense to think of learners independently of the communities in which learning occurs. A learner has to make sense of science through an existing conceptual structure, and whatever science knowledge is constructed will be an interpretation of experience in terms of extant knowledge. Accordingly, three questions are fundamental: first, what experiences should be provided to learners to facilitate their learning; second, how can the learner represent what is known already to give meaning to these experiences; and how should learners be arranged to maximize the learning capital that they bring to the classroom? In a co-participatory classroom, the mediating role of the teacher is focused not only on what students know and how they can represent what they know but also on the identification of activities that can continue the evolutionary path of the classroom community toward the attainment of agreed upon goals. Thus, the concern is beyond representation and also involves mediating the constructions of a discourse that becomes increasingly scientific in character.

This section examines the manner in which the environment can be organized to facilitate student learning. Small-group and whole-class activities are discussed in terms of co-participation and social constructivism to highlight the potential each activity has for promoting the learning of students.

Small-Group Activities

If the route to the facilitation of learning is via co-participation, then it makes sense to organize students for learning such that they can interact with others using a shared language. Linn and Burbules (1993) distinguished cooperative learning (where a task is divided into parts and group members each complete a part), collaborative learning (where two or more students work together to arrive at an agreed-upon solution to a problem), and tutored learning (where one student teaches another). They indicated that any small-group activity might involve a combination of one or more of the above types.

Noddings (1989) examined some of the theoretical and empirical factors associated with small-group learning and concluded that the issues to be considered prior to implementing group activities included the purposes of the groups, group membership, roles of teacher and students, the nature of the activities in which students will engage, and the manner in which group outcomes will be evaluated. Is group learning equally effective for all educational goals? Linn and Burbules identified cognitive, social, and workplace skills as three goal areas often associated with small-group learning. According to Linn and Bubules, group learning is usually effective for brainstorming and generating ideas and is usually ineffective for planning activities. However, they cautioned that successful groups are trained to generate ideas and to accept and elaborate the ideas of others without criticizing them. Learning in a social setting, including a small group, can occur by students appropriating the ideas of others by building on someone else's idea to create an idea they could not have created alone. Linn and Burbules noted that

> Collaboration succeeds when students are effective at communicating their ideas and able to help other group members see why their idea contributes to the group goal. It also depends on group adherence to a form of discourse that values argument, reliance on evidence, and explanation. [P. 112]

Linn and Burbules identified two aspects of life in everyday situations that are unhelpful in making progress toward a scientific form of discourse—a tendency (1) to remain silent about conflicting evidence and (2) to assert with authority on the basis of faith. If students are to make progress by not remaining silent and by not asserting on the basis of faith, then they will need practice in relating evidence to knowledge claims. Such practice will no doubt take place in a variety of activity settings, including small-group activities. Can students accept multiple alternative solutions and then choose the best from among them? There appears no sound reason to expect students to do this automatically, and it is acknowledged that students would have to learn the value of doing this and then learn how to do it. A confounding factor in making progress in this regard would appear to be the perceived status of certain peers and peer pressure to maintain the status quo. For example, an idea generated by a person with the highest status is often accepted without subjecting that idea to tests of its viability. Linn and Burbules commented that often the status accorded an individual has little to do with scientific aptitude. Thus ideas that are not viable may be accepted on the authority of a student who has status for reasons unrelated to his or her knowledge of science. In addition to increasing the probability that students will accept "incorrect" knowledge as correct without first considering other alternatives, there is a danger that group members will reinforce status differences and stereotyped behavior.

Science educators must be concerned about whether students in groups learn and also whether the knowledge the group constructs is viable. Groups might construct a consensus that is at odds with canonical science. To address this potential problem, teachers would need to review the consensuses reached in small groups and facilitate the development of a whole-class-level consensus that can be compared with the views accepted as correct by scientists. Indeed, accessing the knowledge accepted by scientists through texts and other sources of information about science is a necessary part of any science program. Even in a class where small-group work occurs frequently, it is anticipated that levels of consensus will be negotiated and final agreed-upon knowledge claims would be tested with canonical science.

Linn and Burbules commented that students who ask questions that are answered benefit from group learning. They then raised a question about students who are ignored. This question relates directly to research undertaken in mathematics by King (1993), who observed forms of student passivity during small-group cooperative learning, especially among low-achieving students. Low expectations for the performance of low achievers were fueled by self-perceptions and were reinforced by the perceptions of their high-achieving peers. In small-group activities, the engagement of low achievers was mediated by the dominant leadership style of some high achievers, interpersonal relations among group members, their relative inability to make a positive impact on the progress of the group, and the reinforcing effects of their negative self-perceptions with regard to personal progress in mathematics. King noted that because low achievers enjoy learning and working in small groups, educators need to overcome the problems associated with small-group learning. Among the suggestions King made for elementary teachers to allow for the development of cooperative skills were that students should rotate roles within groups; tasks should be selected to enable progression from simple to complex and from short duration to relatively long duration; students should be permitted to practice assigned roles; and success experiences for small groups should be promoted. Teachers were encouraged to closely monitor the progress of low achievers and alter prevailing status differentials with a goal of establishing more equal rates of participation among low and high achievers.

Corno (1992) observed that one reason why students enjoy group activities is that they often mix learning and relationship-building activities. She advocated that teachers provide support and create activities for students to challenge themselves and others while they pursue goals and grow comfortable with criticism. Corno suggested that teachers might mediate less in the learning of students in small-group activities because "the value of peers over teachers in delivering external prompts appears to rest on students' common worldviews at various ages, which lead to developmentally appropriate queries and comments" (p. 79). The suggestion highlights the place of student verbal interaction in the negotiation of a shared discourse. Accordingly, teachers need to strike a balance between effective mediation and over-engineering, by gradually relinquishing control of certain processes and objectives. The assumption is that students will assume responsibility for the control relinquished by the teacher and employ their greater autonomy to pursue activities to enhance their learning and engagement in relevant and meaningful tasks. If the increased autonomy leads to co-participation for students, then small groups can indeed promote meaningful learning.

Whole-Class Activities

During this constructivist era, there seems to be a widespread perception that it is not desirable to employ whole-class activities in science. Rather than adhering to such a generalized assertion, it might be more fruitful to focus on the roles of teachers and learners and inquire as to the types of whole-class activities that might be conducive to learning. The focus of a whole-class activity must be on enhancing the learning of all students, and the roles of students should necessitate active engagement and co-participation in the shared language of the classroom. Analogously, the roles of the teacher ought to be active and focused on mediating the learning of all students.

Experienced elementary teachers will often bring students to sit on a mat together or in a semicircle. The purpose of doing this is to bring the students together in such a way that they can focus on the teacher, whose role is to conduct a whole-class activity. Of course, it is not necessary for the focus to be a teacher; it could just as easily be a peer, as was demonstrated in mathematics education in the problem-centered learning approaches advocated by Wheatley (1991). In the problem-centered approaches in mathematics, students led whole-class discussions in a process of developing negotiated consensuses about what they had learned from earlier small-group work. These whole-class sessions were interactive, continued for up to forty-five minutes, and were productive, presumably because prior problem-solving activities with a peer, for a similar period of time, enabled all students to access the language and participate equitably in whole-class activities.

In my review of the use of an extended wait time in teaching and learning (Tobin, 1987), it was clear that teachers should provide time for students to process speech in whole-class settings. The review suggests that bursts of speech should be punctuated with intervals of three to five seconds of silence, not for others to begin to speak, but for all to think about what has been said and make sense of it. During these periods of silence, students can begin to connect what they are learning to what they already know and identify what else they know that might be relevant to their learning. Thus, they will reconstruct extant knowledge, make connections, identify contradictions and consistencies, and formulate questions that need to be resolved. The arguments that Kuhn (1993) has suggested might characterize science are carried out in the minds of individuals in the silent periods between bursts of speech. During those same intervals of silence, the teacher can reflect on what he or she has already said and consider what is to be said next. In addition, the teacher can monitor the body language of students and formulate strategies for changing the ways in which individuals engage. The inclusion of three- to five-second intervals of silence also increases the potential for noninteractive whole-class activities to become interactive. Students have the time to construct questions and explanations and indicate a willingness to contribute to ongoing conversations.

Wait time is not seen as a mechanical device to be used in a technical way, but as a way to provide time for reflection, to allow the social context to mediate the personal constructions of individuals. As students access the language of the speaker, they need time to assign meaning, reconstruct relevant extant knowledge, and examine the fit of what they are hearing with what they know. The learner has much to do, and a continual barrage of talk from the teacher or another student can interfere with the building of meaningful conceptual relationships. If teachers use wait times of three to five seconds and students do not engage in the processes mentioned previously, then the odds are that they will not learn with understanding. It is important, therefore, for students to have a clear idea of their roles as learners so that they recognize the value of opportunities such as short but regular intervals of silence for such purposes as making sense, elaborating, and clarifying. In addition, if opportunities to reflect are not provided and students understand the significance of regular periods of silence for their own learning, they can request additional opportunities to think things through. To use an extended wait time appropriately is not to pause after every sentence, but to pause when it is appropriate and for a time that is appropriate in the context. Research has shown that on the average the required pause time is three to five seconds, but what an average hides is that there will be times when pauses of ten to fifteen seconds are desirable and other times when less than a quarter of a second is optimal to link sentences to one another.

Rowe (1983), in a series of studies undertaken at college level, and following after her wait-time studies, explored the value of longer periods of time away from the input of a teacher in whole-class settings. Although her initial studies were conducted in college classes, we conducted a set of studies in middle and high school classes (e.g., Tobin and Espinet, 1989) in which we adapted Rowe's 10–2 method to ensure that in every ten minutes of instruction there was at least two minutes for students to look back over what had happened in the previous eight minutes. What we did in those studies was to create groups of two students each in which students discussed questions related to what was covered by the teacher in the previous eight minutes. These review questions allowed students to use their own words to make sense of what had happened previously and also to reconstruct relevant prior knowledge, and examine the fit of what they were learning to what they knew already. Breaks of this type are consistent with building a shared language and creating an environment in which co-participation occurs. Once again, it would not be essential for this to occur for two minutes in every ten minutes in a mechanical way. The 10–2 method serves as a reminder to break up whole-class activities with small-group and individualized activities to enable students to make sense of what is happening.

ASSESSMENT OF LEARNING

Because assessment is a social act that is usually enacted in a classroom, it is important to examine the roles of teachers and students in assessment situations. Teachers often use metaphors to make sense of a role such as assessor. For example, teachers frequently equate their role as an assessor to being a fair judge (Tobin and Tippins, 1996). They perceive their role as one in which they ascertain what students know and weigh the students' knowledge claims against the principal dimensions of canonical knowledge, that is, knowledge accepted as viable by an eminent group of scientists. As a fair judge, it is important for the teacher to ask about the most important parts of the disciplinary knowledge and ensure that his or her own judgment is impartial. Using this metaphor, the judge decides on the focus for the assessment tasks and whether or not performance is adequate. The students' roles are to know what is most important, and thereby prepare to demonstrate what they know about these parts of a course, and to demonstrate their knowledge when called on to do so. If students do not learn what is to be assessed, they rarely have the opportunity to show a fair judge that they learned other things and could have performed adequately on other tasks. The goals of a learner can shape not only what is learned but the manner in which it is learned and how at a later time that knowledge can be enacted in a performance task. The relative importance of learner goals to what is being learned and how knowledge can later be enacted has implications for the design and use of assessment tasks.

One study of a beginning middle/high school science teacher graphically describes the problems associated with assessment practices built on an assessment metaphor of fair judge (Tobin and LaMaster, 1995). Even though Sarah, the teacher in the study, had gained control of her difficult-to-handle students, they had built very negative attitudes toward her because she was holding the line on what she considered to be legitimate standards of learning—standards built from a consideration of the discipline rather than from a consideration of what students knew. The negative attitude toward the teacher was widespread within the class and manifested itself in a latent hostility toward the teacher and the subject of science. On the basis of the metaphor of bargaining work in exchange for grades, it seemed as if Sarah were trying to negotiate too hard a deal, and the workers—the students—were not buying into it. Sarah, like so many teachers we have worked with, had no alternative ways to think about or practice assessment. She had only one conceptualization of assessment, and when it was not working, she had no options to fall back on.

Sarah had strong beliefs about constructivism as a way of thinking about knowing that opened the possibility of trying different approaches to assessment. Initially, Sarah was inclined to try different approaches advocated by those whom she respected in science education. She tried concept mapping, oral interviews, and problem-centered learning; none seemed to be successful. The essence of the difficulty seemed to be how she regarded science itself and how she viewed assessment. Her beliefs about the nature of science were evolving in relation to her beliefs about constructivism. Since she could not construct a metaphor for assessment, the research team suggested to her that it was like a mirror. Although the metaphor appealed to the researchers (student looking into a mirror and seeing her knowledge displayed in her mind), it made no sense to Sarah. Subsequently, we suggested a window into the students' minds, an opportunity for them to show the teacher what they knew. Sarah could see how this would work.

Using the window metaphor, Sarah rethought her assessment policies and practices. She implemented a new approach to the class, and matters began to improve. The interesting aspect of the metaphor that she built was that it transferred power from the teacher to the students. The students now had the responsibility to make decisions about what they knew, how to represent what they knew, and when to schedule time with the teacher to show that they had learned. To Sarah and the students, this seemed like a reasonable approach to assessment. What evolved over a period of time was an approach to assessment that emphasized the autonomy of students and learning with understanding.

The portfolio, conceptualized as a container, can be used as a place for students to display artifacts that show what they have learned. An artifact is evidence of learning and can be the focus for discussions between students or with a teacher and a student. A system of assessment, and learning, that is built around portfolios affords an advantage of providing students with power to decide which artifacts to place in the container, how to describe what each artifact represents, and to engage in an interactive manner about the artifact and what it represents. Via artifacts, students and teachers can engage in rich conversations about what is known and how learning has changed over time. If an artifact is no longer relevant to the understanding of an individual, it can be removed or it can be retained as an example of how learning has occurred over time. Students have considerable power in such a system, but so too do teachers as they focus their attention on ascertaining what students know and how they are making sense of the artifacts that they have chosen to include in their portfolios. Students have the responsibility of describing why an object is in a portfolio and how that object relates to their learning. This description and justification process could take place in writing, orally, or with a combination of each. Because of the difficulty of understanding what an artifact represents, the portfolio would provide a context for discussion where a teacher and a student could negotiate what the artifacts stand for and what progress students had made toward meeting the goals of the course.

The availability of portfolios in classrooms makes it possible for teachers to get in touch with what students know on an ongoing basis. Regular perusal of students' portfolios can provide a basis for a learner-focused dialogue between the students and teacher. Also, portfolios provide opportunities for students to interact with one another about what they know. I can envision a situation where group members spend some time each week examining the portfolios of peers. Some students can assume a tutoring role when others in their group do not appear to have grasped a particular concept, and all group members can provide formative evaluation of the representativeness of artifacts and the extent to which they accurately represent what has been learned. Much of the learning can be centered on portfolios. The use of portfolios is one tangible way of bringing teaching, learning, and assessment closer together, and from a constructivist perspective it is easy to see how these interactive processes could result not only in better assessment, but in better learning as well.

Performance tasks in science usually involve the use of materials to engage a task, identify a problem, and seek solutions. Materials are frequently manipulated, measurements are taken, and calculations are made as data are manipulated in a process of problem solving. Students are given a common task, but they are allowed to seek solutions in their own ways, and they can interact with assessors about the meanings given the tasks, what they mean by their solutions, and how they justify the selection of one solution over another. The potential for interaction diminishes the problems of misunderstanding the intended meanings of the assessor and the assessed but does little to address the power imbalances that are inherent in many assessment system. Thus an essential ingredient of a performance assessment approach is a language that can be accessed and appropriated by both the teacher and students.

CONCLUSIONS

Consideration of science classes as discourse communities brings to the foreground issues associated with participation in the discourse of a classroom. Accordingly, equity and power are tied directly to learning, and an emphasis is placed not just on individual learners but individual learners in a community and the discourse that defines that community. Because this community comprises the actions and interactions of teachers and learners of science, the sign that the community is evolving acceptably is an increasing incidence of knowledge claims being supported by evidence and arguments among participants over the interpretations of data. Co-participation is a critical sign that communication is occurring and that the learning environments are optimal. Thus, a high priority for teachers is to ensure that a shared language is negotiated, shared in the sense that all students in a classroom can access and appropriate that language.

The goal of attaining co-participation for all learners can thus be a benchmark for deciding what activities to plan and implement, when to change from one activity to another, and how best to assess the extent to which students have learned. If the community is defined by doings rather than doers, as Lemke suggests, then the focus of an evaluation of the classroom can be on the discourse of the community, the actions and interactions of each participant in that community.

REFERENCES

Corno, L. (1992). Encouraging students to take responsibility for learning and performance. *The Elementary School Journal*, 93(1), 69–83.

King, L. H. (1993). High and low achievers' perceptions and cooperative learning in two small groups. *The Elementary School Journal*, 93(4), 399–416.

Kuhn, D. (1993), Science as argument: Implications for teaching and learning scientific thinking. *Science Education*, 77(3), 319–337.

Lemke, J. L. (1995). *Textual politics: Discourse and social dynamics.* London: Taylor & Francis.

Linn, M. C., and Burbules, N. C. (1993). Construction of knowledge and group learning. In K. Tobin (Ed.). *The practice of constructivism in science education.* Hillsdale, N.J.: Lawrence Erlbaum and Associates.

National Research Council, (1996). *National science education standards.* Washington, DC: National Academy Press.

Noddings, N. (1989). Theoretical and practical concerns about small groups in mathematics. *The Elementary School Journal*, 89(5), 607–623.

Rowe, M. B. (1983). Getting chemistry off the killer course list. *Journal of Chemical Education*, 60(11), 954–956.

Schon, D. (1985). *The design studio.* London: RIBA Publications Limited.

Tobin, K. (1987). The role of wait time in higher cognitive level learning. *Review of Educational Research*, 57(1), 69–95.

Tobin, K. (ed.) (1993). The practice of constructivism in science education. Hillsdale, N.J. Lawrence Erlbaum and Associates.

Tobin, K., and Espinet, M. (1989). Impediments to change: An application of peer coaching in high school science. *Journal of Research in Science Teaching*, 26(2), 105–120.

Tobin, K., and LaMaster, S. (1995). Relationships between metaphors, beliefs and actions in a context of science curriculum change. *Journal of Research in Science Teaching* 32(3), 225–242.

Tobin, K., and Tippins, D. (1996). Metaphors as seeds for learning and the improvement of science teaching. *Science Education*, 80, 711–730.

Wheatley, G. H. (1991). Constructivist perspectives on science and mathematics learning. *Science Education*, 75, 9–21.

12

"Grain Sizes" in Learning Environment Research: Combining Qualitative and Quantitative Methods

Barry J. Fraser

This chapter considers the idea of "grain sizes" in educational research, shows how qualitative and quantitative methods are applicable at different grain sizes, and reports a learning environment study that illustrates the use of different grain sizes. Although mainly qualitative methods were used in an intensive study of one science teacher, a classroom learning environment questionnaire was used to provide quantitative information, which yielded insights into the extent to which the teacher's class was typical of other science classes in the same school and of a broader group of science classes in a larger group of schools.

GRAIN SIZES IN EDUCATIONAL RESEARCH

Different research studies call for a focus on different levels or grain sizes. In turn, the grain size has implications for the choice of research methods. For example, a fine grain size involving a contrast between two teachers or between several students within a class (as in Tobin, Kahle, and Fraser's *Windows into Science Classrooms* in 1990) calls for intensive qualitative interpretive methods. In contrast, a systemwide evaluation of educational reform would involve a coarse grain size and require economical quantitative survey methods, as in our evaluation of an Urban Systemic Initiative in Dallas involving a survey of over 40,000 students' classroom environment perceptions (Dryden and Fraser, 1996). In many studies, a different grain size will be relevant at different times and for different purposes throughout the particular study.

FIELD OF LEARNING ENVIRONMENT RESEARCH

Over the past two or three decades, the field of learning environment research has become established firmly (Fraser, 1986, 1994; Fraser and Walberg, 1991; Fraser, 1998). Although learning environment research involves a range of observational and interpretive methods, the assessment of learning environment often involves questionnaires that assess students' and teachers' perceptions of dimensions such as Teacher Support, Participation, Task Orientation, Innovation, Cooperation, and Personal Relevance (see Fraser, 1994).

Some advantages of using perceptual measures involving questionnaires are their economy, their involvement of students' experiences over a long period (cf. a single visit to a class by an external observer), and the way in which the pooled judgments of all students in the class are used. Moreover, because students' perceptions are the determinants of student satisfaction and behavior, perceptions can be more important than observed behaviors.

Curriculum evaluators have used learning environment questionnaires as a source of criteria of effectiveness in the evaluation of new curricula or educational innovations (Fraser, 1979). Even when evaluators found no differences between the achievement of students using new and old curricula, they found meaningful differences between the two curricula in terms of student perceptions of the classroom environment. For example, in an evaluation of the Australian Science Education Project, Fraser (1979) found that, relative to a control group, students using the new curriculum perceived their classrooms as more satisfying and individualized and as having a better material environment.

A strong tradition in past research on learning environments involves investigation of associations between students' cognitive and affective outcomes and their perceptions of classroom environment (e.g., McRobbie and Fraser, 1993). These studies span numerous countries, grade levels, school subjects, and outcome measures. Student perceptions consistently account for appreciable amounts of variance in student learning outcomes even after student background characteristics are taken into account. For example, better achievement on a variety of outcomes is found in classes that are more cohesive, satisfying, goal directed, and organized and that have less friction. In science laboratory classes, more integration between theory and laboratory classes leads to improved achievement and attitudes about science.

Researchers have used actual and preferred forms of classroom environment instruments and have investigated differences between students' and their teachers' perceptions of the same classrooms (Fisher and Fraser, 1983). Teachers generally perceive a more positive classroom environment than do their students (the rose-colored glasses phenomenon), and the actual environment is less favorable than what both students and teachers prefer.

Teachers have used assessments of their students' perceptions of actual and preferred classroom environment in practical attempts to improve classrooms (Thorp, Burden, and Fraser, 1994). The five basic steps are *assessment* (students respond to the actual and preferred forms of a classroom environment instrument), *feedback* (teachers score students' responses and draw graphs to show discrepancies between class mean scores on the actual and preferred forms of each scale), *reflection and discussion* (the teacher reflects on these discrepancies, discusses them with colleagues or students, and decides to change specific dimensions), *intervention* (the teacher introduces new classroom strategies aimed at changing the learning environment), and *reassessment* (the questionnaires are readministered to see whether the student-perceived classroom environment has changed).

Fraser and Tobin (1991) recommend the combination of qualitative and quantitative methods in learning environment research. These authors included a classroom environment questionnaire in their case studies of exemplary science teachers. The way in which students of exemplary teachers viewed their classroom environments much more positively than did the students of nonexemplary teachers vindicated the procedure used initially to identify exemplary teachers for the study. In an interpretive study of two science teachers, Tobin, Kahle, and Fraser's (1990) use of a classroom environment questionnaire showed that the student-perceived classroom environment was related to the teachers' knowledge and beliefs, and that differences in teacher expectations and attitudes toward individual students were reflected in differences in individual students' perceptions of the learning environment.

Recently developed questionnaires focus on science laboratory classroom environments (McRobbie and Fraser, 1993), computer-assisted learning environments (Teh and Fraser, 1995) and constructivist-oriented classroom learning environments (Taylor, Fraser, and Fisher, 1997). Currently, we are incorporating classroom environment ideas into school psychology and teacher education (Fraser, 1994).

THE PRESENT STUDY

I was one member of a research team involved in an intensive study of a grade 10 science teacher and her class over a period of five weeks. The school involved provided a challenging learning environment in that many students were from working-class backgrounds, some students were experiencing family problems, and some students had English as their second language. We hoped that valuable insights could be obtained about science teaching and learning by focusing on a challenging learning environment.

We gave particular attention in the study to determinants of classroom environment, especially school culture, teacher beliefs, and constraints (e.g., the prescribed curriculum, time, teacher colleagues, and student gender). Changes in classroom practices and organization depend on factors associated with the communities and cultures in which teaching and learning are embedded. Accordingly, it is important that teachers have the ability and motivation to initiate and sustain school-based research and to learn from it. In the present study, we hoped that collaboration between a teacher-researcher and university-based researchers would enhance our understanding of school reform, as well as give the teacher-researcher some experience in how to conduct school-based research.

Methods

The study involved six university-based researchers collaborating with a teacher-researcher in an intensive study of a grade 10 science class following a chemistry topic. Several of the researchers visited this class each time it met (four times per week) over a period of five weeks.

Our predominant data-collection approach was qualitative and drew on the interpretive methods of Erickson (1986). In addition to classroom observations and the use of student diaries, we interviewed the teacher-researcher, students, school administrators, and parents. We used a videocamera to record the activities of each lesson for later analysis. We made field notes during and soon after each observation. We held team meetings involving all researchers and the teacher-researcher three times per week. All interviews and team meetings were tape recorded and transcribed. We enhanced the "referential adequacy" (Eisner, 1979) of the study by having teachers at the school check written accounts of the researchers' observations and interpretations.

Toward the end of the observational period, we conducted a "peer debriefing" (Guba and Lincoln, 1989). This provided our research group with the opportunity to discuss the study with a group of other university-based researchers and several teachers from the school involved in the study. In addition to short presentations from each researcher, the peer debriefing involved numerous small-group discussions throughout the session and a whole-group discussion at the end.

Our study was consistent with Fraser and Tobin's (1991) recommendation about combining qualitative and quantitative methods in learning environment research. In addition to the qualitative information in our study, we collected quantitative information based on a classroom environment questionnaire designed specifically for the present research and based on understandings derived from the qualitative aspects of the study. The classroom environment questionnaire contained seven dimensions. The first five dimensions were taken from the most recent version of the Constructivist Learning Environment Survey (CLES; Taylor, Fraser, and Fisher, 1997), whereas the other two dimensions were added because they emerged as salient in this teacher's class during classroom observations.

The scales are Personal Relevance (relevance of learning to students' lives), Critical Voice (legitimacy of students' expressing a critical opinion), Shared Control (student participation in planning, conduct, and assessment of learning), Uncertainty (provisional status of scientific knowledge), Student Negotiation (involvement with other students in assessing the viability of new ideas), Commitment (student motivation and effort in relation to learning science), and Teacher Support (helpfulness and friendliness of the teacher towards students).

Typical items are "I learn about the world outside school" (Personal Relevance), "It's OK to ask the teacher 'Why do we have to learn this?'" (Critical Voice), "I help the teacher to plan what I'm going to learn" (Shared Control), "I learn that the views of science have changed over time" (Uncertainty), "I ask other students to explain their ideas" (Student Negotiation), "I pay attention" (Commitment), and "The teacher goes out of his/her way to help me" (Teacher Support). The response alternatives are Almost Always, Often, Sometimes, Seldom, and Almost Never. The questionnaire is presented in Figure 12-1.

We administered the questionnaire to three samples:

1. A selection 11 students who were in Ms. Horton's grade 10 chemistry class in first term
2. A selection of 20 students in two other teachers' grade 10 chemistry classes at the same school during term 1
3. A larger representative group of 494 grade 8 and 9 science students in 41 classes in 13 schools in Western Australia participating in the Third International Mathematics and Science Study (TIMSS).

In the case of the large comparison group, data were available for only the five CLES scales. For the first two samples described above, all seven scales were administered. This design enabled us to ascertain whether this science teacher's class was typical of other science classes in the same school and of science classes in a larger group of schools.

FINDINGS AND CONCLUSIONS

The classroom environment findings can be reported, interpreted, and discussed at various levels or "grain sizes." For example, at the level of the individual student, different students

Figure 12-1
Classroom Environment Questionnaire

DIRECTIONS

1. **Purpose of the Questionnaire**
   This questionnaire asks you to describe important aspects of your science classroom.
   There are no right or wrong answers. This is not a test and your answers will not affect your assessment. *Your opinion is what is wanted.* Your answers will enable us to improve future science classes.

2. **How to Answer Each Question**
   On the next few pages, you will find 42 sentences. For each sentence, circle *only one* number corresponding to your answer. For example:

		Almost Always	Often	Some-times	Seldom	Almost Never
In my science class . . .						
8	The teacher asks me questions.	5	4	3	2	1

   - If you think your science teacher *almost always* asks you questions, circle the 5.
   - If you think your science teacher *almost never* asks you questions, circle the 1.
   - Or you can choose the number 2, 3, or 4 if one of these seems like a more accurate answer.

3. **How to Change Your Answer**
   If you want to change your answer, *cross it out* and circle a new number, For example:

8	The teacher asks me questions.	⊗	④	3	2	1

4. **Completing the questionnaire**
   Now turn the page and please give an answer for *every* question.

in Ms. Horton's class perceived the same class quite differently. For example, Student T perceived much greater levels of Teacher Support than did Student W. The teacher describes Student T as a model student and Student W as a hyperactive student with a genetic disorder.

Figure 12-2 considers the classroom environment of Ms. Horton's class (averaged over all students who responded to the questionnaire) relative to two other "grain-sizes," namely, (1) the average classroom environment as perceived by two grade 10

Learning about the world	Almost Always	Often	Some-times	Seldom	Almost Never
In my science class...					
1 I learn about the world outside of school.	5	4	3	2	1
2 My learning starts with problems about the world outside of school.	5	4	3	2	1
3 I learn how science can be part of my out-of-school life.	5	4	3	2	1
In my science class...					
4 I get better understanding of the world outside of school.	5	4	3	2	1
5 I learn interesting things about the world outside of school.	5	4	3	2	1
6 What I learn has nothing to do with my out-of-school life.	5	4	3	2	1
Learning about science	Almost Always	Often	Some-times	Seldom	Almost Never
In my science class...					
7 I learn that science cannot provide perfect answers to problems.	5	4	3	2	1
8 I learn that science has changed over time.	5	4	3	2	1
9 I learn that science is influenced by people's values and opinions.	5	4	3	2	1
In my science class...					
10 I learn about the different sciences used by people in other cultures.	5	4	3	2	1
11 I learn that modern science is different from the science of long ago.	5	4	3	2	1
12 I learn that science is about inventing theories.	5	4	3	2	1
Learning to speak out	Almost Always	Often	Some-times	Seldom	Almost Never
In my science class...					
13 It's OK to ask the teacher "Why do we have to learn this?"	5	4	3	2	1
14 It's OK to question the way I'm being taught.	5	4	3	2	1
15 It's OK to complain about activities that are confusing	5	4	3	2	1
In my science class...					
16 It's OK to complain about anything that prevents me from learning.	5	4	3	2	1
17 It's OK to express my opinion.	5	4	3	2	1
18 It's OK to speak up for my rights.	5	4	3	2	1
Learning to learn	Almost Always	Often	Some-times	Seldom	Almost Never
In my science class...					
19 I help the teacher to plan what I'm going to learn.	5	4	3	2	1
20 I help the teacher to decide how well I am learning.	5	4	3	2	1
21 I help the teacher to decide which activities are best for me.	5	4	3	2	1

Figure 12-1, continued

"Grain Sizes" in Learning Environment Research

Learning to learn (cont.)	Almost Always	Often	Some-times	Seldom	Almost Never
In my science class . . .					
22 I help the teacher to decide how much time I spend on activities.	5	4	3	2	1
23 I help the teacher to decide which activities I do.	5	4	3	2	1
24 I help the teacher to assess my learning.	5	4	3	2	1
Learning to communicate	**Almost Always**	**Often**	**Some-times**	**Seldom**	**Almost Never**
In my science class . . .					
25 I get the chance to talk to other students.	5	4	3	2	1
26 I talk with other students about how to solve problems.	5	4	3	2	1
27 I explain my ideas to other students.	5	4	3	2	1
In my science class . . .					
28 I ask other students to explain their ideas.	5	4	3	2	1
29 Other students ask me to explain my ideas.	5	4	3	2	1
30 Other students explain their ideas to me.	5	4	3	2	1
Interest in learning science	**Almost Always**	**Often**	**Some-times**	**Seldom**	**Almost Never**
In my science class . . .					
31 I am interested in science lessons.	5	4	3	2	1
32 I am willing to learn.	5	4	3	2	1
33 What we do is important to me.	5	4	3	2	1
In my science class . . .					
34 I try my best.	5	4	3	2	1
35 I pay attention.	5	4	3	2	1
36 I enjoy science lessons.	5	4	3	2	1
Teacher support in learning science	**Almost Always**	**Often**	**Some-times**	**Seldom**	**Almost Never**
In my science class . . .					
37 The teacher is friendly to me.	5	4	3	2	1
38 The teacher helps me with the work.	5	4	3	2	1
39 The teacher is interested in my problems.	5	4	3	2	1
In my science class . . .					
40 The teacher goes out of his/her way to help me.	5	4	3	2	1
41 The teacher moves around the class to talk to me.	5	4	3	2	1
42 The teacher considers my feelings.	5	4	3	2	1

The items in successive blocks of six assess, respectively, Personal Relevance, Critical Voice, Shared Control, Uncertainty, Student Negotiation, and Teacher Support. The circled number is the score for every item except Item 6, which is scored in the reverse manner. Omitted or invalid responses are scored 3.

Figure 12-1, continued

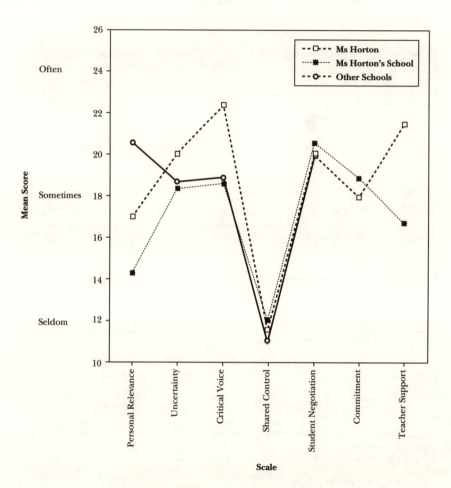

Figure 12-2
Classroom Environment Profiles for (1) Ms. Horton's Class, (2) Other Classes at Ms. Horton's School and (3) a Comparison Group of 13 Schools

chemistry classes of two other teachers at the same school and (2) a large comparison group of science classes.

Two main patterns are evident in Figure 12-2. First, relative to other science classes in her school, Ms. Horton's class is perceived as having greater levels of Personal Relevance, Critical Voice, and Teacher Support. Second, the perceptions of students in other classes at Ms. Horton's school are very similar to those of students in the comparison group, with the exception that Ms. Horton's school was appreciably lower on the Personal Relevance scale.

By drawing on the extensive qualitative data base—consisting of interviews, classroom observations, video recordings, and student diaries—the teacher-researcher was able to provide an account of why the results are consistent and plausible. For example, the high level of perceived Personal Relevance in Ms. Horton's class is consistent with this teacher's practice of devoting one science period per week to things that are of personal interest to her students. Also, the high levels of Teacher Support perceived in Ms. Horton's class are consistent with student interviews conducted by the researcher and are illustrated below:

Interviewer: If you were to compare this teacher with other teachers from the past, in what way does she seem to be different?
Student T: The teacher usually says "Good morning" to me when I walk in. And if you're upset, she asks "What's wrong?"... Most teachers don't really say "Good morning" to you unless they're in a really good mood.
Interviewer: What might be an example of something you like about having this teacher?
Student B: She's always helping us out at the back. I sit in the back row and she reckons it's a bad row, yet she helps.

Significance

This study is unique in that it incorporated a teacher-researcher perspective that has been absent in most past research on classroom learning environments. Also, it provides another example of a study that illustrates the merits of combining qualitative and quantitative methods in learning environment research. Finally, the study provided important insights into the ways in which promoting a favorable classroom environment can be enhanced or impeded by the school culture, teacher beliefs, and various constraints such as the prescribed curriculum and the school timetable.

We hope educational researchers will find that the choice of the appropriate grain size for a particular study—or the choice of which multiple grain sizes should be used within the one study, for what purposes, and at what stages of the study—can be useful in conceptualizing, planning, and reporting their studies of classroom learning environments.

Overall, this study further supports the importance of the learning environment in education and in educational research. Because measures of learning environment outcomes alone cannot provide a complete picture of the educational process, assessments of learning environment also should be used to provide information about subtle but important aspects of classroom life.

REFERENCES

Dryden, M., and Fraser, B. J. (1996, April). *Evaluating urban systemic reform using classroom learning environment instruments.* Paper presented at the annual meeting of the American Educational Research Association, New York.

Eisner, E. W. (1979). *The educational imagination: On the design and evaluation of school programs.* New York: Macmillan.

Erickson, F. (1986). Qualitative research on teaching. In M. C. Wittrock (ed.), *Handbook of research on teaching* (3rd ed., pp. 119–161). New York: Macmillan.

Fisher, D. L., and Fraser, B. J. (1983). A comparison of actual and preferred classroom environment as perceived by science teachers and students. *Journal of Research in Science Teaching, 20,* 55–61.

Fraser, B. J. (1979). Evaluation of a science-based curriculum. In H. J. Walberg (ed.), *Educational environments and effects: Evaluation, policy, and productivity* (pp. 200–217). Berkeley, Calif.: McCutchan.

Fraser, B. J. (1986). *Classroom environment.* London: Croom Helm.

Fraser, B. J. (1994). Research on classroom and school climate. In D. Gabel (ed.), *Handbook of research on science teaching and learning* (pp. 493–541). New York: Macmillan.

Fraser, B. J. (1998). Science learning environments: Assessment, effects, and determinants. In B. J. Fraser and K. G. Tobin (eds.), *International handbook of education* (pp. 527–564). The Netherlands: Kluwer Academic Publishers.

Fraser, B. J., and Tobin, K. (1991). Combining qualitative and quantitative methods in classroom environment research. In B. J. Fraser and H. J. Walberg (eds.), *Educational environments: Evaluation, antecedents and consequences* (pp. 271–292). Oxford, Eng.: Pergamon Press.

Fraser, B. J., and Walberg, H. J. (eds.). (1991). *Educational environments and effects: Evaluation, antecedents and consequences.* Oxford, Eng.: Pergamon.

Guba, E. G., and Lincoln, Y. S. (1989). *Fourth-generation evaluation models.* Newbury Park, Calif.: Sage.

McRobbie, C. J., and Fraser, B. J. (1993). Associations between student outcomes and psychosocial science environment. *Journal of Educational Research, 87,* 78–85.

Taylor, P. C.; Fraser, B. J.; and Fisher, D. L. (1997). Monitoring classroom learning environments. *International Journal of Educational Research, 27,* 293–302.

Teh, G., and Fraser, B. J. (1995). Development and validation of an instrument for assessing the psychosocial environment of computer-assisted learning classrooms. *Journal of Educational Computing Research, 12,* 177–193.

Thorp, H.; Burden, R. L.; and Fraser, B. J. (1994). Assessing and improving classroom environment. *School Science Review, 75,* 107–113.

Tobin, K.; Kahle, J. B.; and Fraser, B. J. (eds.). (1990). *Windows into science classrooms: Problems associated with higher-level cognitive learning.* London: Falmer Press.

13

Technology's Role in Student-Centered Classrooms

Barbara Means and Kerry Olson

There is now a widespread agreement among educators and psychologists that the advanced skills of comprehension, reasoning, composition, and problem solving are acquired not through the passive reception of facts but through the learner's active processing of information (Collins, Brown, and Newman, 1989; Resnick, 1987). This *constructivist* view of learning calls for teaching basic skills within authentic contexts (hence more complex problems), for modeling expert thought processes, and for providing opportunity for collaboration and other external supports that enable students to achieve intellectual accomplishments they could not do on their own. It is this perspective that has provided the wellspring of ideas for many of this decade's curricular and pedagogical reform efforts.

While the vision of a transformed classroom offered by reformers is important for all students, the change in practice is especially dramatic for those who have been variously characterized as "economically disadvantaged" or "at risk." An increasing

---

We wish to thank and to express our admiration for teachers Sonja Ebel and Gail Whang whose class provides the central illustration for the points made in this chapter. We have made extensive use of their ideas and their words, expressed in interviews during our field work at their school.

proportion of the children in schools across America come from homes with incomes below the poverty line. Many have been raised in homes where English is not the dominant language or is not spoken at all. Statistically, students with these characteristics are more likely to fall behind academically, to drop out of school, or to turn off from the whole process of education. The conventional view for these students has been one of diminished expectations—schools try to teach them basic skills but do not expect them to attain high levels of accomplishment in the advanced skills of problem solving, scientific inquiry, or composition (Knapp and Shields, 1990). As a result, they are provided less instruction on advanced skills and fewer opportunities to develop capabilities in these areas than their more economically advantaged peers (Allington and McGill-Franzen, 1989; Oakes, 1986).

A constructivist approach calls for a dramatically different kind of classroom for economically disadvantaged students. Table 13-1 summarizes recommendations for teaching students at risk drawn from the research literature on constructivism. Rather than focusing on the deficits of learners from poor or culturally different backgrounds, instruction would build on the strengths that students bring and would treat cultural diversity as a resource. Instead of treating basic skills as a hurdle that must be surmounted before attempting more complex tasks that involve reasoning, problem solving, and composition, schools would give students opportunities to learn basic skills in the context of working on challenging, authentic tasks (Means and Knapp, 1991). This change would mean fewer spelling and punctuation worksheets and more involvement in composition, comprehension, and applications of skills. Instead of working in isolation, often in ability groupings or pull-out classes for compensatory instruction, students would work in mixed-ability groupings. They would be judged on their ability to perform a complex task and to reflect on and describe the thinking that went into it rather than on their facility with multiple-choice tests. A fundamental role for the teacher would be modeling powerful thinking and problem-solving strategies. The central form of discourse would be dialogue rather than lecture.

Table 13-1
Principles of Constructivist Approaches of Teaching Advanced Skills to All Students

Taking a New Attitude Toward Economically Disadvantaged Learners
- Appreciate intellectual accomplishments that all learners bring to school
- Emphasize building on strengths rather than just remediating deficits
- Learn about students' cultures to avoid mistaking differences for deficits

Reshaping the Curriculum
- Focus on complex, meaningful problems
- Embed instruction on basic skills in the context of more global tasks
- Make connections with students' out-of-school experiences and culture

Applying New Instructional Strategies
- Model powerful thinking and problem-solving strategies
- Encourage multiple approaches
- Provide scaffolding to enable students to accomplish complex tasks
- Make dialogue the central medium for teaching and learning

Source: Means, B., and Knapp, M.S. (1991).

TECHNOLOGY'S ROLE IN EDUCATION REFORM

In this chapter, we will make the argument that technology can support this transformation in teaching. We take this position despite the poor track record of earlier generations of technology (television in the 1960s, computers in the 1970s, videodisc and artificial intelligence in the 1980s) relative to the grandiose expectations for their impact on education. We believe that technologies being introduced in many schools today have much higher potential—not because of their greater power and capabilities—but because so much has been learned about designing constructivist learning activities and the ways in which technology can support those activities.

Earlier efforts at introducing technology within schools failed to have profound effects because they were based on an inappropriate model of teaching with technology. Technology developers believed in the worth of their knowledge of content areas or of pedagogical techniques and in the power of technology to convey that knowledge and instructional approach to students. Technology developers pointed with satisfaction to "teacher proof" instructional programs. Despite the intelligence and good intentions of their developers, most of these instructional technology applications did not receive prolonged use. Technology will never be able to perform important teacher functions relating to role modeling, provision of social rewards, and skilled diagnosis of the needs of the "whole child." Moreover, technology applications designed for classroom use have a real problem trying to match the local core curriculum, which varies considerably not just from state to state or district to district but often even among classrooms within a given school.

Until recently, most of the software market has been dominated by computer-assisted instruction, which tends to focus narrowly on isolated drill and practice on specific basic skills, which are easily presented in the highly structured format of that medium. The exposure of students from economically disadvantaged backgrounds to technology has been particularly likely to be confined to this kind of software, often in the form of an integrated learning system located in a separate computer laboratory. At the other end of the spectrum, instructional games, simulations, and intelligent tutoring systems have tended to convey more challenging material, but to cover only a very narrow slice of a subject domain, and often a slice that is a poor match to state curriculum guidelines or individual teacher preferences. Such technology-based activities have tended to get used with students who finish their "regular" course work early, with gifted students, or with those in some of the more innovative schools serving affluent neighborhoods. These technology applications have had little effect on what most teachers do with the bulk of their students for the majority of the school day (Cohen, 1988).

There are, however, a good number of "existence proofs"—teachers who organize their classrooms around collaborative, technology-supported projects, with multiple groups working concurrently on different aspects of their tasks (Means and Olson, 1994). These teachers find that technology's chief benefit is its use as a tool to support student thinking and productivity. Technology has tremendous power to help students in obtaining, organizing, manipulating, and displaying information. Students use word processing, database, design, and graphing software in the same ways as do professionals in business, communications, and research. Such tool uses of technology contrast sharply with the more didactic technology applications designed explicitly for instruction (see Means et al., 1993, for a discussion).

When technology is used as a tool, there is not an issue of the match of technology content to curriculum. Technology tools can be used to organize and present information in any content domain. Moreover, the teacher does not need to know everything about a new technology application; students and teachers can acquire those skills in the course of using the technology on their projects. In fact, one of the best things teachers can do with technology is to model the thinking processes and the experimentation of the intrepid learner who approaches a new technology as a problem to master.

As part of a project funded by the Office of Educational Research and Improvement within the U.S. Department of Education, SRI conducted case studies in schools using technology as part of a concentrated program of school reform. Within those schools, we looked for classrooms in which constructivist teaching approaches were supported by technology. To illustrate the powerful role of technology as a supporting tool within a broader instructional context designed and orchestrated by effective teachers, we will describe a fifth/sixth-grade classroom in an inner-city school. Before providing a description of the ways in which technology enabled and extended various aspects of the curriculum, we begin with brief overviews of the setting and implementation process. As with most classrooms, the integration of technology with these teachers' pedagogy was a gradual process.

AN ILLUSTRATIVE CASE

The School

Located in a low-income neighborhood of a Western city, Hawthorne Elementary School serves 1,400 students in grades K–6. The area surrounding the school has a reputation for crime, drugs, and gang activity. Approximately 85 percent of the school's students are eligible for free or reduced-price lunches. Ethnically, 57 percent of the students are Hispanic; 19 percent are African American; 23 percent are Asian/Pacific Islander; and 5 percent are Caucasian, Non-Hispanic. An influx of immigrants each year brings the school an increasing proportion of limited-English and non-English-speaking students (59 percent of students).

The Technology

CSILE (Computer-Supported Intentional Learning Environments) functions as a "collaborative learning environment" and a communal database, with both text and graphics capabilities.[1] Within this networked multimedia environment, students generate "notes" containing an idea or piece of information relevant to the topic under study. Notes are available for other students to comment on, leading to dialogues and an accumulation of knowledge. Students have to label their notes in order to be able to store and retrieve them; over time, they come to appreciate the value of precise, descriptive labels. In addition to receiving writing practice as they create their own notes, students get practice reading the notes generated by others. The idea behind CSILE is that through such communication, students will gain skills in making their understandings explicit, critically analyzing multiple perspectives, and working in collaborative groups.

CSILE was developed by Marlene Scardamalia and Carl Bereiter at the Ontario Institute for Studies in Education (Scardamalia and Bereiter, 1993). It has been used in a research program within Toronto schools for over five years. Apple Computer provided support for introducing CSILE to a number of American schools, including Hawthorne. Each participating classroom was equipped with 8 Macintosh computers, enough to allow each student to have a minimum of one-half hour per day of CSILE access. Hawthorne's CSILE classrooms were linked to one another via a local area network (LAN), permitting communication and joint projects across classrooms. The participating teachers were sent to an introductory three-day training session in St. Louis, where they were introduced to the CSILE model of collaborative knowledge building and where they had the opportunity to meet other CSILE teachers from across the country.

---

[1] CSILE is now available as Web Knowledge Forum. A demonstration can be found on the World Wide Web at http://csile.oise.on.ca/demo.html.

The first year of implementation, school year 1991–92, was difficult, given the general lack of familiarity and expertise with the system on the part of the teachers, as well as problems and limitations associated with the early versions of the software. System changes required constant adaptation and learning of new sets of procedures. Teachers did enjoy the opportunity that they were given to provide feedback and to have input in the development of the software, however.

Because of funding problems, outside technical support and teachers' electronic-mail accounts had to be discontinued at the end of the first year of CSILE implementation at Hawthorne. Relatively little was done with the CSILE system through the 1992–93 school year, but in 1993–94, Scardamalia and Bereiter began sabbaticals at a research center not far from Hawthorne. Two of their graduate students were assigned to spend two days a week at Hawthorne providing direct technical assistance and facilitating the integration of CSILE into the curriculum. In addition to their individual classroom support, the graduate assistants met with Hawthorne teachers as a group twice a month. These interactions with outside resources were critical in revitalizing teacher interest in CSILE and in providing the technical support teachers needed to feel confident about planning classroom activities that depended on use of the technology.

The Classroom

During school year 1993–94, Sonja Ebel and Gail Whang shared a job (each working half time) teaching a class of 31 fifth and sixth graders. With more than six languages spoken by their students, Ebel and Whang had the most ethnically and linguistically diverse class in a very heterogeneous school. These teachers took the linguistic and cultural diversity of their students not as a burden but as an opportunity. Ebel and Whang shared a similar educational philosophy, emphasizing collaborative learning and a constructivist approach. They decided to make the study of culture and the development of a positive classroom culture for learning as their unifying theme for the year. The class began by talking about the things that make culture, features such as housing, language, food, transportation, and government, which Ebel and Whang call "cultural universals." First the class examined these universals within the mainstream American culture, and then they worked on developing a hypothetical ancient culture, as part of the DIG Project.

The Project

Ebel and Whang's class was one of two Hawthorne classes that decided to implement the DIG Project curriculum. Developed by *Interact*, this curriculum unit is an extended activity in which each participating class constructs its own hypothetical culture. In outline, the DIG curriculum calls for students within each class to work in small groups to develop different aspects of a hypothetical culture (e.g., housing, language, and food), based on a set of overarching values and a geographic location selected by the class as a whole. Students produce artifacts for their culture, and then each class buries their artifacts for the other class to excavate. After excavating the other class's materials, each class reasons about the culture that would have produced those artifacts.

The DIG Project was not designed as a technology project, and Whang and Ebel did not immediately plan to incorporate technology into this unit, even though they had experience in using CSILE the prior year. They were attracted to the project because of the curricular content, the way in which it built on cooperative learning skills, and its power to give students a conceptual framework for thinking about their own and other cultures. It was through interactions with the CSILE developers that the teachers realized the potential for the system to support what they were trying to do. As Whang expresses it:

> When we first learned CSILE, I was trying to have my curriculum fit in with CSILE... creating units so that it would be compatible with CSILE, which now I think is backwards. Now what I want is for the technology to support what we are doing in the classroom. And that was a realization that I had this year when we were discussing CSILE with the creators, and that idea came out. We are the "experts" on what we're doing in the classroom, so why don't we have a discussion about the archeology project, let the CSILE people listen in and then they, being experts on CSILE and how the technology operates, can give us suggestions for how we can integrate CSILE into what we're doing and how it would enhance our curriculum.

Once Ebel and Whang began to think of CSILE as a tool that could help their students achieve the instructional goals they were aiming for, they moved wholeheartedly into using CSILE for the DIG Project. The class selected the care of the environment as their culture's overriding theme, and they located their culture in the rain forest. Using CSILE as a shared database, students wrote text and created graphics that described and depicted their cultural universals. They created links between entries that were connected conceptually—most often linking a piece of text with a corresponding graphic image. For example, the toucan was selected as a symbol for the rain forest culture. The text note describing the values represented by the bird was connected to a beautiful computer graphic. Many of the Spanish-speaking students entered their notes in their primary language, which they then linked to an English translation. The alphabet for the language invented for the culture—"Slaminian"—was shown with its English equivalent in a sort of electronic Rosetta Stone.

> For the DIG project, a lot of [the students] wrote messages in Slaminian, which is the language they created, and they were able to access this immediately. There was no way that the two students who created it would have been able to meet with everyone and explain it, so it made it easy and quick. Students were using it to work on their own universals, which were all connected in some way. So students working on dance could access what the costumes should look like. Through the computer, they were able to communicate all this with one another.—Gail Whang

As each small group created its piece of the culture (e.g., clothing, language, housing), it needed to determine whether their concept was consistent with the overall culture. The groups documented their work in CSILE notes, which could be instantly shared with all the other groups. Students used the CSILE network and database in much the same way that people in office environments use electronic mail and intranets to keep abreast of each others' activities.

> Student groups created graphic and text notes to explain what their cultural universal was. Then other students could access that and comment back right away, and say, "Wait a minute, you can't make a boat out of a tree because our culture doesn't cut down trees!" So then they could enter into a discussion about other materials. Students in this way could analyze and discuss what was being developed.—Sonja Ebel

Students examined each others' notes and provided assistance and feedback, providing "helpful, thoughtful" comments.

Examining the computer record of student exchanges, Ebel and Whang could see how students were helping each other advance their thinking. In one exchange, for example, students posted their invented number system and received a cogent critique from their classmates in another group:

CSILE entry on the number system:

> This is the slaminan's number system. It is a basic
> 10 number system too. It has a pattern to it. The
> number of lines increase up to five then it goes
> upside down all the way to 10.

[Above text entry is linked to an illustration of the number system]

Comment posted on CSILE from the "ritual group":

> We all like the number system, but we want
> to know how the number 0 looks like, and you can
> do more numbers not just ten like we have right now.

Figure 13-1 provides an example of a more extended interchange across student groups.

Other technology tools were incorporated into the project when appropriate. Early on, students studied images of animal and plant life on a videodisc about the rain forest to make sure that the flora and fauna incorporated into their clothing, food, and artwork would be compatible with a rain forest habitat. The students videotaped the rituals they developed for rites of passage, marriage, and burial, using scripts they had written and wearing costumes designed and created by the group in charge of clothing. The videotape was buried along with the artifacts made of clay and plant materials in the plot outside the classroom for the other class to excavate and interpret.

Archeology graduate students from a nearby university helped Hawthorne students with the preparation of topographical maps, and with the burying and retrieval of the artifacts. The excavation site was prepared to scale, with the students staking out the lot and dividing it up. Once all of the artifacts were buried, the two participating classes excavated one another's sites. Each artifact was carefully removed, cleaned, and recorded, using standard methods of archeology. Once the site was completely excavated, students met in small groups with the archeology graduate stu-

Technology's Role in Student-Centered Classrooms

Figure 13-1
CSILE Dialogue on the Subject of the Marriage Ritual

CSILE entry on marriage ritual:

TOPIC: Archeology Marriage & Family Groupings
MARRIEG CE. BY MAXIL
CEREMONY: THE MAN FALL IN LOVE WITH THE GIRL AND HE OFFERS HER A POT WITH A JAVA SEED IN IT AND IF SHE EXCEPT IT THEY CAN GET MARRIED, BUT THERE IS A CATCH TO THIS. YOU MUST BE ASKING WHAT THE POT IS FOR. THE JAVA SEED MUST HAVE DEVELOPED A JAVA LEAF WITHIN A MONTH, BUT IF IT HASN'T DEVELOPED A LEAF THEY CAN'T GET MARRIED, WITH THE SAME PERSON. YOU DON'T HAVE TO GET MARRIED WITH SOME ONE THAT YOU DON'T WANT TO MARRIE AND IF YOU DON'T FIND THE PERSON THAT YOU WANT TO GET MARRIED WITH THEN YOU DON'T HAVE TO GET MARRIED AT ALL.

[*Text is linked to illustration of "Engagement Plant"*]

Linked comment note:

comments
I thik the marrig saramony is intisting but what if it grows befr the end of the moth we thik you
shold keep this idea.

frrom jamedra and Emmanuel

Linked response note:

to Jemmedra and Emanuel
Dear Jamedra and Emmanuel,
I think you have mistaken the way the ceremony
goes if the leaf doesn't grow in a month then they
can't get married, if it grows then they can get
married.

Sincerely,
Video Group

dents to discuss their findings and to begin generating theories about the newly discovered culture. They entered and responded to one another's theories through text notes on CSILE. As a final activity, the two participating classrooms were brought together to discuss their theories and to present their respective cultures.

Follow-up Projects

After completing the DIG project, Whang and Ebel's class continued to study the phenomenon of cultures, turning to the study of the ancient Egyptian civilization. The students' increased familiarity with the concepts of culture, with cooperative learning, and with the use of CSILE enabled them to produce more extended interchanges focusing on various lines of inquiry (e.g., Why did they build pyramids? Why were cat gods so important?). Following are CSILE entries in response to a teacher's question on the ancient Egyptians: "Why did they build pyramids?"

> I think that they build the pyramids is because So
> the theifs can't steel their golds. (JL)

> I don't think that they just build pyramids so that
> they wouldn't steal there gold. I think that they also
> build them for like homwes for the dead people. and I
> don't think that the Egyptian just thought about
> stealing only... (MM)

> I agree with you because right after I finish
> typeing on csile I went to Research and I read a book
> on pyramids. It says that they build the pyramids for
> keeping theifs away from their golds and stuffs
> that meen alot to them. And the pyrmids are for
> the Kings and Queens. When the kings or Queens die...
> In the pyramid has a tomb. You know whats a
> tomb right? then you know what happens.

> ... I disagree with you about you writing about the
> pyramids. Pyramids are build not for theifs so that
> they couldn't still. They are build to put things that
> are important to them. They wouldn't think that their
> people would do that to them. (PS)

As this interchange indicates, students who were still struggling with English (and certainly with the mechanics of spelling and grammar) were able to use writing in extended discussions about important curriculum concepts. The technology motivated students to do more writing, and drew students who normally said little in class into the group discussion. Working at a computer, students who needed more time to state their arguments in English could take the time they needed, and still be part of the group discourse. Peers could help a student translate an argument from Spanish to English, or correct spelling and punctuation in situations where language mechanics were a concern. We are not making the argument that students should not work on spelling, grammar, or punctuation skills, but rather that an incomplete grasp of these skills should not preclude students from engaging in meaningful intellectual activity or from experiencing writing as a powerful means of communication.

In Whang and Ebel's class, the study of ancient civilization was then followed by an examination of the cultures from which the students had come. One wall of the classroom was covered by silhouettes of each student with yarn connected to the point on a world map from which the student's family had come to America. The teachers believe that their unit on cultures gave their students a conceptual framework for looking at their own cultures and for appreciating the reasons for differences among those different cultures:

> It has given them the tools with which to look at the different cultures represented in our class, which is fabulous. It's like a kid picking up a National Geographic magazine and looking at a culture in the Amazon and seeing something that is so different—they laugh and make fun of it. Now they look and they know there has got to be a reason . . . What is the reason they have this ceremony or that jewelry? . . . So it's given them the tools to look at cultures around the world and within the class, which is a goal for our class, to appreciate the diversity.—Gail Whang

Additional Activities

Throughout the year, CSILE was used for other activities in addition to the curriculum on culture. One of the most productive areas was an on-line literature circle ("Book Talk") in which students provided reviews of the books that they had read. Students in all the CSILE classrooms built a communal database that could be searched to find specific kinds of books and then to read reviews of books they were considering reading. Students could also engage in dialogues with students in their own class or another CSILE class about books they had both read. Sonja Ebel comments on the way this activity provides an authentic context for skills such as summarizing and choosing key words:

There's a lot of high-level knowledge embedded in the "Book Talk" that they're not even aware that they are using. They have to produce summaries... All these things you used to teach out of a workbook and it didn't make any sense. Here it's a direct application. They need to be able to do this in order to access something. So it's automatic that they learn how to do it because they want to be able to access the information. Like with the Book Talk, they apply key words to their summaries, so that someone can scroll through and see. "Now here is a book on family problems...." So making that kind of link, being able to synthesize your thoughts... there's actually an application on CSILE for linking, so they can link one note to another, talk about what the connection is.

As in their units on culture, the students' research and book discussions with CSILE showed increasing sophistication and skill over time. Whang and Ebel reported that their students became more skilled at using keywords and at identifying the type of entry they were making (e.g., statement of fact, opinion, inquiry). They gained skill also in asking and responding to intellectually challenging questions and issues, and became more likely to cite one another as references in their research. This growth process was facilitated because the teachers were able to monitor students' discussions through the ongoing review of CSILE files, which enabled them to focus individualized and group instruction on the specific areas in need of support.

The CSILE-DIG Project as an Exemplar of a Constructivist Approach

Table 13-1 shows a set of guidelines for taking a constructivist approach to teaching advanced skills to all students, including those from impoverished or culturally or linguistically diverse backgrounds. The technology-supported DIG Project, as it was enacted in Ebel and Whang's classroom, exemplified many of the principles in that table.

Attitude Toward Economically Disadvantaged Learners. From the beginning, Whang and Ebel were committed to treating the diversity of their students as a resource rather than a drawback. Unlike many teachers who sought to limit at least the linguistic diversity in their classes, Whang and Ebel lobbied to have all of the cultural and linguistic groups at Hawthorne represented. When culture was made a topic of study, the knowledge possessed by different students about diverse cultures gave the group a rich body of information from which they could draw inferences about cultural universals and about the things that are culture-dependent. African-American, Cambodian, and Filipino cultures, for example, were open to comparison. The kind of reasoning that Whang and Ebel's students engaged in is often not encountered until college-level anthropology classes (if at all).

Reshaping the Curriculum. The study of culture in general, and the DIG Project in particular, provided students with a complex, long-term set of tasks. Designing a hypothetical culture in such a way that it fits a particular habitat and that all the pieces are logically consistent requires both thinking and collaboration skills. The importance of systematicity and keeping careful records became apparent during the excavation of the other class's archeological site. Piecing together a conception of the other class's hypothetical culture, using the artifacts that had been excavated, called on inference-making skills. The curriculum connected with students' out-of-school experiences and culture as they compared their various cultures in order to understand that there are different ways in which different cultures can provide for communication, housing, and rituals that bind a society together. Within this complex project, the students received practice also in more basic skills, such as finding information, reading English text, and writing.

Applying New Instructional Strategies. Both the organizational structure for the unit (in small cooperative learning groups) and the CSILE technology promoted dialogue among students as the central medium for teaching and learning (rather than teachers lecturing to students). Students acquired knowledge and tested their ideas through interactions with each other. Scaffolding was provided by teachers and by technology. The teachers prepared the students for cooperative learning through discussions of what "helpful, thoughtful" comments are and the reasons why they should respond to each other with comments that provide information as well as encouragement. The teachers modeled powerful reasoning processes as the groups worked on designing their culture and on interpreting the meaning of the other culture's artifacts. Further modeling of reasoning in this domain was provided by the archeology graduate students who came in to help with the excavation and analysis of artifacts. The CSILE technology provided scaffolding by offering (1) a communal database of the work that had been accomplished and (2) an implicit structure that prompted students to think about the relationships among their ideas, to analyze the nature of what they were contributing and what they needed to advance their thinking, and to label content in a logical way that would support retrieval. Students were encouraged to approach the content in multiple ways. They not only wrote about the culture but also created graphical designs, concrete objects, and rituals to represent its key features.

REFLECTIONS ON THE RELATIONSHIP OF TECHNOLOGY TO CONSTRUCTIVIST TEACHING

As illustrated by the DIG Project, the model of technology use we advocate is one in which the curriculum rather than the technology is at the center of the activity. Much of what happened in the DIG Project did not involve computers at all. Whang and Ebel led off-line discussions on the nature of constructive feedback. Students used papier mache and clay to construct eating utensils, jewelry, and other artifacts from their hypothetical culture. They went out to the school yard with shovels to bury their artifacts, and used stakes, string, measuring tapes, and paper worksheets to systematize their excavation of the other class's cultural artifacts.

CSILE and video technology were used as tools to support the project, but the project was not about learning to use technology, and it could have been conducted without technology. In our view, this is perfectly appropriate. Almost any complex real-world task is likely to have components that can be executed more efficiently or effectively with technology supports and aspects that occur without technology. Technology use enhances the students' motivation and their sense that they are performing something important in the way that professionals would, but its use is not an end in itself.

A major reason that CSILE worked so well as part of Whang and Ebel's curriculum unit is that it was designed to foster the kind of learning through interaction that the teachers were striving to establish in their classroom. In contrast to the kinds of software economically disadvantaged students are usually exposed to, in which individual students are assessed on a set of learning objectives and then given exercises to perform independently until they can pass a mastery test, CSILE supports collaborative learning. The students create a group repository of knowledge and seek to maximize not what individuals can do in isolation but the collective wisdom of the class. The objective is to support what Brown (Brown et al., 1993) and others have called a "community of learners." Under this model, it is perfectly acceptable for different students to make different contributions—some specializing in computer graphics, some in managing the linking of different parts of the database, and others excelling in scriptwriting or video production. This diversification of roles reflects practice in the world of work and fosters the development of specialized areas of expertise.

CSILE helps to foster collaborative skills not only by providing a communal database and a medium for the exchange of ideas, but also by facilitating the participation of a wider range of students. Computer-based communication facilitates fuller participation for several reasons. First, students are excited about the prospect of using the computer and, at least in this classroom, did not have any preconceptions about their inadequacy in its use:

> It seems like students feel equal around a computer—there's something about it, maybe because it's new and they haven't been tracked ... They haven't identified who is good and who is bad on the computer, so they all still feel relatively equal around it.—Sonja Ebel

Second, the computer provides a safe channel for communication with individuals a student might not normally talk to. Much has been written about the power that wide area networks offer in bringing students into communication with distant experts or other students thousands of miles away. Much less has been written about the phenomenon that Whang and Ebel observed: communicating through a computer made students feel comfortable about discussing important issues with students in their own school from different cultural groups, grades, or genders. For this reason, the different perspectives available in the classroom came through much more clearly when students could express themselves within CSILE notes:

> They [are] able to communicate. They do comment, "your idea made me think about this aspect ..." [They hear] different voices and different

> perspectives through the computer where they might not be able to talk to each other [face to face] in such an intimate way.—Gail Whang

Finally, as noted here previously, the ability to engage in discussions over the computer makes it easier for students with differing levels of English facility to engage in serious intellectual dialogue. Some students may take more time to compose their note or some may first compose it in Spanish, but they are not kept out of the computer-based discussion the way they would be in an oral class discussion where talk must keep moving in real time. Moreover, students can help explain what they mean by using graphic representations, as many students did within the unit on cultures.

While we have argued that the CSILE technology improved collaborative learning in Whang and Ebel's class, we would also stress that the transition to using CSILE was made much easier because both the students and the teachers had already worked on communication and collaborative learning skills. An earlier schoolwide program stressing conflict resolution and norms for respectful communication gave the teachers something to build on in preparing the students for participating in CSILE dialogues.

> First of all... social skills are explicitly taught and stressed—what it looks like and feels like to attentively listen and to share and to cooperate. Secondly, when we introduce CSILE and the concept of a comment, we have overheads that we developed and use which go through nice comments, put downs and helpful, thoughtful comments. We make it clear that we don't just want nice comments. We ask students if disagreeing is a put down. We talk very specifically about helpful, thoughtful comments—that they push people's thinking, they question things, they disagree if that's necessary, they give support. But they do it in a helpful way. They don't just say "that's stupid," which is not very helpful, or "that's nice," which is also not very helpful. Because some of the kids have been with us for three years, they're outstanding at commenting... ninety percent of the comments are helpful, thoughtful.—Sonja Ebel

Many studies of classrooms in which there is extensive use of technology have found an impact on student and teacher roles, with teachers doing less lecturing and acting more as a "coach" for students as they work on technology-based activities (e.g., Dwyer, Ringstaff, and Sandholtz, 1990). Students tend to collaborate more when working on technology-supported project (Baker, Gearhart, and Herman, 1994).

Whang and Ebel were already proponents of collaborative learning and student-centered approaches before they became involved with technology. Nevertheless, once they committed to using CSILE in a serious way as part of their core classroom activities, they found that they were propelled much farther along the continuum toward a student-centered classroom structure. Whereas before whole-class instruction had been interspersed with small-group activities, the need to give every student at least a half hour a day at the computer for CSILE activities meant that they needed to be in rotations all the time. The teachers felt that the technology prompted them to give up the last vestiges of teacher-focused instruction.

A final important contribution of the CSILE technology is the implicit supports it provides for certain kinds of thinking. CSILE's designers worked from a cognitive psychology perspective to develop a system that is flexible and open to any content but nevertheless prompts certain thinking skills. Students label their notes as a request for information, an opinion, or a statement of information, based either on their personal understanding or on an outside information resource. Information sources are referenced, and students are encouraged to reference each other's notes in building their arguments. Building links among notes requires an analysis of the relationships among arguments, information, and illustrations. This understanding takes some time to develop and is an important part of the foundation for more advanced reasoning and composition skills.

Implications for Teachers

Our extended description of the DIG Project is offered as a demonstration of how technology can, within the context of a larger, teacher-designed activity, support constructivist teaching approaches. The point is not that technology can bring these changes about by itself, but rather that technology offers the skillful teacher a powerful new set of tools that can be used to support learning and collaboration.

Complex technology-supported projects of the sort we have described require teachers to have multiple skills. The subject matter itself is challenging and because it is open-ended, can never be totally mastered. At the same time, the teacher's new role poses challenges. The teacher must be able to launch and orchestrate multiple groups of students, intervening at critical points to keep the group on track, to diagnose individual learning problems, and to provide feedback. At least initially, the technology itself adds a degree of difficulty as students and teachers try to learn how to set up equipment, remember software commands, and troubleshoot system problems. Teachers require a high degree of skill, confidence, and perseverance to adopt constructivist teaching practices with technology. But rising to this challenge offers real opportunities, not only by dramatically changing students' school experiences but also by enhancing teachers' professional growth.

> I see so often what I consider incredibly wasted opportunities with the computer.... Why put all that money into a computer when a workbook does just fine ... It's such a linear way of thinking, to take exactly what you already do and put it on the computer. My view of technology is ... complicated. It's not smooth and the outcomes are not predictable. There is no prescription. We're constantly experimenting, and we're not always sure what's going to happen with the experiment. There is a loss of control, but out of that some every exciting things happen!—Sonja Ebel

What does it take to bring teachers to the point where they can use technology to support constructivist learning activities? A considerable body of research on pioneer technology-using classrooms and schools suggests that a major requirement is time—time for the teachers themselves to become comfortable using a new technology and time to think about their practice and to try out instructional uses of technology with their students (Means et al., 1993). Estimates of the amount of time required for novice teachers to become skilled and comfortable in using technology within their classrooms range between three and five years (Office of Technology Assessment, 1995; Sheingold and Hadley, 1990). The likelihood that teachers will attain this level of skill appears to be higher in settings where there is a critical mass of other technology-using teachers, where technical assistance is readily available on site, where teachers have opportunities within the regular school day to collaborate with each other, and where external sources of inspiration and support (such as the CSILE research team in our example) engage with teachers on an extended basis (Means and Olson, 1995).

REFERENCES

Allington, R. L., and McGill-Franzen, A. (1989). School response to reading failure: Chapter 1 and special education students in grades 2, 4, and 8. *Elementary School Journal, 89,* 529–542.

Baker, E. L.; Gearhart, M.; and Herman, J. L. (1994). *The Apple Classrooms of Tomorrow: The UCLA evaluation studies* (CSE Technical Report 353). Los Angeles: UCLA Graduate School of Education, CRESST.

Brown, A. L.; Ash, D.; Rutherford, M.; Nakagawa, K.; Gordon, A.; and Campione, J.C. (1983). Distributed expertise in the classroom. In G. Salomon (ed.), *Distributed congitions: Psychological and educational considerations* (pp. 188-228). New York: Cambridge University Press.

Cohen, D. K. (1988). Educational technology and school organization. In R. S. Nickerson and P. P. Zodhiates (eds.), *Technology in education: Looking toward 2020* (pp. 231–264). Hillsdale, N.J.: Erlbaum.

Collins, A.; Brown, J. S.; and Newman, S. E. (1989). Cognitive apprenticeship: Teaching the craft of reading, writing, and mathematics. In L. B. Resnick (ed.), *Knowing, learning, and instruction: Essays in honor of Robert Glaser* (pp. 453–494). Hillsdale, N.J.: Erlbaum.

Dwyer, D. C.; Ringstaff, C.; and Sandholtz, J. (1990). *The evolution of teachers' instructional beliefs and practices in high-access-to-technology classrooms.* Paper presented at the annual meeting of the American Educational Research Association, Boston.

Knapp, M. S., and Shields, P. M. (1990). Reconceiving academic instruction for the children of poverty. *Phi Delta Kappan, 71* (10), 752–758.

Means, B.; Blando, J.; Olson, K.; Middleton, T.; Morocco, C. C.; Remz, A. R.; and Zorfass, J. (1993). *Using technology to support education reform.* Washington, D.C.: U.S. Government Printing Office.

Means, B., and Knapp, M. S. (1991). Introduction: Rethinking teaching for disadvantaged students. In B. Means, C. Chelemer, and M. S. Knapp (eds.) *Teaching advanced skills to at-risk students: Views from research and practice.* (pp. 1–26). San Francisco: Jossey-Bass.

Means, B., and Olson, K. (1995). *Technology's Role in Education Reform: Findings from a National Study of Innovating Schools.* Menlo Park, Calif.: SRI International.

Means, B., and Olson, K. (1994). "Tomorrow's Schools: Technology and Reform in Partnership." In B. Means (ed.), *Technology and Education Reform* (pp. 191–222). San Francisco: Jossey Bass.

Oakes, J. (1986). Tracking, inequality, and the rhetoric of school reform: Why schools don't change. *Journal of Education, 168,* 61–80.

Office of Technology Assessment. (1995). Teachers and technology: Making the connection. Washington, D.C.: U.S. Government Printing Office.

Resnick, L. B. (1987). *Education and learning to think.* Washington, D.C.: National Academy Press.

Scardamalia, M., and Bereiter, C. (1993). Technologies for knowledge-building discourse. *Communications of the ACM, 36*(5), 37–41.

Sheingold, K., and Hadley, M. (1990). Accomplished teachers: Integrating computers into classroom practice. New York, N.Y.: Center for Technology in Education.

Index

Achievement,
   of English language learners, 173-177
   influences on, 64-72
   international comparisons of, 206
   labeling and, 29-30
   learning environment and, 287
   teacher-student interaction and, 164-165
Assessment,
   international comparisons of, 219-221
   metaphors for, 280-282
   portfolios and, 282-283
   and science education, 280-283
At-risk students, constructivist approach to learning and, 298-299, 310-311

Beginning teachers, 45. *See also* Teacher education
   content knowledge of, 49-50
   research on, 48-57
   self-evaluation of, 53-55
   support and supervision of, 50-53, 54, 69
Behavior management. *See* Classroom management
Biographies and autobiographies, and research on teaching, 44-45. *See also* Narrative research

Characteristics of teachers. *See* Teacher characteristics
Classroom Environment Study, 213, 214, 215, 219-220
Classroom environment, 23, 140, 218-219
Classroom Interaction Analysis Scale (Flanders'), 21

Classroom management, 138, 207
  behavioral approaches to, 252
  beliefs about, 261-262
  definitions of, 249-251
  and desists, 252-253
  expert teaching, and 45
  future research on, 265-266
  of groups, 252-255
  history of, 251-255
  instructional content and, 256, 259-260, 263-264
  principles of, 262-264
  room arrangement and, 253
  rules and procedures and, 253, 254, 260, 265
  small-group activities and, 274-277
  sociocultural studies and, 255-260
  student accountability and, 253
  teacher-student interactions and, 161-163
  techniques for, 36, 37
  and withitness, 161
Classroom observation research
  descriptions of, 108-109
  identifying, 112-113
  instructional inequities and,
  instructional processes and, 110-112
  limitations of, 117-121
  methodological concerns about, 118-
  new directions for, 121-123
  pragmatic concerns about, 120-121
  purposes of, 109-116
  shadowing and, 121-122
  strengths of, 109
  teacher education and, 113-115
  teaching practices and, 115-117
  technology use and, 110-112
  theoretical and epistemological criticisms of, 117-118
Cognitively guided instruction, for English language learners, 177-180
Comprehension teaching, 84-85

Constructivism
  defined, 297
  technology use and, 299-301, 310ff
Computer-Supported Intentional Learning Environment, 302ff
Computers. *See* Technology
Content knowledge, of beginning teachers, 49-50
Contexts of teaching, current research on, 42-48
  biographies and autobiographies, 44-45
  expert teachers, 45-46
  metaphors, 42
  stories, 43
  voice, 47-48
Cooperative learning, 137, 179-180
  English language learners and, 185-187
  lesson structure and, 216
  science education and, 276-277
  technology use and, 184-185, 303, 305, 308, 311, 312-313
Co-participation, and learning science, 270-272, 274, 277
Correctives and reinforcement, 82
Cues, 79-80
Culturally diverse students, constructivist approach to learning and, 305, 308, 310-311
  labeling and, 30
Culturally responsive instruction, 180-182
Curriculum, effectiveness correlates for, 136
Cycles, of teaching, 24

Desists, and classroom management, 252-253

Effective schools
  effective instruction in, 131-133
  conditions for, 137-142
  correlates at the classroom level, 133-137
  criteria for, 143
  curriculum materials and, 136, 139

Index

Effective schools, *continued*
  framework for, 142-145
  future research for, 145-148
  goals and, 139
  grouping and, 139
  instructional theories for, 135-137
  international studies of, 133-134, 148
  organizational aspects of, 139
  policy for, school-level, 140-142
  school board role in, 139-140
  time and, 140
Engagement, 81
English language learners
  cognitively guided instruction for, 177-180
  cooperative learning and, 185-187
  culturally responsive instruction for, 180-182
  effective teaching practices for, 177-189
  future research on teaching of, 193-194
  instructional conversation and, 187-189
  problematic approaches to teaching, 175-177
  teacher education programs and, 191-193
  teacher expectations of, 174-175, 192-193
  technology use and, 182-185, 305, 308-309, 314
  underachievement of, 173-177
Expectations of teachers. *See* Teacher expectations
Expert teachers, research on, 45-46
Explicit teaching, 83-84

Gage model, research on teacher effects, 34-35
Grain sizes, in learning environment research, 285-286, 290, 294-295
Grouping, of students
  effective schools and, 139

effectiveness correlates for, 137
science education and, 274-277

Hierarchical linear modeling, 119-120
Home environment, and student learning, 70
Homework,
  international comparisons of, 220
  and time use, 140

Inner-city schools
  effective, 112
  technology use in, 111
Instructional processes, classroom observation and, 110-112
Instructional strategies, and teacher-student interactions, 161-163
Instructional systems
  adaptive instruction, 89-90
  computer-assisted instruction, 90
  cooperative learning programs, 93-94
  effects of, 87-103
  individualization, 88
  mastery learning, 89
  mathematics effects, 99-100
  programmed instruction, 87-88
  reading effects, 94-95
  science effects, 96, 97-98
  social environment, effects of, 93-94
  special populations programs, 100-101
  student grouping, 91-93
  writing effects, 96, 97
Interaction, student-teacher, 21-30. *See also* Teacher-student interaction
  labeling students, 29-30
  nonverbal communication, 26-28
  teacher expectations, 28-29
  verbal communication, 22-26
International Association for the Evaluation of Educational Achievement, 205-206
International research on teaching, 205-222
  allocated time and pacing, 214-215

International research, *continued*
  assessment and evaluation, 219-221
  conceptual framework for (lesson), 206-211
  classroom environment, 218-219
  lesson activities, 215-217
  lesson purpose, 212-214
Interpersonal relationships. *See* Teacher-student interaction

Labeling students, 29-30
Language-minority students. *See* English language learners
Learner autonomy in science, 86-87
Learner-centered classrooms, and classroom management, 255-260, 265
Learning environment
  grain sizes and, 290-291, 294, 295
  questionnaires for, 286-288, 291-293
  research on, 286-296
  student perceptions of, and achievement, 287
Learning, influences on, 64-72. *See also* Achievement
  student aptitudes, 67
  classroom instruction and climate, 68-69
Limited English proficient. *See* English language learners

Management. *See* Classroom management
Master teacher, 38-39
Mastery learning, 137
Measurement instruments, and teacher-student relationships, 156-157
Mentor teachers, 51-52
Meta-analysis, of research findings, 64-67
Metacognitive teaching. *See* Comprehension teaching

Metaphors, to describe teachers' work, 42
Minority students. *See also* Teacher-student interactions; English language learners
  and teacher expectations, 28, 39
  labeling and, 29-30
Model for Interpersonal Teacher Behavior, 156, 159-160, 162

Narrative research, 42-44, 229-246
  advantages of, 234
  conceptual frameworks of, 234-237
  conceptual roots of, 239-241
  definition of, 230-233
  epistemological issues, 237-241
  future directions for, 241-243
  interpretation of, 237-239
  limitations of, 235-237
  teacher education and, 236
National Science Education Standards, 273-274
National Science Foundation, 86, 96, 99, 101
Nonverbal communication, 26-28
Novice teachers. *See* Beginning teachers

Observation, of classrooms. *See* Classroom observation
Open education, 85-87
  effects of, 87

Patterns of teaching, 82-83
  effects of, 83
  explicit teaching, 83-84
  open education, 85-87
Portfolios, in student assessment, 282-283
Principals, as instructional leaders, 139
Process-product research, 33-35, 37, 41, 152
  criticisms of, 39-41

Index

Professional development. *See* Teacher education
Program design, 70
Psychological elements of teaching, 76-78

Question-Answer Relationship, 179, 180
Questionnaire on Teacher Interaction, 157, 158, 163-164

Reciprocal teaching, 179, 180
Reflection, of beginning teachers, 55-57
Room arrangement, and classroom management, 253

Scaffolding
  for English language learners, 179
  technology use and, 311-312
School boards, and effective schools, 139-140
School organization, 71
Schools for Thought, 259-260
Science education
  assessment of learning and, 280-283
  constructivism and, 272-283
  co-participation, 270-272, 274, 277
  National Science Education Standards, 273-274
  wait time and, 278-280
  whole-class activities and, 277-280
Self-evaluation, of beginning teachers, 53-55
Self-fulfilling prophecies, 28-29
Shadowing, 121-122
Sociocultural studies and classroom management, 255-260
State and district characteristics, 71-72
Steering groups, and instructional pacing, 215
Story research. *See* Narrative research

Strategies for successful teaching, 35
Student teachers. *See* beginning teachers; Teacher education
Student-centered classrooms. *See* Learner-centered classrooms
Student-teacher interaction. *See* Teacher-student interaction

Teacher behavior. *See also,* Teacher style; Narrative research
  current research on, 41-48
  effectiveness correlates for, 137.
Teacher characteristics, 30-33
Teacher education, 102-103
  English language learners and, 191-193
  improving through classroom observation research, 113-114
  narrative education in, 235
  teacher-student interaction and, 167-169
Teacher effects, 33-41
  Gage model, 34-35
  Emmer and Evertson model, 37
  Master teacher model, 38-39
  research on, 18-19, 33-41
Teacher expectations, 28-29
  of English language learners, 174-175, 192-193
Teacher-student interaction, 151-169
  characteristics of, 158-163
  classroom observation research and, 115-117
  effective, 163-165
  ethnicity and, 113
  instructional strategies and, 161-162
  Model for Interpersonal Teacher Behavior, 156, 159-160, 162
  nonverbal, 158-161
  patterns of, 153-155

Teacher-student interaction, *continued*
  perceptions of, instruments for exploring, 156-157
  professional development and, 166-167
  Questionnaire on Teacher Interaction, 157, 158, 163-164
  sex-related, 112-113
  student achievement and, 164-165
  systems approach to, 153-155
  teacher education implications of, 167-169
  and technology use, 185
  theory of, 155

Teaching style,
  behavior, 152, 156, 159-160
  definition of, 18-22, 152
  indirect instruction, 20-22
  model for interpersonal teacher
  nonverbal communication and, 26-28
  psychological elements of, 76-78
  research on, 20-22, 69, 152
  teacher-student interaction and, 21-30
  types of, 20-22
  verbal communication and, 22-26

Technology
  classroom observation research and, 110-111
  Computer-Supported Intentional Learning Environment, 302ff
  constructivist approach and, 310ff
  cooperative learning and, 184-185, 303, 305, 308, 312-313
  education reform and, 299-301
  English language learners' use of, 182-185, 305, 308-309, 314
  implications for teachers, 315-316
  limitations of, 299-300
  scaffolding and, 311-312
  teacher-student interactions and, 185

Verbal communication, 22-26
  teaching cycles and, 24-25
Voice, research on, 47-48. *See also* Narrative research

Wait time, in science education, 278-280
Withitness, 161
Write to Read Program, and English language learners, 183
  Instructional conversation, and English language learners, 187-189